PONTIFICAL INSTITUTE OF MEDIAEVAL STUDIES

Studies and Texts
No. 29

WARBOYS

TWO HUNDRED YEARS IN THE LIFE
OF AN
ENGLISH MEDIAEVAL VILLAGE

J. Ambrose Raftis

Pontifical Institute of Mediaeval Studies
Toronto
1974

ISBN o 88844 029 4

Printed in the Netherlands by Royal Van Gorcum Ltd., Assen

TABLE OF CONTENTS

MAPS:

VI

LIST OF TABLES

PREFACE

This is the second in a series of monographs on the mediaeval English village. Louis Henri has argued convincingly for studies of individual villages as prerequisite to understanding the history of the early modern villagers. As one pushes back into the Middle Ages this argument for the history of individual villages becomes even stronger. For it is impossible to identify the mediaeval villager except against the unique historical qualities of his village.[1]

Despite the long lists of names, this is not an exercise in romantic antiquarianism or even in geneological studies. Rather, there has been no historiography of the mediaeval villager as such; even more, the possibility of nominal identification of the villager has been traditionally denied by historians and furthermore continues to ge denied. The following study is presented primarily as a model for the methodology that may be followed for the study of the mediaeval villager. As a fairly substantial village with a well balanced collection of account rolls and court rolls, Warboys was an obvious selection for this model. The great bulk of this volume, therefore, is directed towards the detailed presentation of village personnel in the manner of personal identification and then in the relation of individuals to time, place and social groupings or families. For the student investigating a single village this tedious listing of names is enlivened by his growing acquaintance with various families and personalities. In the following study, the last part has been directed towards exemplifying the many ways by which villagers gradually stir to life as the historian pieces together these few remains.

In a number of ways the surviving records do not serve well the history of Warboys. Information about the material resources of Warboys is much less than that for some of her neighbouring villages. On the other hand, the very good information available for the fen economy is better left to a wider study of this economy since inter-

---

[1] This is not all to suggest that these studies should stop at the village level. For a useful criticism of this inadequacy of local studies, cf. *American Anthropologist*, 75, 1973.

commoning prevailed throughout the Huntingdonshire fenland. One must also leave to regional studies the more detailed study of the role of the lordship in the life of the villagers and the analysis of the history of various Warboys individuals and families throughout the whole region of West Huntingdonshire.

While the author assumes full responsibility for this methodology, I would like to thank colleagues for many helpful criticisms of my work and that of my students in developing this approach to village history. Unfortunately, the work of Dr. Patricia Hogan on the villager of Wistow will not appear before this study of Warboys, but I would like to acknowledge here the pioneer work that she has done in setting out the various ways of isolating village generations. Special thanks are also due to Dr. Edwin DeWindt for making available his exhaustive index to the fifteenth century Ramsey Court Book. Finally, a special debt of gratitude must be acknowledged to Miss Beryl Wells who not only typed the whole manuscript but undertook the tedious work of setting out the tables and drawing the maps. Owing to the fact that most personal names appear already in the volume in alphabetical order in tables, that places referred to are indicated on the two maps and that tables and lists cover most topics, an index has not been considered necessary.

PART I

INTRODUCTION

CHAPTER I

Those men must remain silent to the historian who for more than a millenium would have trudged along the wooded escarpment of Warboys in order to skirt the soggy fen some fifty feet below. By the time of its first appearance in history, as a foundation property of Ramsey Abbey in the tenth century, the Huntingdonshire township of Warboys was already a well established settlement with the substantial assessment of ten hides. The inhabitants themselves only received their first recognition in history as the anonymous parish priest, thirty-four villagers and thirteen bordars of Warboys in Domesday Book. In view of the fact that Warboys was said to have twenty geldable ploughlands at the time, this Domesday population count could have indicated only the largest tenants, for these figures would not at all represent an adequate working personnel for such a productive village.

One hundred years later a village extent[1] listed the Christian names of the tenants of Warboys. At the most there were 116 tenants. As only 16 of these were given any further identification, and in 8 cases simply by the parental Christian name, it remains impossible to determine the separate identity of the many Roberts (12), Williams (11), Richards (8), Johns (6), and Walters (4). Nevertheless, that Warboys was well populated by this time is indicated in several ways. First, about a dozen "tofts" had been rented from the demesne by persons who appear to be distinct from the villagers holdings in villeinage. Secondly, of the thirty-six full virgates listed in villeinage, twenty-five were held jointly by two tenants. Thirdly, the eight cotlands and two dozen tofts held from the villeinage would also appear to have for the most part tenants who were not virgators. Finally, four natives of Warboys were seeking their fortunes elsewhere. Indeed, if Reginald the son of Ingeram was the brother of William the son of Ingeram who held a full virgate, at least one of these émigrés came from a prominent family.

---

[1] *Carts*, III, pp. 253-257.

Some two generations later, in 1251, four local inquisitors presented another report on the tenurial situation at Warboys.[1] In this very detailed extent the villagers are for the most part carefully identified by surnames. Perhaps the more exceptional tenancy by women and the rare appellation explains why it was not considered necessary to further identify Beatrix, Botild (Matilda?), Katerina, Tubernus, Duraunt, and Lucas. In the more stable core of the village, the larger holdings in villeinage, a good number of tenants are still considered to be adequately identified by their father's Christian name. But for all others a remarkably wide variety of distinctive first and surnames had been applied.

Of the 144 names associated with tenements, some are repeated and this may be taken as an indication of plural holdings. Thus Matilda the Widow was said to hold a virgate jointly, with Godfrey the son of Adam, but twice she was also listed as holding an entire virgate by herself. Nicholas Turbern held one virgate and was later listed as holding a messuage and croft. William Faber, Thomas son of Robert, Simon son of Walter, Alexander Puttock, and Alexander the Clerk were also holders of two tenements each. But the more interesting feature is the spread of tenure among more than 130 persons. Even when the surname is common, there is an adequate variety of Christian names to allow separate identification of tenants. In the following table these names have been arranged in alphabetical order.

TENANTS AT WARBOYS IN 1251[2]

Adam, Godfrey son of	Baldyne, Alexander
Adam, Beatrice widow of	Baseley, Simon
Alexander, Ralph son of	Basille, Ralph
Alexander, William	Beatrix
Alger, Walter son of	Benedict, Thomas son of
Anthony, William son of	Berengarius, Richard
Arnulph, John	Bole, Richard
Arnulph, Godfrey	Bonde, Simon
Avenel, Godfrey	Boscum, Richard ad

---

[1] *Carts*, I, pp. 305-320.

[2] In this, as with following tables, the spelling of common Christan names has been modernized. Some common trade and occupational surnames, such as Carpenter and Carter, have been put in English, for convenience of identification and comparison since many of the names were rendered in English in local records from the early fourteenth century. One may suspect corruptions in the text, so that Albinus son of Ranulph may be the same as Albinus son of Ralph, but the problem of identification cannot be further pursued.

Boltild'
Brandon, Emma wife of Richard de
Buk, Richard

Carpenter, Simon
Carpenter, William brother of Simon
Carter, William
Clerk, William
Cromebred, Cecilia

Duraunt'

Edwin, Robert son of
Edwin, Ralph brother of Robert son of

Faber, William
Faber, Bartholomew son of John
Faber, Walter
Faber, William son of Ralph
Faukus, William
Fekere, Walter
Fine, Robert
Fraunceys, Alice

Gerold, Richard
Gerold, Christina
Goatherd, Richard the
Godeman, Richard
Godfrey, John son of
Godfrey, Nicholas son of
Gosse, Godfrey

Harsyne, William
Harsyne, Richard
Hatynge, Ralph
Hawot, John
Hayward, Richard
Heline, John
Henry, Robert son of
Henry, Thomas son of
Herbert ad finem ville
Herbert, Cecilia
Herbert, Robert son of
Herbert, Robert
Hervy, Thomas
Hunfridi, heirs of William son of

Jagge, William
John, Richard son of

John, William son of
John, Walter son of
John, Martin son of
John, Nicholas son of

Katerina
Knyt, John
Knyt, Ralph
Knyt, Alexander

Love, Robert
Lucas

Matilda the widow

Noble, Richard the
Noble, William brother of Richard the

Oty, John

Pakerel, William
Pilche, Ralph
Pilche, William
Pilgrim, Ralph
Pilgrim, William
Pyntel, Matilda
Plumbe, Alan
Plumbe, Simon
Puttock, Alexander

Ralph, Albinus son of
Ralph, Henry son of
Ranulph, Albinus son of
Ranne, Matilda
Raven, Robert
Reeve, Richard the son of Ralph the
Reeve, Benedict the, dictus Haliday
Richard, Albinus son of
Richard, Thomas son of
Richemanni, Richard son of
Richemanni, Alexander
Richemanni, Hawysia daughter of
Robert, Walter son of
Robert, Thomas son of
Roger, Godfrey son of

Scim, Cecilia
Sculle, Richard
Sebiry, Godfrey, of Caldecote

Segelina, the Widow
Selime, Adam
Semare, Godfrey
Semare, Martin
Shepherd, Stephen
Simon, Herbert son of
Simon, William
Skyny, Osbert
Soute, Robert
Sperver, Ralph
Sperver, Hugh
Swift, Adam

Turbernus
Turbernus, Nicholas
Turbernus, Ralph son of

Valentyn, Matilda
Vicarius, Hugh

Walse, Godfrey
Walter, Simon son of
Walter, Herbert son of
William, John son of
William, Simon son of
Wodekoc, Cristina
Wodekoc, Henry

Subtenants of Walter son of Algeri
    Bartholomew de Grangiis
    Robert (his?) brother
    Ivo de Hyrst
    William the Miller
    John son of Henry
    Simon Fuylet
    William de Grafham
    William de Higney
    Tropeschaunt
    Pakerel
    Sarra de Brehylle

Despite this long list of tenants, these villagers of Warboys remain relatively isolated individuals. There are a few indications of the names of wives and daughters, of fathers and sons, but the near as well as the more distant blood ties of these tenants are not revealed to us. Obviously from the nature of the name entries in the late twelfth-century extent comparison of the two extents is of little further assistance. The continuation of property in the families of Humfridus (Hunfridus, 1251) and Alger is the most that can be clearly ascertained. Indeed the casual manner by which names were still handled in the mid-thirteenth century is well illustrated from the difficulty of identifying the four inquisitors from the village in the extent itself. Of these four named at the beginning of the 1251 extent, Thomas the son of Robert and Thomas the son of Henry are found among the tenants. Godfrey of Caldecote is very likely the Godfrey Sebery of Caldecote listed at the head of the virgators. But the fourth inquisitor, William the son of Arnulph, cannot be seen as a tenant unless he is to be taken as William Arnulph.

It comes as no great surprise, therefore, that the considerable variety of records that become available for village history from the thirteenth century actually do not bring us much closer to individual villagers. In the 1250 account roll[1] for Warboys, Benedict is reeve, William Miller,

[1] Add. 34903.

Simon Fulet (Fulyet) and Robert de Aula receive rent discounts for services. There are several new entries to land for that year: the son of Benedict the reeve—one-quarter land in Caldecote (4 s.), Ralph Turbern —one-quarter land (5 s.), Albinus the son of Richard—one-quarter land (5 s.), William the son of John—one-quarter land (5 s.), John the son of Godfrey—one-half virgate (6 s. 8 d.), Nicholas the son of Agnes—one-half virgate (8 s.) and Adam Swift for his father's land (10 s.); Nicholas the son of Agnes is the only name of this group that cannot be identified in the extent.

In the same account roll licences to marry were listed for the widow of Adam Feker (2 s.), the daughter of Godfrey of Caldecote (4 s.), Juliana Marger (12 d.), Matilda Denuld (15 d.), Agnes Sculle (6 d.) and Matilda Richeman (6 d.). The names of none of these women appeared in the 1251 extent.

The account roll for 1254-55[1] indicates that Benedict the Reeve is still responsible for the account. Three names are given in the list of entry fines to property. The first of these, William Pilgrim, is found in the 1251 extent. The other names, John le Fraunceis and Nicholas Berynger, are new and very likely indicate heirs of Alice Fraunceys and Richard Berengarius. Of the only other personal names mentioned in this substantial account roll, that of William le Ponder who pays a small fine "to have protection of the lord", may indicate a newcomer to the village, while no other information is available for the Richard the Cowherd whose land has fallen into the lord's hands, and John of Drayton whose land was sown by the reeve.

The public records are equally impersonal. Of such records the most detailed for the thirteenth century is the Hundred Rolls, coming about a generation after the large Warboys extent. In the Hundred Roll[2] for Warboys where possible the name of only one representative is given for each category of tenant. That is, Albinus of Caldecote is taken to be typical of the full virgator, Simon Plumbe of the semi-virgator, William Lucas of the akermanlander, Godfrey ate Wode of the *coterellus*. Godfrey Clerk was said to hold jointly with six "peers" three and one-half virgates of maltland, while four other crofters held by the same condition as Richard ate Wode, and three others held a messuage and

---

[1] Add. 39669.
[2] The unedited Hundred Roll for Hurstingstone Hundred to be found in the Public Record Office, London (Sc 128/56) adds nothing to the version edited by the Record Commissioners.

lot in the same fashion as William Haliday. The holdings of Henry Sutor, Robert Schayl and Richard Schamer did not come under common categories. Those larger freeholds of William of Higney from Bartholomew of H'ame, of Hugh of Ramsey, William of London, Richard le Bonde, John of Cotenham, and John Berenger had also to be listed separately. Finally, it was noted that Ivo of Hurst held land of William of Higney, John the Chaplain of Ivo of Hurst, John Foliet and Katherine Gosebell of Ivo of Hurst, Robert Cook of William of Higney, Amabelle the Gardener of both William of Higney and Ivo of Hurst, and Richard Caton of Roger of Glatton, parson of Sawtrey. Beyond evidence for the continuation of some surnames, the Hundred Rolls adds little to the 1251 extent.

About a decade later, in November, 1290, there begins at last a series of records for Warboys that introduces us to the individual villager as something more than a tenant. In this 1290 court roll, personal names are given 138 times, in reference to the following activities: juror, chief pledge, debt, assize of ale, defamation, avoidance of work on the demesne, failure to be in tithing, failure to distrain, bearing children out of wedlock, trespassing with beasts in the meadow, digging turf wrongly, cutting wood wrongly, selling reeds to outsiders wrongly, outside the demesne with or without licence, false plea, trespassing on ditch and road, receiving an outsider not in tithing, sale and purchase of land, and homicide. Some villagers' names appear several times, as with Richard Bonde who was a capital pledge, juror, defendant in a debt suit, and pledge for Luke Bonde who was licenced to leave the lord's demesne,

Undoubtedly some villagers' names would not appear in the Warboys court roll for 1290 since not all would have been involved in the above-mentioned activities. But the series of court rolls for Warboys that begins at this time is such that the vast majority of the villagers do come to our attention. Preliminary studies of the Warboy's court rolls have indicated the more than five thousand entries for the pre-1350 period, embracing more than four hundred families and over one thousand personal names.[1] While it is difficult to speak of averages, as we shall see, when so many families disappear and others appear anew, and responsibility does tend to concentrate about certain families, still for more than three-score main families much evidence has been found

[1] J. A. Raftis, "Social Structures in Five East Midland Villages", *The Economic History Review*, 1965, p. 100.

available for the first half of the fourteenth century.[1] In addition there is proportionate information available for lesser categories of families.

From this series we can discover more about Richard Bonde: he was involved in a plea and as a pledge in 1292, three times as a pledge in January, 1294, as a juror and twice as a pledge in November, 1294, as a juror in 1299 and 1301, as a taster, a pledge four times, and with pasture in the fen in 1301, as a juror and in concord over a suit in 1305, three times as pledge in 1306, as a juror and charged with purpresture while ploughing in 1309. But we also obtain information about Bonde's with the first names of Martin, Juliana, Nicholas son of Richard, Benedict son of Richard, Ralph, Joan wife of Hugh, William son of Robert, Stephen, Robert, Alice, Maurice, Matilda wife of Paul, Margaret daughter of Paul, Emma and Paul. Richard Bonde had a relatively short span of life in the period of the extant court rolls. Others, like Ralph Fine, can be traced over a longer period, from 1290 to 1322 (1290 sues for debt, 1292 was a pledge, 1294 January, was pledge and sold land,November 1294 trespassed on the lord's land, was pledge, and defendant in a debt suit, 1299 was pledge twice, early 1301 was pledge four times, and trespassed in the lord's wood, later in that year he was pledge again, in 1305 he was pledge three times, in 1306 pledge once, at various times over 1313 pledge four times, and for breaking warren once, in 1316 he took in unkown outsiders without licence, was pledge twice, failed to perform his work once for the lord and did not have his pledgee once, in 1322 he again failed to perform his work services on one occasion, and finally in 1322 he was a pledge and had the hue and cry raised against him.) There were also some dozen other persons appearing in the court rolls with the surname of Fine.

It seems possible, therefore, to attempt a reconstitution of the village population of Warboys from this time.[2] The following list of the court rolls available to this reconstitution indicates the month of the year when this is known.

---

[1] J. A. Raftis "The Concentration of Responsibility in Five Mediaeval Villages", *Mediaeval Studies*, 1966. It should be noted that the chronology covered in this article differs somewhat from that employed in this volume so that the data from the article cannot be directly employed for this study.

[2] For a description of the method of reconstitution as first applied to such materials, cf. the unpublished doctoral dissertation of P. M. Hogan, *Wistow: A Social and Economic Reconstitution in the Thirteenth and Fourteenth Centuries*, University of Toronto, 1971.

EXTANT COURT ROLLS FOR WARBOYS[1]

1290	(Nov.)	(39754)	1332	(Dec.)	(34363)	1390	(July)	(34815)
1292	(?)	(34335)	1333	(?)	(39470)	1390	(Oct.)	(34814)
1294	(Jan.)	(39597)	1333	(Dec.)	(34919)	1391-2	(Oct.)	(179/43)
1294	(?)	(34894)	1334	(Nov.)	(39762)	1398	(July)	(34817)
1294	(Nov.)	(39755)	1337	(Jan.)	(34899)	1400	(Oct.)	(179/45)
1299	(Dec.)	(179/10)	1339	(Dec.)	(39853)	1402	(July)	(179/47)
1301	(Oct.)	(179/11)	1343	(?)	(179/31)	1403	(Oct.)	(179/48)
1301	(Oct.)	(39850)	1347	(?)	(39856)	1404	(?)	(179/49)
1305	(?)	(34774)	1349	(Nov.)	(39763)	1405	(July)	(39862)
1306	(?)	(34895)	1350	(Oct.)	(179/34)	1410	(Oct.)	(39768)
1306	(Nov.)	(39756)	1353	(?)	(179/35)	1411	(July)	(179/53)
1309	(Dec.)	(34342)	1360	(Oct.)	(39764)	1412	(Sept.)	(39769)
1313	(Jan.)	(34910)	1363	(?)	(39857)	1418	(Nov.)	(179/55)
1313	(Jan.)	(34324)	1365	(?)	(39860)	1421	(Oct.)	(39770)
1316	(Jan.)	(34897)	1369	(July)	(39473)	1423	(Nov.)	(39864)
1316	(Jan.)	(34896)	1369	(July)	(39765)	1424	(April)	(39865)
1318	(Jan.)	(39757)	1371	(?)	(39858)	1427	(Dec.)	(34370)
1320	(Jan.)	(39758)	1372	(Oct.)	(39766)	1428	(Oct.)	(179/59)
1320	(Nov.)	(34918)	1372-3	(Oct.)	(179/39)	1430	(June)	(39480)
1320	(Nov.)	(39759)	1375-6	(Nov.)	(179/40)	1434	(July)	(179/62)
1322	(Jan.)	(179/20)	1382	(Nov.)	(34306)	1440	(Jan.)	(39771)
1322	(Oct.)	(34777)	1384	(Oct.)	(34901)	1440	(Jan.)	(39772)
1325	(?)	(34898)	1386	(Sept.)	(34902)	1448	(Oct.)	(39773)
1326	(?)	(39760)	1386-8	(July)	(179/42)	1455	(Oct.)	(39774)
1331	(?)	(39761)	1387-8	(Oct.)	(39474)	1458	(Oct.)	(179/68)

[1] The five letter numbers with stroke are from ministers' accounts (Sc 6) in the Public Record Office, London; the other five letter numbers are for Additional Rolls in the British Museum. Court sessions were held twice a year, early in the calendar year without view and late in the year with the view of frankpledge. The second report for 1294 is likely a skin separated from one of the other 1294 court rolls; the two October 1301 rolls are likely parts from the same court, as are the two rolls for January 1313, January 1316, and November 1320. References to the 'above year' for 1372-3, 1375-6, 1387-8 and 1391-2 may refer to either of the two years indicated.

PART II

NUMBERS, GENERATIONS AND MOVEMENT OF VILLAGERS

Chapter II

THE LOST VILLAGERS

WARBOYS VILLAGERS APPEARING IN THE COURT ROLLS 1290-1458

The process whereby the individual villager is discovered in the court roll is painfully slow and tedious,[1] yet possible. Surnames, distinctions within one generation by Christian names as well as by the designations junior and senior, patterns of involvement in the court, as well as changes with chronology are the main factors that allow collections of a "bank" of data about villagers.[2] The following table presents a simple list in alphabetical order of those villagers identified in the court rolls of Warboys. While individual families do not necessarily parallel one another in their chronology of generations, there is a certain convenience in breaking down the first sixty-year period of the court rolls into two roughly equal periods or generations. It has long been known by historians, and there is special evidence of this for Huntingdonshire,[3] that a considerable break occurred in the population after the famine years in the second decade of the fourteenth century. For this reason, the Warboys court rolls for 1290-1318 are gathered under one generation.[4] The second generation may be practically terminated with the Black Death, that is, for these court rolls, 1320-1347.

After the Black Death the first period is determined as 1349-1376 both by the break in surviving records after 1376, as well as the fact that more

---

[1] For this reason no doubt court rolls have been the last major historical record to be critically exploited for the study of the villager. For a general survey of the historiography of the villager confer E. B. De Windt, *Land and People in Holywell-cum-Needingworth* (Toronto, 1972), Introduction.

[2] For further discussion of methodology, cf. my articles cited below in the bibliography, and De Windt, *op. cit.*, Introduction.

[3] De Windt, *op. cit.*, p. 167.

[4] The 1318 court roll is actually a mere fragment with only a score of entries, so for all practical purposes this generation is 1290-1316. On the other hand, apparently the reeve of Warboys did not have court rolls available over 1288-1289, 1289-1290, so that court fines still owing for these two years were entered in the account roll for the corresponding year. As a result, we can obtain some three-score entries from these account rolls (Add. 39671, 39672) to supplement the court rolls, although these account rolls include so few new names that court rolls remain the basis for the first generation.

permanent changes begin in village social life from the 1380's.[1] These changes assume dramatic proportions after 1400, so that the fourth period is limited to 1382-1398. The final two periods 1400-1425 and 1426-1458, are more balanced chronologically, although much the highest concentration of records survive for 1400-1412. This is most fortunate since, as we shall see below, there is corraborative evidence from account rolls that the greatest changes in village life for the first 60 years of the fifteenth century occurred for a few years after 1400.

For these six periods the following numbers of individuals have been identified from the court rolls. Only a few of the servants and others not personally identified are listed in this table for the sake of illustration. Their number does not represent the dozens of unkown outsiders, servants, etc. who were not identified in any way.

PERIOD	MEN	WOMEN	TOTAL
1290-1318:	469	162	631
1320-1347:	406	122	528
1349-1376:	308	70	378
1382-1398:	134	39	173
1400-1425:	203	47	250
1426-1458:	137	24	161

Table I

Warboys villagers appearing on court rolls 1290-1347

NAME	1290-1318	1320-1347
Above the Town, Henry	–	1326
Agath, (Egath, Egace), Robert	1294-1320	–
—, Richard	1306-1313	–
—, John, servant of Robert	1320	–
—, father of John, servant of Robert	1320	–
Ailmer, Adam	–	1326
Alan, (Alayn, Aleyn), Agnes	–	1334
—, Ralph, son of	1306-1313, 1343	–
—, Richard	–	1343
—, Robert	–	1320, 1333
—, William	1299	–

[1] Cf. *Estates of Ramsey* Abbey, and below pp. 218 ff.

NAME	1290-1318	1320-1347
Albyn, (Aubyn, Albini), Alice	—	1320-1322?
—, Beatrice	—	1320-1322
—, Cecilia	—	1320
—, Hugh, son of Robert	—	1322-1347
—, John, son of	—	1309-1339
—, Martin	—	1325-1347
—, Matilda	—	1343-1347
—, Nicholas	1294-1301	—
—, Ralph	—	1333
—, Richard	1301-1334	—
—, Robert	1305-1322	—
—, Robert, son of	—	1322-1339
—, William	—	1326-1347
Alot, Robert	—	1333-1339
Akerman, Stephen	1316	—
Ande, John	1306	—
Arnold, Thomas	1294	—
Aspelon, John	—	1334
Assebech, Beatrice	—	1339
—, John	—	1347
Ategate, John	—	1334
—, William	—	1334
Atehall, William, servant of Thomas	1316	—
Atewold, John	—	1334
Attewode, Adam	1301-1313	—
—, Agnes	—	1322-1347
—, Joan	—	1347
—, Matilda	1306	—
—, Richard	1306-1331	—
—, Robert	1313-1322	—
—, Roger	1313-1322	—
—, William	—	1320-1339
Aula, Hugh de	1289	—
—, Stephen de	1294–1301	—
—, Peter, shepherd of Stephen de	1301	—
Bailiff, Thomas, servant of	—	1334
Balde, John	—	1334
—, Thomas	—	1334
Balentyn, Simon	1301	—
Ballard, John, of Broughton	1294	—
Balle, Stephen	1306	—
Baroun, Elena	1313	—
—, John	—	1339-1343
Barre, Williiam	—	1333
Bartholomew, Godfrey, son of,	—	1326-1331

NAME	1290-1318	1320-1347
Bartholemw, Simon, son of	1305-1306	–
—, William, son of	1294	–
Bas', Nicholas	1313	–
Baseley, Agnes	1294-1299	–
Bateman, Richard	–	1347
—, Robert, of Pidele	–	1347
Beadle, Godfrey	–	1325
—, John, son of Thomas	1299-1306	–
—, Reginald	1313	–
—, Richard	1294	–
—, Richard, son of Richard	1288	–
—, Simon	1292	–
—, Thomas	1294	–
Beggar, Robert the	–	1334
Ben (r), Lawrence	–	1333
Beneyt, Cecilia	1299-1313	–
—, Hugh	1294-1347	–
—, John, son of Thomas	1294	–
—, John	–	1347
—, Nicholas	1320	–
Beneyt, Reginald	1305-1337	–
—, Richard	–	1343
Berenger, Agnes	–	1339-1347
—, Alice, wife of Robert	1320	–
—, John	1301-1309	–
—, John, son of Robert	–	1332-1347
—, Richard, son of John	1316-1334	–
—, Robert	1313-1347	–
—, Roger	–	1322
—, William	1290-1326	–
—, William, junior	–	1333-1334
—, William, son of John	1301	–
Bereshers, Nicholas	1316	–
Bernewell, John of	–	1334
Beste, John of The	–	1326
Bettes, Godfrey	–	1333-1339
Beuge, John	–	1334
Bewford, William	–	1347
Bigge, John	–	1334
Bissop (Bishop), Beatrice	1316	–
—, Emma	1316-1331	–
—, Agnes, wife of Robert	1290-1320	–
—, Robert	1288-1294	–
—, Sarra	–	1339
Blosme, John	–	1334

NAME	1290-1318	1320-1347
Blosme, Juliana	1301	–
Bodyngton, John of	–	1339
Bokeland, Henry of	–	1339-1347
Bok (Worth?), William of,	1292	–
Bolby (Boltby, Bulbe), Cristina	–	1331
—, Hugh	–	1322-1234
Bon, John le	–	1334
Bonde, Alice	–	1331
—, Benedict, son of Richard	1313-1322	–
—, Emma	–	1320
—, Joan, wife of Hugh	–	1322-1325
—, John, servant of Stephen	–	1337
—, John, son of Robert	–	1318-1339
—, John, son of Paul	–	1332
—, Juliana	1290-1316	–
—, Luke	1290-1301	–
—, Martin	1290-1294	–
—, Matilda, wife of Paul	–	1320-1322
—, Matilda	–	1339
—, Margaret, daughter of Paul	–	1320
—, Maurice	–	1320
—, Nicholas, son of Richard	1301	–
—, Paul	–	1320-1322
—, Ralph	1316-1339	–
—, Richard	1288-1309	–
—, Robert	1299-1339	–
—, Stephen, (son of Richard?)	–	1316-1339
—, William	1326-1343	–
—, William, son of Robert	–	1326
—, William, servant of Ralph	–	1334
Botelar, John	–	1334
—, John, of Broughton	–	1334
Boty't, Richard, of Fenton	1305	–
Brancaster, Alan of	1301	–
Brandon, Alice	–	1332-1334
—, John	–	1320-1331
—, William	1313-1316	–
Brgge, John atte	–	1334
Bronning, Godfrey	1309	–
—, Joan	–	1343
—, John	–	1326-1347
—, Nicholas	–	1316-1339
—, Robert	1290-1320	–
—, Simon, son of Simon	1290-1292	–
—, Simon	1288	–

NAME	1290-1318	1320-1347
Broughton, Agnes	–	1339
—, Cristina, wife of Robert	1294	–
—, John Robert, of	1294	–
—, John of	1294-1305	–
—, John, son of William of	1299	–
—, Henry of	1306	–
—, William Henry of	–	1320
—, Thomas of	1292, 1327	–
Brownote (Bronnote), Adam	–	1347
—, Robert, of Wistow	1288-1299	–
Brumeswater, (Brumes), Andrew	–	1347
—, John of	–	1343
Brun, Alice,	1289-1322	–
—, Henry	1306-1347	–
—, Joan	–	1334
—, John	–	1332-1347
—, John, servant of Henry	1318	–
—, Lawrence, son of William	1292-1294	–
—, Nicholas	1294-1325	–
—, Richard	1294	–
—, Thomas	1294-1301	–
Bryd, Cristina	–	1331-1343
—, Emma	–	1313-1343
—, Godfrey	–	1322-1325
—, Michael	–	1337
—, Richard	–	1316-1339
—, Simon	–	1320-1343
—, William	–	1337-1347
Bugge, (Bukge) Amitia	1306-1322	–
—, Godfrey	1299-1316	–
—, John	1299	–
—, Matilda	1301	–
—, Nicholas	1290-1316	–
—, Richard	1294-1334	–
—, William, son of Ralph	1294	–
Buk (Bok), Agnes	1294	–
—, Thomas	1294	–
—, Robert	–	1331-1333
—, Simon	–	1347
Bulloc, Robert	1316	–
Bumbel, Alice	–	1339-1347
—, Simon	1325	–
—, William	1316-1339	–
Buntyng, John	–	1331-1339

NAME	1290-1318	1320-1347
Burg, (Byr), John of	1294	–
—, Alice	1306	–
—, Godfrey	1306	–
—, John, son of Godfrey of	1306	–
Bus', William son of William	1313	–
Bynethetun, Richard	1301	–
Cam, John of	–	1320
—, John of, of Long Stanton	–	1320
Canne, William, of Woldhirst	–	1343
Cappe, Edward	1316	–
Carpenter, Alice, wife of Roger	1301	–
—, Reginald	1301	–
—, master Richard	1292-1301	–
—, Roger	1288-1301, (1325?)	–
— Simon,	1299	–
—, Thomas, of Woldhirst	1294	–
Carter, Alexander	1294	–
—, Joan, daughter of John	–	1322
—, John	1294	–
—, Henry the	–	1334
—, Richard	1313	–
—, Robert	1301-1305	–
—, Roger	1299	–
—, William, of the lord	–	1333-1334
—, Richard, of Broughton	–	1337
Catoun, Alice	1301-1339	–
—, Beatrice	1306-1325	–
—, Cristina	1288-1294	–
—, Hawy's	1292-1322	–
—, Hugh, son of Richard	1294-1301	–
—, John	1301-1326	–
—, John, son of John	–	1309-1347
—, Margaret, wife of John	1322-1326	–
—, Richard	1290-1333	–
—, Robert, son of Margaret	–	1326
Cecilia, Beatrice (Braciatrix)	1292-1301	–
—, Agnes, daughter of	1301-1306	–
—, Godfrey, son of	1299-1326	–
—, John, son of	1316-1333	–
—, Stephen, son of	1301-1306	–
Chamberlain, Alexander	1294	–
Chapman, Emma le	1306	–
—, Thomas	–	1347
—, William	1306-1320	–
—, wife of William	1313	–

NAME	1290-1318	1320-1347
Chatteris, Agnes of	1301	–
—, Alice of	1299-1316	–
—, Juliana of	1316	–
Chaumon, (Chamun, Cham, Champyn),		
Cristina	1313-1316	–
—, Goscelin	1294	–
—, John	–	1322-1339
—, Margaret	1306-1316	–
—, Richard	1294-1306, (1322?)	–
—, Thomas	–	1347
—, William (Taylor?)	–	1320-1347
Chop, William	1294	–
Chose, Godfrey, son of Robert	1305	–
—, Robert	1305	–
—, Roger	1305	–
Chycheley, John	–	1326-1334
—, Stephen	1306	–
Cissor, Joan	–	1320
—, Nicholas	1320-1322	–
—, Richard	–	1320
Clerk, Alice	1292-1333	–
—, Amitia, wife of Simon	1322	–
—, Beatrice, servant of William	–	1347
—, Cristina, daughter of Robert	1294	–
—, Dionysia	1306	–
—, Gilbert	–	1331-1333
—, Godfrey	1290-1301	–
—, John	1305-1343	–
—, Margaret, wife of John	–	1320-1337
—, Mariota	–	1322
—, Ralph	1292	–
—, Reginald, son of Godfrey	–	1313-1339
—, Robert of Caldecote	1294	–
—, Robert, son of Alexander	1290-1294	–
—, Robert	1290-1303	–
—, William	–	1333-1347
—, Simon	1316-1322	–
Clervaux, John	1318-1322	–
—, Michael	–	1334
—, William, son of John	–	1318-1326
Cobe, (William)	–	1343
Collesson, (Colle), Robert	–	1347
—, —, Roger	–	1333
—, —, William	–	1347
Cook, Amitia, wife of Ralph	1320	–

NAME	1290-1318	1320-1347
Cosyn, (Colyn), John	–	1333-1337
—, Thomas	–	1333-1334
Couper, Richard the	1309	–
—, Robert the	1309	–
Cous, (Cons?), Alice	–	1339
—, William	–	1322-1326
Cowherd, Agnes, daughter of Ralph	1305-1325	–
—, Agnes, daughter of Simon	–	1322
—, Emma	–	1326
—, Henry	1294	–
—, Isabella, wife of Henry (or Nicholas?)	1292-1294	–
—, Juliana	–	1347
—, Matilda	–	1322
—, Nicholas	1289-1322	–
—, Richard	–	1333
—, Robert	1290-1294	–
—, Simon	–	1320
—, William	–	1339-1347
—, William	1316-1322	–
Crane, Mariota	–	1322
—, William	–	1322-1334
—, ( )	–	1334
Cranfield, John of	1290	–
Cros, Thomas atte	–	1334
Curteys, Robert, of Wistow	1316	–
Dalebrok, (Delbrok), Andrew	–	1320
Dam, Simon ate	–	1334
Decoun, (Dekne), Mabel	–	1337
—, Simon The	1306	–
Derward, (Derworth, Derwurth), Alice	1306-1313	–
—, Beatrice	–	1331
—, Henry	–	1334-1343
—, John	1313-1320	–
—, Richard	1294	–
Dike, Alice, wife of Godfrey	–	1322-1343
—, Godfrey	–	1325-1326
—, John	–	1325-1347
—, Simon	–	1325-1347
Dourdonn	–	1331
Drake, Cecilia	–	1320
Draper, John the	–	1337
Drayton, Cristina, of	1299	–
—, husband of Cristina of	1299	–
Drewes, Lillian	–	1331

NAME	1290-1318	1320-1347
Duncepere, John	–	1337
Dunheved, Edmund	–	1337
Durant, (Durand, Derend), Cristina	–	1331
—, Emma	–	1322-1226
—, Hugh, of Warboys	1299-1316	–
Duton, William	1290	–
Dyt', Nicholas	1309	–
Ecclesiam, William, ad, of Wistow	1299	–
Edmund, William, son of	–	1320
Edward, Juliana	–	1326
—, 2 Sons of Juliana	–	1326
—, Nicholas	1305	–
—, Robert, son of Robert	1305	–
—, Roger	1305	–
—, William, son of	–	1333
Edwyne, Robert	1305-1316	–
—, Robert son of Ralph	1306	–
Elington, Alice of	–	1347
Eliot, William	–	1325
Ellsworth, Simon of	1291, 1299, 1320	–
—, John of	1320-1331	–
—, Joan, wife of John, of	1320	–
—, Nicholas, son of John, of	–	1334
Ely, John of	–	1331
Emma, Richard, son of	1301	–
Engyne, John	–	1334
Encrord, John	–	1333
Est, William, of Fenton	–	1337
Everard, Agnes, daughter of Ralph	1294	–
—, John	–	1334
Eydon, Godfrey, servant of Hugh of	1313	–
—, Hugh of	1292-1309	–
—, John, son of Hugh of	1306-1320	–
—, Matilda, widow of Hugh of	1318	–
—, Stephen of	1299	–
Faber, Agnes, wife and widow of William	1292-1322	–
—, Agnes	–	1334
—, Benedict, son of Thomas	1316-1339	–
—, Emma, wife of William	–	1339
—, Hugh	1294	–
—, Juliana, wife of Stephen	1294	–
—, Mariota	–	1339-1347
—, Matilda, wife of William	1318	–
—, Richard, son of Henry	1292-1343	–

NAME	1290-1318	1320-1347
Faber, Sampson	–	1320-1326
—, Stephen	1290-1343	–
—, William	1290-1294	–
—, William, son of William	1299-1343	–
Fabyn, (Fabian, Fabion), Edmund	–	1322
—, Edward	1316	–
—, William	1316	–
Faconn, John	–	1334
Fannel (Fennel, Fan'), John	–	1320-1343
Fekere, Alan le	1294-1299	–
—, Thomas le	1294	–
Fenreve, Simon the	1313	–
Fenton, John Aleyn, of	–	1333-1334
—, John, son of Edward of	–	1333
—, William, son of John of	1294	–
Fersonater, Stephen of	1294	–
Fikeis, John	–	1322-1334
Fine, Agnes	1301	–
—, Alan, son of R(alph)	–	1334
—, Alice, daughter of Ralph	–	1322-1325
—, Cecilia	–	1325
—, Emma	1306	–
—, John	–	1334-1347
—, Margaret	1299-1316	–
—, Matilida	1306	–
—, Phillipa	–	1347
—, Ralph	1290-1322	–
—, Richard, son of Ralph	1306-1313	–
—, Richard	1316-1333	–
—, Richard, father of Richard	1316	–
—, William	1290-1325	–
Fleming, John	–	1347
Folbe, John, son of William	–	1333
—, William	1316	–
Folyet, (Foliot, Foillet), Cristina, wife of John	1292-1294	–
—, John	1289-1309	–
—, Richard	1301-1322	–
—, Roger	–	1320
—, William	1301	–
For', Richard	1294	–
Fot, Alice	–	1343
—, Beatrice, wife of William	1305-1306, (1339!)	–
—, Godfrey	1288-1301	–
—, Hugh	–	1333-1343

NAME	1290-1318	1320-1327
Fot, Richard	–	1343
—, Robert	1305-1326	–
—, William, son of Godfrey	1294	–
—, William	1306-1333	–
Fraunceys, John, son of John	1294	–
—, Nicholas	1316	–
—, William, brother of John	1294	–
Freman, Caterina	–	1332-1334
Frere, John, son of Alexander	–	1337
Freyl, John	–	1333
Frost, William	1299	–
Gagon, Stephen	1306	–
Galewey, Thomas	–	1320
—, Walter	1294-1322	–
Galyon, Thomas	1316	–
Gardener, Matilda	–	1322
—, Nicholas	1316	–
—, Godfrey, (son of Nicholas?)	1292-1309	–
Gardener, Ralph	1294	–
—, Richard	1299	–
Gerneys, William	1306	–
Gernoun, John	–	1334
Gerold, Agnes, wife of Simon	1316-1347	–
—, Emma	1305-1306	–
—, Godfrey	1313-1347	–
—, Godfrey, jun.	–	1347
—, John, (son of Richard)	–	1333
—, Richard, sen.	1288-1290	–
—, Richard, jun.	1292-1334, (1340?)	–
—, Simon	1288-1337	–
—, Thomas	–	1333-1347
—, William	1299-1326	–
Gille, Roger	1301	–
Gocelyne, son of Godfrey of Little Raveley	1299	–
Goscelyn, Stephen	–	1325
Goselin, Thomas	–	1333
Gouceyn, Alexander	1290	–
Godfrey, Alice	1306-1331	–
—, Alice, daughter of John	1288	–
—, Hawysia, dau. of John, son of	1294	–
—, John	1313	–
—, John, son of	–	1333-1347
—, Reginald, son of	–	1325-1334
—, Richard, son of	–	1337-1347
—, Roger, son of	1301	–

NAME	1290-1318	1320-1347
Godfrey, Simon, son of	–	1331-1347
—, Sarra	1289	–
Godrych, Robert, of Woldhurst	–	1326
Godwyne, Andrew, son of Richard	1305-1306	–
—, Cecilia	1305	–
—, Matilda, wife of Richard	1306	–
—, Richard	1299-1313	–
—, ?	1290	–
Gore, John, of Broughton	1313	–
—, Thomas	–	1347
Gosse (Gost, Gosce, Gase), Alice	1313-1339	–
—, Beatrice	–	1325
—, Emma, daughter of Richard	1306	–
—, John	–	1320-1347
—, John, servant of Hayward	–	1320
—, Richard	1316	–
—, Robert	1290-1313	–
—, Simon	1292-1301	–
Gouler, Margaret, dau. of Stephen	1299-1301	–
Gray, Robert, of Niddingworth	1305-1306	–
Grendale, Agnes of	1299	–
—, Alan of	1299-1316	–
—, Joan of	–	1320-1339
—, Richard of	1305-1306	–
Grobbe, Joan	1306	–
Haliday, Margaret, wife of William	1290-1299	–
—, William	1290-1294	–
Hamemaker, Margaret the	1301	–
Harsine, Agnes, wife of Robert	1318	–
—, Cristina	–	1331-1339
—, Godfrey	1294-1320	–
—, John, (son of Cristina 1339)	–	1333-1347
—, Robert, (son of Richard, 1301, 1305)	1294-1334	–
—, William	1313	–
Haugate, (Hawegate), Alice	–	1313-1331
—, Alan ad le	1290-1322	–
—, John de	1299-1339	–
—, John, brother of Roger son of John de	1294	–
—, Margaret de	1294	–
—, mother of Roger de	1299	–
—, Ralph	1313	–
—, Ranulph	1316	–
—, Roger, son of John de	1294	–
—, Thomas	1299-1326	–
Hawys, Richard	–	1339-1347

NAME	1290-1318	1320-1347
Hayward, Alice de	1313-1331	—
—, (Hey'), Emma	1301-1322	—
—, Isabella	—	1334
—, (Messor), Richard	1294	—
—, (Hy), William	1305-1313	—
—, (Messor'), William	—	1337-1339
Henry, Richard	1316	—
—, Stephen, son of	1306	—
—, William	—	1334
Herbert, (Herberd), Alice, wife of John	1301	—
—, Godfrey	1288-1309	—
—, John	1299	—
—, Reginald	—	1333
—, Robert	—	1322-1339
—, William	1294-1313	—
Hering, John	1290-1299	—
—, Matilda	1288-1322	—
—, Matilda's husband	1306-1320	—
—, Nicholas	1301	—
Herny, Constance	1294	—
Hiche, junior, Emma	—	1322
Hill, John of the	—	1331
Hobbe, John	—	1333
—, William, of Broughton	1305	—
Hockley, Richard	1288-1290	—
Homificii (Hornsici), William	1288-1290	—
Horseman, John	1320	—
Hugh, of Upwood	1292	—
—, William, son of	—	1322
—, ? son of	—	1334
Hundreder, Alan the, of Kirkeby	1294	—
Hunne, Gilbert the	1313	—
Hunter, Emma the	1316-1322	—
—, (Godfrey) the	—	1325
Hygeney, Alice of	1325	—
—, Allotta (Tillota), of	—	1322
—, Amicia, widow (to 1299) of Robert	1294-1320	—
—, Beatrice	—	1331
—, Cecilia, wife of Roger of	— (1290)	1325-1326
—, Cristina	1294-1301	—
—, Hugh	—	1320-1326
—, John of	1292-1316	—
—, Matilda	—	1343
—, Richard	—	1332-1339

NAME	1290-1318	1320-1347
Hygeney, Roger	1294-1334	–
—, William (son of Roger, 1343)	–	1325-1347
—, William, freeman	–	1347
Hyrst, Ivo of	1290-1313	–
—, Roger of (son of Ivo, of 1320)	–	1320-1337
—, Robert, brother of Roger of	–	1332
—, William of	–	1322
—, William, son of John Raven of	–	1326
Ingram, Richard	1309	–
Isabel, Agnes	–	1331
—, Henry	1290-1320	–
—, John	1290-1294	–
—, John, son of Henry	–	1322
—, Matilda, wife of William	–	1347
—, Richard, son of Henry	–	1313-1326
—, William, son of Henry	–	1326
Jekysson, (Jekkissone, Jeksson) John	–	1343
Jewel, Juliana	–	1339-1343
John, Gilbert, son of	–	1325
—, father of Gilbert son of	–	1325
—, Nicholas, son of	1294-1309	–
Jordan, Beatrice	1299	–
Juliana, Richard, son of	1292-1299	–
? , William, son of Richard	1299	–
Justice, Adam	–	1334-1343
—, John	–	1334
—, Katherine	1289-1292	–
Katherine, (Catherine), Richard, son of	1313	–
—, William, son of	1316	–
Kaunt, Alice	–	1347
—, Andrew, son of Nicholas	1306	–
—, Henry	1292-1320	–
—, Juliana	–	1320-1331
—, Lawrence	1290-1320	–
—, Nicholas	1299-1316, (1343?)	–
—, William	1292-1301	–
—, (Yold')	–	1343
Kaye, Agnes	–	1333-1343
—, Beatrice	1306	–
—, Richard	–	1343
Keston, Matilda of	–	1333
—, husband of Matilda of	–	1333
Kocis, Robert of	–	1322
Lacy, Roger, of Houghton	1313	–
Lane, Emma in the	–	1339

NAME	1290-1318	1320-1347
Lanerok, Thomas	1316	—
Lauwe, John	—	1326
Lawrence, Andrew	—	1333
—, Benedict, son of	—	1316-1345
—, John, son of	—	1325
—, Richard, son of	—	1326
—, Simon, son of	—	1322
Lenot, Alice	—	1333-1343
—, Allota	—	1320
—, Anabella, wife of Robert	1309-1326	—
—, Benedict	1309-1332	—
—, John	(1301)	1331-1347
—, Robert	1301-1334	—
—, William, son of Robert	—	1347
Lerhert, John	—	1337
Little, John	—	1333
Lomb, William	—	1337
London, Alan of	1299	—
—, Emma, wife of William of	1290-1301	—
—, John of, porcarius	—	1322
—, Ralph, son of William of	1290-1301	—
—, Robert of	—	1339
—, Rosia of	—	1322
—, Stephen, son of William of	1301	—
—, William of	1290-1294	—
—, William (son of William of, 1301)	—	1322-1343
—, William of, at Fenton	—	1326
—, servant of William of	1290	—
Lone, Margaret	—	1347
—, Nicholas	1299-1305	—
—, Robert, son of Simon	—	1320-1322
—, Simon	1290-1316	—
—, servant of Nicholas	1301	—
—, William	—	1339-1347
—, wife of Simon	1313	—
Long, Richard	—	1339
—, Robert the	—	1337-1347
—, William the	(1294), 1316-1343	—
—, Richard, of Little Raveley	1299-1305	—
Longe Curte, Roger	1294	—
Lonik, Richard	—	1334
Lord, Emma the	—	1331
Lucas, Alice, daughter of William	1306-1322	—
—, John	1294	—
—, John, servant of Richard	1318	—

NAME	1290-1318	1320-1347
Lucas, Richard	1313-1326	–
—, Thomas	–	1347
—, William	1290-1313	–
Lytemold, Robert	1305-1306	–
Lyrtebrok (Lurtebrok, Lundbrok, Loytebrok), William	–	1339-1347
Mabel, Robert son of, of Caldecote	1301	–
Mably, Roger	1305	–
—, Robert	1316	–
Malitraz, Agnes	1313	–
Malyn, Alice	–	1333
March, William	–	1337
Margarete, (Magge, Margery), Nicholas	1290	–
—, Richard, son of Nicholas	1299-1313	–
—, Robert, brother of Richard	1299	–
—, Robert	–	1320-1347
—, Richard, son of Simon	1313-1331	–
—, Simon	1290-1301	–
—, William	–	1331
Mariot, Cristina	1288-1292	–
Martyn (Martin), Agnes	–	1339-1347
—, Henry	–	1320-1339
—, John	1292-1294	–
—, John	–	1347
—, Richard	–	1320-1347
—, Thomas, son of Benedict, of little Raveley	1299	–
Mercator, Henry	1290-1294	–
—, Hen(rietta?), wife of Henry	1290	–
—, Emma, daughter of Henry	1292	–
—, William, son of Henry	1294-1309	–
Mice, (Mise), John	–	1347
—, William	–	1339
Miller, (Molendarius, Milner), Emma, daughter of Ralph	1294	–
—, Elena, daughter of Robert	1301	–
—, sister of Elena	1301	–
—, Godfrey	–	1333-1347
—, Hugh	1294	–
—, Nicholas	1305-1306	–
—, Nicholas	–	1318-1331
—, Ralph	1290-1305	–
—, wife of Ralph	1301	–
—, Richard	1292	–
—, Robert	1301	–
—, Roger	1292	–

NAME	1290-1318	1320-1347
Miller, Walter	1313	–
—, William	–	1326-1347
—, ?	–	1331-1347
—, servants of	–	1337
—, servants of Nicholas	–	1325
Mohaut, Thomas	–	1334
Molk, Richard	–	1334
Mold (Molt), Alan	–	1326
—, Godfrey	–	1325-1350
—, Reginald, son of Godfrey	–	1334
—, William	–	1326-1339
Moke, John	1326-1339	–
—, Matilda, servant of John	1339	–
Mory, (Morite), Robert	1306-1333	–
— ? William of	–	1347
Mousichet, John, servant of John	–	1325
Mowyn, William	–	1325
Nel, (Neel), Agnes wife of Richard	1316	–
—, John	–	1316-1347
—, Juliana	–	1343
—, Richard, sen.	1294-1306	–
—, Richard	1301-1316	–
—, Simon, of Broughton	–	1334
Neweman, Robert the	1316	–
Nicholas, Godfrey, son of Matilda	1316	–
—, Joan	–	1334-1337
—, John	–	1331-1337
—, Matilda	1320	–
—, Nicholas, son of	–	1343
—, Richard, son of	–	1326-1343
—, Robert, son of	–	1337-1347
—, William, servant of John	–	1337
Noble, Agnes	1322	–
—, Alice, wife of Godfrey	–	1322-1347
—, Godfrey the	–	1320-1337
—, Richard, son of Godfrey	–	1320
—, Richard, servant of Godfrey	–	1322
—, Richard, sen.	1290-1320	–
—, Richard, jun.	–	1306-1334
—, Simon, brother of Godfrey the	–	1320-1334
Norreys, Alice	1313-1337	–
Norton, John of	–	1339
Nunne, (Nonne), Dionysia	1316-1325	–
—, Nicholas, son of William	–	1347
—, Richard, brother of William	1325-1326	–

NAME	1290-1318	1320-1347
Nunne, Robert	1313-1326	—
—, William	1299-1325	—
—, William	—	1325-1347
Odyham, Stephen of	1299-1301	—
Onty, Cristina	1294-1299	—
—, Emma	1294	—
—, John	—	1326-1333
—, Richard	1299	—
—, William	—	1334
Osbern, Cristina, sister of Nicholas	1313	—
—, Nicholas	—	1313-1344
—, Richard, father of Nicholas	1294	—
Othehill, Richard	—	1334
Pakerel, Agnes	1294	—
—, Alice	1288-1294	—
—, Alice, daughter of Lawrence	1290	—
—, Benedict, son of Lawrence	—	1320-1343
—, Cristina, daughter of Richard	1294	—
—, Gratia, daughter of Richard	1305-1306	—
—, Henry	1306-1343	—
—, Hugh	1294-1306	—
—, Lawrence	1290	—
—, Matilda	1306	—
—, Nicholas	—	1322
—, Richard	1290-1316	—
—, Richard, son of Lawrence	1309	—
—, Simon	1313-1322	—
—, William	1290-1299	—
—, William	—	1316-1347
Palfreour, (Rydeman), William the	1294-1299	—
Palmer, Agnes	—	1337-1343
—, John	—	1331-1350
—, Richard	—	1347
—, Thomas	—	1326
—, William	—	1334
Parewe, Stephen	—	1334
Patrick, Adam, of Wistow	1288	—
—, Alice, sister of Margaret	—	1334
—, Margaret	—	1334
Pellage, Thomas	—	1334
Peny, Henry	1313-1325	—
Peres, Robert	1299-1306	—
Phihe, Nicholas	—	1337
Pigman, (Porcarius), Joan, daughter of Reginald the	1294	—

NAME	1290-1318	1320-1347
Pigman, John, son of Benedict the	1313	–
—, Reginald the	–	1337
—, Robert	1294	–
—, William	–	1322
Pilche, Agnes	–	1326-1343
—, Alice (daughter of William, 1292)	1292-1325	–
—, Bartholomew	1292-1294	–
—, Emma	1292-1334	–
—, Godfrey, Hayward	1301-1305	–
—, Hugh	1299	–
—, John	–	1333-1347
—, John, son of Godfrey	–	1337
—, John, son of Simon	–	1347
—, Margaret	–	1339
—, Matilda	1299-1306	–
—, Matilda, daughter of William	–	1313-1331
—, Richard	1299-1313	–
—, Richard, servant of John de Temesford	1305	–
—, Richard	–	1337-1343
—, Robert, son of William	1301	–
—, Sarra	1309	–
—, Simon	–	1331
—, William, son of Godfrey	–	1320-1347
Pilgrim, Agnes (sister of Hawysia, daughter of William)	1292-1299	–
—, Agnes	–	1339-1347
—, Alice	1290	–
—, Alice	–	1347
—, Cristina, sister of Agnes	1292-1301	–
—, Hawysia	1299-1301	–
—, John	–	1339-1347
—, Matilda	–	1331-1343
—, Nicholas	–	1339-1348
—, Richard	1299-1339	–
—, Robert	–	1331-1333
—, Stephen	1313-1339	–
—, William	1289	–
Plumbe, Alan, servant of Richard	1306	–
—, Alice, wife of Nicholas	–	1339
—, John	–	1343-1347
—, John, jun.	–	1347
—, Nicholas	1294-1339	–
—, Richard	1306-1309	–
—, Simon	–	1339-1343

NAME	1290-1318	1320-1347
Plumbe, William	1320	–
Ponder, Alice, daughter of John, the	1305	–
—, Margaret the	1294	–
—, John the	1288-1313	–
—, Pauline, servant of John the	1294	–
Potter, William the	1306	–
Powel, Margaret	–	1320
Prat, John	1305-1309, 1339	–
Proudhele, John	–	1332
Puttok, Beatrice	1299-1339	–
—, Emma	–	1337
—, Henry	1288	–
—, Richard	1299-1320	–
—, Thomas	–	1320-1343
—, servant of Thomas	–	1331
—, Simon	1290-1309	–
Pidley, Richard of	1306	–
Querdunmyng, William	1299	–
Ralph, Robert son of	1309-1316	–
Ramsey, Robert le Glover of	–	1333
—, Nigel of	–	1325
—, Nigel Ailward of	–	1326
Raveley, William	–	1331
Raven, Alice	–	1322-1347
—, Joan	–	1331
—, John, servant of Thomas	–	1325
—, John, of Woldhurst	–	1347
—, John	–	1331-1333
—, Katherine	–	1343
—, Mariota	–	1333-1339
—, Nicholas, stepdaughter of Thomas	1316	–
—, Robert	–	1325-1347
—, Roger	–	1322-1347
—, shepherd of Thomas	–	1337
—, Thomas (sen.)	1294-1326	–
—, Thomas (jun. 1325-1326)	–	1325-1347
—, Thomas, brother of Robert	–	1326
—, Thomas, son of Hugh	–	1347
—, William	1305	–
—, William	–	1322-1347
Rede, Agnes	–	1333
—, Dulc', wife of? le	–	1334
—, John le	–	1313-1339
—, Juliana le	–	1333-1339
—, Richard	–	1343-1347

NAME	1290-1318	1320-1347
Reeve, (Prepositus), Albinus	1290	–
—, John the, of Wistow	1316	–
—, Hugh (Benyt)	1292-1299	–
—, Mabel, widow of Godfrey reeve of		
Caldecote	1290	–
—, Godfrey	1290	–
—, Thomas	1316-1326	–
—, William	1290-1334	–
Reginald, John, son of	–	1334
—, Richard, son of	1306-1322	–
—, William, son of	1309	–
Reynoke, Alice	–	1331
Reynold, Richard	–	1334-1337
—, William	–	1320-1339
Richard, Godfrey, son of	(1306)	1316-1337
—, son of Godfrey, son of	–	1325
—, John, son of	–	1339
—, Simon, son of	–	1325
Robert, Hugh	–	1334
—, Maurice, son of	1301	–
—, Richard, son of	1290-1301	–
—, Simon, son of	1301	–
—, Thomas, son of	1299-1305	–
—, William, son of	1292	–
Robyn, Beatrice		
(wife of Simon Robisson, 1322)	–	1313-1333
—, Hugh, son of Thomas	–	1333-1347
—, Margaret	–	1347
—, Robert	–	1332-1347
—, Robert, son of Thomas	–	1334
—, Thomas	1313	–
Roger, Cristina	1309	–
—, Nicholas	–	1334
—, Simon	1299	–
[Ronge Cunce], Richard	1294	–
Rolf, Cassandra, wife of William	1309-1339	–
—, Hugh	–	1343
—, John, son of William	–	1326
—, John	–	1334-1350
—, Robert, son of William	–	1320-1322
—, William	1305-1325	–
Rooleg (Rewleg'), Walter	–	1347
—, William	–	1347
Roper, Beatrice le	1318	–
—, William le	1316	–

NAME	1290-1318	1320-1347
Russel, Alan	–	1334
—, John, of Broughton	1313	–
—, Thomas	–	1334
Salbe, William	1294	–
Sarra, Emma, daughter of	1294	–
Sawere, Robert	1322-1334	–
—, William	1322	–
Sbnger, Joan	–	1343
Sculle, Alice, daughter of Juliana	1305-1306	–
—, Beatrice	1320	–
—, Robert	1294-1299	–
—, William	1294-1306	–
Scut, (Scot, Schut), Agnes, wife of (Edmund)	1320	–
—, Agnes	1309, 1322-1326	–
—, Elena	1292-1204	–
—, Godfrey	1290-1306	–
—, Godfrey	–	1331-1333
—, Henry	1288, 1316	–
—, John	1290-1333	–
—, John, jun.	–	1333-1350
—, Margaret	–	1333
—, Ralph	1288-1322	–
—, Richard	–	1333
—, Robert	1301	–
—, Thomas	–	1322-1339
—, William, son of Godfrey	1299-1316	–
Segely', (Sesely, Seteby), Albinus	1290-1301	–
—, Alice, daughter of John	1313	–
—, Benedict, brother of William	–	1322
—, John	1288-1313, (1333)	–
—, Mariota	–	1322
—, Richard	–	1313-1347
—, Robert	1316-1326	–
—, William	–	1322
—, William, son of (Richard?)	–	1347
Selome, Alexander	1309	–
Semar, Albinus (Alan?, 1305, 1313)	1290-1313	–
—, Cecilia, wife of Albinus	1290-1305	–
—, Henry	1290-1322	–
—, Juliana	1292-1343	–
—, John	–	1333-1334
—, Martin	–	1322-1339
—, Reginald	1313-1347	–
—, Richard	–	1320-1350
—, Robert	1313-1337	–

NAME	1290-1318	1320-1347
Semar, William	–	1325-1343
Seuster, John, son of Alice	–	1339
Sewar, William	–	1331
Sewyne, Richard	1305-1316	–
—, Thomas (of Woodhurst)	1316	–
Shepherd, Alice, daughter of John	–	1331
—, Emma, wife of John	1322-1332	–
—, Henry	–	1313-1339
—, John	1313-1331	–
—, Phillipa, wife of Robert	1316	–
—, Robert	1294, 1333	–
—, Roger	1299-1322	–
—, Thomas	–	1325
—, William	–	1322-1331
Simon, William, servant of	–	1332
Skynner, Alice	1288	–
—, Agnes	–	1333
—, Elena	1301-1313	–
—, John	–	1322-1343
Smart, Richard	–	1347
—, Robert	1290-1347	–
—, William, son of Robert (1320)	–	1320-1347
Smult, Emma	1294	–
Somersham, John, servant of the forester of	–	1332
—, John	–	1337
—, John, son of John of	–	1325
—, Margaret of	–	1322
—, cowherd of	1320	–
Soper, Constance the	1294	–
—, Emma the	1294-1305	–
—, William, the hayward of infirmarian	1294-1313	–
Sparhawk, Alice, wife of William	1316	–
—, William	1292-1322	–
Sperner, Bartholomew	1294-1320	–
—, Cristina	1290-1294	–
—, Juliana	1294	–
—, Lawrence	1299-1316	–
—, Matilda	1322	–
—, Margaret	1294-1301	–
—, Philippa	1306-1316	–
—, Richard	1294-1322	–
—, Robert	1292-1294	–
Sperwe, (Sparwe), Stephen	1294-1306	–
Stilke, John	–	1333

NAME	1290-1318	1320-1347
Stowe, Baldewyn of	1289	–
Stratford, Robert of	1309-1313	–
Sudbury, John of	–	1333
Sutor, Alexander	1294-1325	–
—, Henry	1294	–
—, Hugh	–	1339-1343
—, John	–	1326
—, John, son of John	–	1326
—, Reginald	1299	–
Sutton, Andrew of	?	–
—, Godfrey of	1299	–
—, Juliana of	1316	–
—, Master Lawrence	1316	–
—, Margaret, daughter of Reginald of	1301	–
—, Reginald of	1292-1294	–
—, William of	–	1343
Swan, John the (son of Robert)	1294-1299	–
—, John	–	1334
—, John, son of Henry	1292	–
—, Reginald the	–	1334
—, Richard	–	1347
—, Robert	1294	–
—, Thomas, of Wistow	–	1337
Syneker, Nicholas	–	1322
Tabard, John	1309	–
Taillour, Agnes, daughter of Nicholas	–	1339
—, Godfrey	–	1332
—, Henry	–	1347
—, Nicholas	–	1333
—, Robert	–	1334
—, Roger	–	1347
Tannator, John	1288-1306	–
Temat', Ascelin	–	1325
Temesford, John of	1322-1325	–
Thacher, Alexander	–	1322
—, Thomas the	–	1334
Therngg', (Thyringg'), Quena?	1294	–
—, Reginald of	1305	–
Thomas, John, son of	1306-1316	–
Thresher, (Threche), William	–	1334
—, (?)	–	1347
Thurberne, Ralph	1288-1290	–
—, Walter, son of Ralph	1290	–
Thurkyld, (Thurkyle), John	1313-1316	–
—, wife of John	1316	–

NAME	1290-1318	1320-1347
Tixtor, Alexander	1294-1313	–
Top, Agnes	–	1334-1343
—, Alice	–	1337
—, Cristina	1320	–
—, Godfrey, brother of Valentine	1294	–
—, John	–	1334-(1353)
—, Thomas	–	1347
—, Valentine	1294	–
—, William	1290-1294	–
—, William	–	1339-1347
Toperhyl, Thomas	1306	–
Tortorin, (Tanteryn, Tarterin), Alexander	1289-1294	–
—, John, son of Alexander	1301	–
Tra, ? Ralph	–	1322
Trille, Juliana	–	1332
Trobe, Adam	–	1320
Tymme, (Hawys?)	–	1343
—, John	–	1320-1347
—, Nicholas	–	1339
Unfrey, (Humphreys), John	1299-1320	–
—, John, (Wistow?)	–	1332-1333
—, William	–	1320-1322
Uphele, Hugh	–	1331-1334
Vicory, (Vicar), Richard	–	1326
—, William	–	1334-1347
Wake, Thomas	–	1322
Waleboy, Thomas	–	1334
—, William	1313-1316	–
Walsh, (Walys, Walse, Walche, Waysch, Whassh, Walshe), Godfrey	1294	–
—, Nicholas	1318	–
—, Reginald	–	1318-1332
—, Richard	1316-1322	–
—, Thomas	–	1331-1347
Walsoken, Margaret of	1301	–
Walter, Alice	1316	–
—, Emma, wife of William	–	1320-1339
—, Godfrey, son of Simon	1299	–
—, John, son of	1290-1313	–
—, Juliana	–	1347
—, Nicholas, son of Walter	1290-1320	–
—, Simon	–	1334
—, Thomas, son of Walter	–	1331
—, William	–	1320-1322

NAME	1290-1318	1320-1347
Warboys, John of	1316	–
—, (Boys), John of	–	1332-1337
—, Richard (Ebe) of	1292	–
—, Richard of	–	1343
—, William of	–	1331-1337
Warin, John, of Wistow	–	1326
Warwyk, Thomas of	1299	–
Webester, Agnes, daughter of Alexander	–	1343
—, Hugh the	–	1316-1347
—, John, son of Richard	–	1320-1332
—, Robert the	–	1331-1337
—, Walter	–	1334-1347
—, William	–	1339
Welle, (Dille?), William	–	1343
Wennington, John, son of Robert of	–	1316-1339
—, Ralph of	–	1339
—, Richard of	1313	–
—, Robert of	1294-1332	–
—, William of	–	1333
Weston, Thomas, servant of John	–	1334
Wilkes, Agnes	–	1331-1339
—, Henry	–	1339
—, Hugh, son of Richard	–	1320-1331
—, Joan	–	1343
—, Juliana, wife of Richard	–	1320-1347
—, Reginald	–	1331
—, Richard	–	1320-1337
—, Roger	–	1333
—, William	1299	–
—, William	–	1334-1350
William, John, son of	1299	–
—, Thomas, son of	1294-1313	–
Wilmot, William	–	1334-1347
Wistow, Adam, reeve of	1316	–
—, Agnes of	–	1339
—, Godfrey Faber (of)	1316	–
—, John, Reeve (of)	1316	–
—, Stephen, Reeve, (of)	1316	–
—, Thomas, Lanerok (of)	1316	–
—, Alexander Chamberlain (of)	1316	–
Wodekoc, Emma	1309-1322	–
—, Godfrey	1301-1331	–
—, Hawys (wife of Richard?)	1290-1294	–
—, John, son of William	1301-1339	–
—, John, jun.	–	1339-1347

NAME	1290-1318	1320-1347
Wodekoc, Richard, son of Henry (1290)	1290-1305	—
—, Richard	—	1331-1333
—, William	1290-1313	—
—, William	—	1331-1347
Wodeward, Alexander the	1288-1290	—
—, Adam, servant of Lawrence	1313	—
—, Godfrey, son of Godfrey	—	1332
—, Henry, forester of the lord	1301	—
—, Lawrence	1313-1316	—
—, Richard the	1294	—
—, Simon	—	1334
—, Walter of Glatton	1294	—
—, William, servant of	—	1322
—, William, servant of Lawrence	1316	—
Wolfeye (Wulfeye), farmer of	1306	—
—, Reginald, servant of farmer of	—	1331
Wolney, Edmund of	—	1320
Woodhurst, Nicholas, reeve of Hurst, of	1316	—
—, Robert Godrych of	1316	—
—, Robert Oky of	1316	—
—, Roger Edward of	1316	—
—, Simon the Colyer of	1316	—
—, Thomas Sewyne of	1316	—
—, William Ulf of	1316	—
—, William Sewyne of	1316	—
Woyne, John	—	1339
Wrek, Ralph	1294-1306	—
Wrench, Godfrey	1306	—
—, John	—	1320
—, Nicholas	—	1322
—, Ralph	1313	—
Wright, Thomas	—	1347
Writte, William the	1322	—
Wulle, John of	—	1332
Wymar, Agnes	1299	—
Wymark, Alice	1306	—
Wyne (Wene?), John	—	1337-1339
Wynt', Gratia	1306-1313	—
Wynton, Alice, daughter of Stephen of	1299	—
Wyr, Nicholas	1294	—
(Wycher, Godfrey, son of Simon)	1294-1313	—
(Wych, Godfrey)	1299-1313	—
Wyttawere, Thomas	—	1331
Ychener, Nicholas	—	1325

Table I

Warboys villagers appearing on court rolls 1349-1398

NAME	1349-1376	1382-1398
Abbot, William	1363	–
Adam, William	1360	–
Albyn, Agnes	–	1382
—, Emma	–	1382-1386
—, John	1349	–
—, Hugh	1350-1360	–
—, Nicholas	–	1386
—, Robert	1350-1369	–
—, Robert, servant of Robert	1365	–
Alcok, John	1360	–
—, William	1369	–
—, Richard	1353	–
Alderne, Simon of Hurst	–	1386
Alexander, John, son of	1369	–
Aleyn, Lawrence	–	1391-1392
Alot, Alice, wife of John	–	1382-1390
—, dau. of John	–	1386-1388
—, John	–	1382-1392
—, Richard	1349-1392	–
Aspelon, John	1369	–
Attecrouch, Thomas	–	1375-1376
Attegate, Robert	–	1386-1388
—, Stephen	1363	–
Attehill (Ofthehill), Agnes	–	1371-1386
—, John	–	1382-1392
—, Richard	1369	–
—, Richard, servant of John	–	1386
—, Robert	–	1384-1386
—, William	1353-1386	–
Attewell, ( )	1369	–
Attewode, John	–	1371-1390
Aubus, ( )	1369	–
Augustyn, John	1369	–
—, Simon	1369	–
—, William	–	1384
Badburgh, Robert of	1353	–
Bachelor, Ralph	1371	–
Balde, Robert	1376	–
Balle, Andrew	1365	–
—, (Alan, of Pidele)	1350	–
—, John	1369	–
Barnwell, John	–	1382

NAME	1349-1376	1382-1398
Barre, William	1349	–
Baroun, John	1349-1376	–
—, Richard	1349-1388	–
—, William sen.	1349-1388	–
—, William jun.	–	1386-1388
Basyng, William	1369	–
Bele, Alice	1360	–
—, Thomas	–	1384-1390
Beneyt, John	1349, 1375-1382	–
—, Robert	–	1375-1384
Bennesson, Richard	–	1360-1398
Bercar', John, of Wistow	–	1398
—, Roger	1369	–
Berenger, Agnes, wife of Richard	(1349), 1384-1388	–
—, Agnes, wife of John	–	1387-1388
—, Joan, dau. of Robert	1365-1369	–
—, John	1349-1388	–
—, John, of Caldecote	–	1384
—, John, of Warboys	1360-1376	–
—, Margaret	1360	–
—, Mariota	1371-1376	–
—, Richard	–	1386-1390
—, Richard, of Caldecote	–	1387-1390
—, Robert	1349-1369	–
—, William	–	1386-1392
Bettes (Bete), Joan	–	1386-1392
—, William	1353, 1387-1388	–
Bigge, John	1369	–
—, William	1372-1373	–
Bithewater, John	–	1386-1388
Bishop, Agnes	1349	–
Bochild, Godfrey	1350	–
Bodeseye, William	–	1391-1392
Bokelond, John	–	1384-1386
—, Henry	1349-1353	–
Bokkisson, John	1353	–
Bonde, (Bowde), Agnes	1375-1376	–
—, Andrew	1349-1376	–
—, husband of Juliana	–	1382
—, John	1369-1386	–
—, Juliana	–	1382
—, Robert	–	1384
—, Stephen	1350	–
—, William	1353, 1371-1376	–
Bost, (Boost'), (Boccior?), John	1363-1369	–

NAME	1349-1376	1382-1398
Botiller, William	1375-1376	–
Botild', Joan	1360	–
—, John	1360	–
Boys, (Bois), Alice	–	1382-1392
—, Ralph	1365-1398	–
—, Sarra	1349	–
Braban, Lucy	–	1390
Brampton, Robert	1371	–
Brayn, John	–	1384
—, Roger	1363	–
Brennewol, (Brennewater), John	–	1375-1382
Breustr, Beatrice	–	1390
Briesson, John	–	1375-1382
Bronnote, John	1369-1384	–
—, William	–	1391-1392
Bronnyng, John	1349-1353	–
—, John jun.	1360-1388	–
—, John sen.	–	1386-1398
—, Robert	1349-1350	–
—, Roger	1349-1350	–
Broun, (Brown), Adam	1354-1369	–
—, Alice	–	1382
—, Christina	1349-1353	–
—, Felicia	1353	–
—, father of Alice	–	1382
—, Godfrey	–	1372-1390
—, John	1369	–
—, John jnr.	–	1387-1388
—, Philipa	1353	–
—, Richard	–	1382-1390
—, Roger, servant of Christina	1360	–
—, William	1365-1371	–
Bryd, William	1349-1353	–
Buckwell, (Buckworth), Agnes	–	1390-1392
—, Thomas, servant, of Wm.	–	1382
—, William	1369-1398	–
Bunte, Thomas	–	1391-1392
Burbrigge, Joan	1350-1360	–
—, Steven	1350	–
By, Simon	–	1387
Bym ( ), Thomas	1369	–
Carter, Joan	1371	–
—, John	1349, 1363-1371	–
—, Simon	1365	–

NAME	1349-1376	1382-1398
Catoun, Joan	1371	–
—, John	1349-1392	–
—, John, of Broughton	1363-1373	–
—, servant, of John	–	1390
—, Thomas	–	1384
—, William	1349	–
Caunt, Agnes	–	1386-1392
—, Thomas	–	1390
Cecilia, Letitia	1353	–
Channtely, John	–	1384
Chapman, John	1363-1390	–
—, John jun.	–	1386-1392
—, Thomas, servant of John	–	1398
Chaumsson, (Chomissone), Agnes	1371	–
—, John	1371	–
—, William	1360	–
Child, Alice	–	1390-1392
Clampyon, John	1363	–
Clerk, Alice	1349-1353	–
Colle, Henry	1369	–
—, Richard, servant of Robert	–	1382
—, Robert	1371-1392	–
—, Thomas	1375-1376	–
—, William	1347-1363	–
Colleson, Robert	1349-1350	–
Colyer, (Collier), Alice	1360-1392	–
—, John	1349-1390	–
—, servant, of John	1350, 1365	–
Colville, William	–	1390-1398
Cotalio', Godfrey	1353	–
Cott, Thomas	1363	–
Cowherd, Peter	1350	–
—, (Joan)	1349	–
Crane, John	–	1384
—, Robert	1363	–
Croxton, John	1363	–
Dally, John	–	1387-1392
—, Thomas	1363	–
Derworth, Gilbert	1372-1391	–
—, Hugh	1353-1392	–
—, Katerina	–	1382-1392
—, William	–	1390
Dicoun, Thomas	1369	–
Dike, Alice	1349-1353	–
—, Richard	1353	–

NAME	1349-1376	1382-1398
Edward, Henry	1369, 1386	–
—, John	–	1386-1398
—, Robert	1369	–
—, Thomas	–	1398
Elington, Alice of	1349-1353	–
Elliot, John	1353, 1360	–
—, Richard	1372	–
—, Thomas	1369	–
Euge, (Eugene), John	1353, 1365	–
Eyr, Rose	–	1390-1392
—, Thomas	–	1382-1398
Farendon, ( )	1369	–
Faron, John, shepherd of Richard	1369	–
Fenton, Nicholas (Al--n), of Fenton	1363	–
—, Roger, son of Edward, of Fenton	1365	–
Ferour, William	1349	–
Fikes, John	1353	–
Fishere, John	1360	–
—, Robert	1369-1392	–
—, Simon	1363	–
Flexhower, Nicholas	1371	–
Flexman, William	1369	–
Flemyng, John	1349-1392	–
—, William	–	1375-1388
Fot, Hugh	1353, 1360	–
Forester, John	1372-1398	–
Fox, John	1369	–
—, Roger	–	1386-1388
Free, Agnes	–	1390
Fyne, (Fyn), Agnes	1349	–
—, John jun.	1353, 1360-1372	–
—, John sen.	1350-1360	–
Gandissen, Thomas	1365	–
Geffreyson, (Godfrey?), John	1372-1373	–
Gernoun, John, of Wistow	1369	–
(Gernon), Roger	–	1387
Gerold, Agnes	1349-1353	–
—, John	1349-1360	–
Gildesowe, Robert	1365	–
Godfrey, (Molt?), John, son of Godfrey	1349-1376	–
—, Alice, wife of John, son of	1350	–
—, Nicholas, of Niddingworth	1360	–
Gore, Thomas, of Broughton	1365	–
Gosse, Agnes	–	1391-1392
—, Mariota	1370	–

NAME	1349-1376	1382-1398
Gosse, Thomas	1375-1376	–
—, William	–	1382
Gouler, Benedict	1369	–
Grubbe, John	1372-1373	–
Hacon, (John?)	1369	–
Haliday, John	1363	–
Haring, John	–	1390
Harregate, Margaret	1369	–
Harsene, Alice	–	1390
—, John	1353-1376	–
—, John sen.	1360-1371	–
—, John jun.	1369-1371	–
—, William	–	1386-1392
Haulond, William, of Broughton	1365-1376	–
Hawegate, John	1372	–
Hawkinnsson, (?)	1369	–
Hawys, Richard	1349	–
Haukyn, John	1369	–
Henene, Margaret	–	1386
Henry, John	1369-1388	–
Herbin, Thomas	1369	–
Hering, John	–	1386-1398
—, John sen.	–	1390
—, John jun.	–	1392
—, (Alice)	–	1390
Herressone, (Herrisson), John	1371-1392	–
—, John jun.	–	1390
—, John sen.	–	1390-1392
—, William	1372	–
Herrow, Nicholas	1369	–
Herry, Robert	1360	–
Hervy, John	–	1386-1390
—, Thomas	–	1386
Heven, Margaret	–	1384
Hiche, Henry	1369	–
—, John, son of Robert	1375-1376	–
—, Stephen	1369	–
Hygh, (Hy), Alice	–	1386-1388
—, John	1369-1390	–
—, John jun.	–	1382-1390
—, John sen.	–	1382-1388
—, Juliana	1371-1376	–
—, Richard	1360-1390	–
—, Simon	–	1382-1398
—, William	1372-1373	–

NAME	1349-1376	1382-1398
Higeneye, Agnes	1350, 1360	–
—, William	1349-1382	–
Hikkesson, Hugh	–	1387-1388
—, John	1353-1392	–
—, John sen.	1369	–
Hirst, Roger	1349-1350	–
Hny, (Huy), John	1369-1398	–
Hobbe, Richard	1371-1372	–
Horwode, Richard	–	1390
Hugh, Thomas, son of Hugh	1363	–
Hunter, Emma	–	1390
—, Joan	–	1387-1392
—, John	1375-1376	–
—, Robert	–	1382
—, Simon, servant of Thomas	–	1386-1388
—, Thomas	1349-1350, 1363-1392	–
—, William, son of Thomas	–	1386-1388
Hythe, John of the	–	1386-1388
Janne, Agnes	1360	–
Jekkisson, John	1350, 1360-1365	–
Juesson, John	1363	–
Kaye, John	1360	–
—, Richard	1353, 1363	–
Khisson, John	1369	–
Kilpesham, John	–	1387-1388
Kirkeley, Thomas	1372-1373	–
Ladde, John	1369	–
Lambehirde, Robert	1371	–
—, Walter	–	1390
Lambt', Robert	1372	–
Lawshill, John	–	1387-1392
Lenot, Agnes, wife of John	1353, 1369	–
—, Emma	1349-1360	–
—, Gilbert	–	1391-1392
—, Joan	1350, 1382-1392	–
—, John	1349-1392	–
—, John jun.	1350-1353, 1398	–
—, John, fissher	1371-1372	–
—, Matilda	1349	–
—, servant, of John	1369	–
Lirtebrook, (Laytebrooke), William	1353-1372	–
London, (Lonedene), Richard	1360	–
—, John	1353	–
—, William	1365	–
Lone, Agnes, wife of William	1353	–

NAME	1349-1376	1382-1398
Lone, Emma	–	1386
—, John	1369	–
—, William	1349-1373	–
Lowe, William	1372	–
Lyvedon, Robert	1349	–
Make a Mayden, Alice	–	1386-1388
Margerette, ( )	–	1390
Martin, Agnes	1349-1373	–
—, John	–	1391-1392
May, Alan	1365	–
Merton, Agnes	1369-1372	–
Miles, John	1369	–
Miller, Collon	–	1382
—, John	1372-1373	–
—, Ralph	1350-1353	–
Milner, Alan	1371	–
—, John	1369	–
—, John jun.	1369	–
Molt, (Mold), Agnes	1349	–
—, Godfrey	1349-1373	–
—, John	1353-1392	–
—, John jun.	–	1382-1392
—, Richard	1350-1388	–
—, Thomas	–	1386-1388
Mons, Walter	–	1390
Nedham, John	–	1386-1398
Newell, Joan	1369	–
—, John	1371	–
Newman, Thomas	1369	–
—, William	1369	–
Nicholas, the chaplain	–	1391-1392
Niddingworth, Nicholas	1360	–
Norreys, Sarah	1350	–
—, John	1375-1376	–
Northbourgh, Henry	–	1398
—, Hugh	–	1372-1390
Nunne, Richard	1350-1388	–
—, Richard jun.	–	1390
—, Richard sen.	–	1386-1392
—, William	1372-1373	–
Oky, John	1369	–
Oliver, Agnes	1360	–
—, Henry	–	1371-1388
—, Robert	1363-1388	–
—, William	1360-1365	–

NAME	1349-1376	1382-1398
Oliver, William, servant of William	–	1398
Olneye, Henry	1372	–
Onty, John	1369	–
Orewell, John	1365-1369	–
Oryne', Mariota	1369	–
Othehiche, Thomas	–	1382
Othewold, John	1375-1376	–
Palmer, John	1350	–
Pakerel, John	1365-1376	–
—, Robert	1353	–
Payne, William	1369	–
Pege, (Page), John	1369	–
—, William	1353-1371	–
Peny, Robert	1369	–
Porcar, John	1369	–
Perrot, William	1350	–
Person, (Personage, Personous), Thomas	–	1387-1388
—, William	1363-1390	–
Phobe, Richard	1371	–
Pike, William	1371	–
Pikeler, Matilda	1369	–
Pilgrim, Alice	1360	–
—, John	1350-1363	–
—, Nicholas	1350-1373	–
—, William	–	1387-1388
Pontisbury, Richard	1363	–
Plumbe, Beatrice	1353, 1360	–
—, Joan	1375-1376	–
—, John	1365-1398	–
—, Richard	1365-1398	–
—, son of Richard	–	1391-1392
—, Thomas	–	1386-1388
Pook, son of John	1369	–
Pappeworthe, Alice	–	1391-1392
—, John	–	1386-1388
Porc', Roger	1363	–
Poulyn', Amitia	1369	–
Prat, John, of Broughton	1375-1376	–
Prestycosyn, John	–	1386-1390
Randolf, John	1369	–
Raven, Alice	1349	–
—, Godfrey	1363-1372	–
—, John	1360-1390	–
—, John, of St. Ives	–	1390
—, John, of Holywell	–	1390

NAME	1349-1376	1382-1398
Raven, John, son of Ralph	1350	—
—, John, son of Alice	1350	—
—, Katherine	1349	—
—, Richard	1363-1392	—
—, Robert, son of Thomas	1360	—
—, Thomas, servant of (Hugh)	1360	—
—, Thomas	1349-1382	—
—, Thomas jun.	1365-1371	—
—, William	1350-1363	—
—, William, son of Alice	1349-1350	—
Raveley, John	1363-1392	—
—, Robert	—	1390
Rede, Robert	1369-1373	—
—, Robert, of Wistow	—	1382
Redhoved, John	1369	—
Reginald, John	1353	—
Renale, Agnes	—	1382
Reeve, William	1360	—
Revisson, Richard	1369	—
—, Robert	—	1390
Rewall, John	1369	—
Richard, John, son of	1360	—
Rising, William	1371-1372	—
Robyn, John	1369	—
—, Margaret	1349-1369	—
—, William, husband of Margaret	1349	—
Roger, Cristina	1372	—
Rolf, Agnes, wife of John	1369	—
—, Alice	1363	—
—, Bochardus	1350	—
—, Hugh	1349-1360	—
—, Isabella, wife of Robert	1350-1360	—
—, Joan	1360	—
—, John	1350, 1369	—
—, Matilda, wife of Hugh	1353	—
—, Robert	1349-1369	—
—, William	1365	—
Ronale, Baldewyn	—	1387-1390
Rooleg, Walter	—	1382-1384
Ropere, John	—	1391-1392
Sadeler, William	1375-1376	—
Sande, Agnes	—	1372-1392
—, John	—	1371-1390
—, William	—	1372-1373
Sandisson, John	1353-1371	—

NAME	1349-1376	1382-1398
Sarrisson, Isabel	1369-1376	–
—, John	1372-1373	–
—, Ralph, son of	1363-1373	–
Saundra', John	1371	–
Sawe, John	–	1387-1388
Say, John	–	1387-1388
—, Robert	1371-1376	–
Sceme, Robert, of Fenton	–	1386-1388
Scut, Agnes	1349	–
—, John	1350-1382	–
—, Richard	1353-1392	–
—, Ralph	1372-1373	–
—, Thomas jun.	1360-1392	–
—, Thomas sen.	1349-1373	–
Segrave, Alan	1363-1371	–
(Segeley), John	1375-1376	–
Semar, Agnes, wife of William	1369-1372	–
—, Richard	1350-1398	–
—, Thomas	1349-1363, 1386	–
—, Thomas, of Caldecote	–	1382
—, William	1350-1373	–
Sewyne, Thomas	1363	–
Shepherd, Clemens	–	1390
—, Hugh	–	1386-1388
—, John, of Broughton	–	1390
—, Nicholas	–	1390
—, Richard	1360	–
—, Roger	1360-1392	–
Skite, Thomas	1363	–
Skynner, Agnes	1369	–
—, Alice	1369	–
—, Joan	1360	–
—, John	1365	–
Smart, Alice	1349	–
—, Robert	1349-1350	–
—, Simon	–	1371-1392
Smyth, William	1350-1392	–
Simon, John, son of	1353	–
Sperner, John	1375-1390	–
—, Richard	1349-1369	–
Stotenill, Godfrey	1363	–
Stukeley, Nicholas	1350	–
Strynge', John	–	1387-1388
Sudbury, Roger	1349	–
—, William	1353-1365	–

NAME	1349-1376	1382-1398
Sutor, (Soute), Agnes	1350-1371	–
—, Hugh	1371-1372	–
—, (Sewester), Joan	–	1386
Swafham, Edward	1365	–
Swan, Alice, wife of Robert	1353	–
—, Agnes	1371	–
—, Bartholomew	1349-1369	–
—, John jun.	–	1382
—, John sen.	1365-1382	–
—, Robert	1353-1373	–
—, Thomas	1353	–
Symond, William	1369	–
Taylor, Beatrice	–	1387-1388
—, Godfrey	1371-1376	–
—, Richard	–	1390-1398
—, Robert	–	1391-1392
Tame, John	1360	–
Tasker, Emma	–	1384-1388
—, John	–	1382-1390
Thacher, Alice	1375-1376	–
—, John	1371	–
Thomisson, John	1369-1376	–
—, William	1369	–
Thresher, Thomas	1360	–
—, John	–	1386
—, William	1360	–
Tineman, Roger	1350	–
Top, Richard, of Somersham	–	1386-1388
—, John (Tappe)	1353	–
Vernoun, John	1363	–
—, Richard	1363-1364	–
Vicori, Alice	–	1390
—, Robert	–	1372-1390
Walsh, Agnes, wife of John	–	1372-1390
—, John	1350, 1382	–
Walter, John	1360	–
Warboys, Richard	1369	–
Webbester, (Webbister), Agnes, wife of Thomas	–	1391-1392
—, Edwin	–	1387-1388
—, Hugh	–	1384-1388
—, John	–	1382
—, shepherd, of Hugh	–	1390
—, William	–	1382-1392
Wennington, (Wenygton), John	1369-1390	–

NAME	1349-1376	1382-1398
White, Roger	1375-1376	–
Wilkes, Beatrice	–	1382
—, John	1365-1392	–
—, John jun.	–	1383-1398
—, John sen.	–	1386-1398
—, John, son of William	1375-76 (jun?)	–
—, John, in the Lane	–	1384
—, Juliana	1350-1353	–
—, Richard	1353-1373, 1386	–
—, William	1350, 1353-1376	–
—, William, servant of John	–	1391-1392
Wilkynesson, Alexander	1371	–
William, John, son of	1369	–
—, Alexander, son of William	1371	–
Willimot, Joan	–	1371-1392
—, John	–	1371-1390
—, Thomas	1360-1392	–
Willis, ( )	1363	–
Wodekoc, William	1349-1353	–
Wolney, Henry	1369-1373	–
Wright, Agnes	–	1382-1388
—, Robert	–	1386
—, John	1375-1376	–
Wyngood, Thomas	1375-1376	–

Table I

Warboys villagers appearing on court rolls 1400-1458

NAME	1400-1425	1426-1458
Albyn, Nicholas	1404-1405	–
Alm', John, of Wistow	–	1448
Almer, Thomas, of Hemmingford	1424	–
Alot, Joan	1410	–
—, John	1402-1405	–
Altheworld, Alice, wife of William	–	1428
—, William	1403	–
Andrew, John jun., of King's Ripton	1424	–
—, John, of Somersham	–	1448
Asplond, John	–	1428
—, Richard	–	1427
Asshewode, John	–	1458

NAME	1400-1425	1426-1458
Asswell, Robert	–	1440
—, William	–	1440
Attegate, Robert	–	1428
—, Steven, of Wistow	–	1440
Attehill, (Othehill), John	1400	–
Attetownsende, Thomas	–	1440
Attewode, John	–	1448
—, Simon	1424	–
Austin, John, of Bluntisham	–	1448
—, Thomas, of Bluntisham	–	1448
Baker, John, of Huntingdon	1424	–
—, Richard, of Wistow	–	1448
Barbat, Thomas	1400-1405	–
Barford, John	–	1448
Barker, Richard	–	1448
Baroun, (Baron), John	–	1430-1458
—, John sen.	–	1458
—, John jun.	–	1458
—, Thomas	1418-1458	–
—, William	1400-1418	–
Berenger, Cristina, dau. of John	–	1440-1448
—, Joan, dau. of John	–	1440-1458
—, Joan, dau. of William	1405-1428	–
—, Joan	–	1455
—, John, son of William	–	1448-1455
—, John, medicus	–	1440
—, John, son of Richard	1418-1458	–
—, John, in the Lane	–	1448
—, John, of Hirst	–	1448
—, John, farmer	–	1455
—, John	1402-1458	–
—, John, sen.	1424-1428	–
—, John, of Caldecote	–	1440
—, John, jun.	–	1423-1448
—, Katherine, dau. of Richard, of Caldecote	1402	–
—, Katherine, dau. of Richard	–	1455-1458
—, Margaret	1400	–
—, Richard	1400-1458	–
—, Richard, son of William	–	1458
—, Thomas	–	1423-1440
—, Thomas jun., son of Richard	1418-1427	–
—, Thomas Attestownsende	–	1448
—, William, brother of Thomas Attetownsende	–	1440
—, William, son of Richard	1418-1421	–

NAME	1400-1425	1426-1458
Berenger, William	1400-1440	–
—, William	–	1458
Bek', John	1405	–
Bekewell, (alias John Fisher)	1418	–
Bele, John	–	1448-1458
—, Thomas jun.	1418-1428	–
Bene, Thomas	1424	–
Benet, John	1400-1440	–
—, Robert	1410-1421	–
—, Thomas	1404-1428	–
—, William	–	1455
Benson, (Bennesson), Alice dau. of Richard	1404-1405	–
—, John	1402-1440	–
—, John, of Caldecote	1421	–
—, Matilda	1403, 1418	–
—, Nicholas	1424-1430	–
—, Richard	1400-1448	–
—, Richard, of Caldecote	–	1430-1434
—, Thomas	–	1427-1458
—, William	1400-1428	–
—, William	–	1440-1458
Berker, Richard, of Wistow	–	1427
Blackwell, Thomas	–	1427
Bocher, Nicholas	1423	–
Bokelond, Ralph	1410-1412	–
Bokeswell, John	1410-1412	–
Boleyn, John	–	1458
Bonde, (Bounde), John, son of William	1424	–
—, John	–	1440-1458
—, Robert	1400	–
—, William	1400-1440	–
Bone, Thomas, of Wistow	–	1448-1455
Botiller, Hugh	–	1440
—, Thomas	1423	–
—, William	1400-1428	–
Bouller, Thomas	1423	–
Bowes, John	1421	–
Boys, Alice	1400-1403	–
—, John	1400-1440	–
—, Margaret, dau. of (Thomas)	1403	–
—, Richard	–	1448-1458
Brampton, John	1418-1424	–
Braseer, Thomas	–	1440
Brgge, Robert, of Wistow	–	1448

NAME	1400-1425	1426-1458
Bronnyng, (Brownyng),		
Agnes, dau. of John jun.	1418	–
—, Alice, dau. of John jun.	1418	–
—, Emma, dau. of John jun.	1418-1428	–
—, John	1400-1412	–
—, John, of Caldecote	1400-1402	–
—, John jun.	1418-1424	–
—, Margaret, dau. of John jun.	1418	–
Broun, (Brown), Agnes	1405-1421	–
—, Godfrey	1405-1421	–
—, Richard	1402-1428	–
Brt, (Brd, Byt, Byrd, Bird), Henry	–	1440-1458
Brynnewater, (Brennewater), Alice	1400-1418	–
—, John	1400-1414	–
Bukworth, Agnes	1400-1403	–
—, William	1400-1405	–
Buntyng, Thomas	–	1424-1455
—, William	–	1428
By the Water, William	1423	–
Byrere, Richard	1410	–
Caldecote, Thomas	1424	–
Catoun, John	1400-1410	–
—, John jun.	–	1440-1458
Chapman, Alice	1410-1418	–
—, John	1400-1427	–
—, Katherine	–	1455-1458
—, Simon	–	1427-1458
—, William	1424	–
Chiple, John	–	1448
Clynt, John, of Brech	1418	–
Cobbe, (Cob), Emma	–	1427-1448
—, John jun.	–	1427-1440
—, John	–	1440
Colevyll, (Coleville), John	1405-1412	–
—, Richard	1400-1428	–
—, William	1402-1455	–
Colle, John jun.	1405	–
—, Richard	1410	–
—, Robert	1400-1414	–
Colles, John	1423	–
Coppynghalle, ( )	–	1458
Corner, John jun.	1424	–
Cristyne, John, of Brech	1418	–
—, John	1413-1414	–
Dalby, John	1410	–

NAME	1400-1425	1426-1458
Dally, John jun.	1405	–
Dallyng, John	1421	–
—, Simon, parson of Holywell	1424	–
Delboys, John	1410	–
Derworth, Walter	1400	–
—, William, butcher	1400-1427	–
Edham, John	1405	–
—, Robert	1405	–
Edward, John	1400-1414	–
—, Thomas	1405-1448	–
Elys, John	–	1428
Elmesle, John	–	1427
Eyr, (Eyre), Alice, dau. of Thomas	1405-1448	–
—, Joan, dau. of Richard	1423-1424	–
—, Katherine, dau. of Richard	1423-1424	–
—, Richard	1410-1421	–
—, Thomas	1400-1423	–
Fisher, John	–	1440-1458
—, John jun.	1421	–
Flemyng, John, son of William	1405-1411	–
—, John	1412-1430	–
—, Thomas, son of John	1403	–
—, Thomas, son of William	1403-1458	–
—, William	1405-1410	–
Fordyngton, Hugh	1418	–
Fornyngton, Thomas	–	1458
Forester, John	1400-1412	–
Fraunceys, Thomas	1400-1428	–
Freeston, Agnes	–	1428
Freman, Thomas, son of William, of Ramsey	1403-1421	–
—, Thomas	1418	–
—, William	1418	–
Frere, John, of Wistow	–	1427-1448
George, Katherine	1421	–
Gerold, Emma, dau. of John	1403-1405	–
Goderke, Clemens, of Wistow	–	1448-1458
Gooselowe, John	–	1455-1458
—, Juliana	–	1455-1458
Gyles, Agnes	–	1427
—, John	–	1428
Harpour, Thomas	–	1458
Harseys, John	1403	–
Harsine, John	1402	–
—, Agnes	1405	–
Haukyn, John	–	1458

NAME	1400-1425	1426-1458
Herresson, John	1402	–
Heryng, John	1403-1427	–
—, John sen.	1402-1410	–
—, John jun.	1400-1421	–
Hethe, Roger of the	1405	–
Hry, son of Thomas, of Houghton	1403	–
Hervy, John sen.	1400-1428	–
—, John jun.	1410-1428	–
—, John, of Caldecote	1410-1411	–
—, Richard	1423-1424	–
—, Thomas	1400	–
—, William	–	1423-1440
Hewe, Thomas	–	1458
Hiche, Agnes, dau. of (Thomas)	1418-1448	–
—, John sen.	–	1427
—, John jun.	–	1427
—, Robert, of Wistow	–	1427
—, William, of Wistow	–	1427-1428
Hichesson, Agnes, dau. of Thomas	–	1440
—, John	1402	–
—, Margaret, dau. of Thomas	–	1455-1458
—, Thomas	1402	–
Hird, John	–	1428
—, Thomas	1421-1424	–
Hirst, Roger of	1402	–
Hoberd, William	1400-1410	–
—, William, of Caldecote	1411	–
Hobt, William	1405	–
Horewode, Agnes	–	1427-1448
—, Joan	1400-1428	–
—, John	1410-1458	–
—, John, constable	–	1455
—, Richard	1400-1428	–
—, William	–	1427-1430
—, William, son of John	–	1440
Horne, John, of Broughton	1423	–
Hsethe, Agnes	1403	–
Hunne, Godfrey, of Wistow	–	1428-1448
Hunter, Emma	1421	–
—, Robert	1404-1458	–
Huy, John jun. de	1403	–
Hyd, John	1411	–
Hygh, (Hy, Hye), Alice	–	1448
—, John	1413-1458	–
—, John sen.	1400-1423	–

NAME	1400-1425	1426-1458
Hygh, John jun.	1410	–
—, Katherine	1424	–
—, Simon jun.	–	1423-1440
—, Simon sen.	–	1440-1458
—, Simon	1400-1421	–
—, Thomas jun.	1421	–
Kay, John	1410	–
Lambard, Godfrey	–	1455-1458
Lavell, Richard	–	1455
Lawshill, John	1400	–
Leffen, John	1412	–
Lenot, John	1400-1418	–
—, John sen.	1400-1408	–
London, Robert	–	1434
—, William	–	1424-1458
Maddyngle, John, of Herford	1424	–
Margaret, Agnes, dau. of Richard	–	1427-1455
—, John	1413-1414	–
Martin, John	1403	–
—, John, Chaplain	–	1427
Mayke, John, Chaplain	–	1427
Merton, Lawrence	–	1434
Miller, John	1400, 1448	–
Milner, John	1403-1412	–
—, Richard	1424	–
Molt, Agnes, dau. of Thomas	1404	–
—, Agnes, dau. of John	1403, 1448	–
—, Alice	–	1448
—, Alice, dau. of Thomas	1404-1428	–
—, Alice, dau. of John	1405	–
—, John	1402-1410	–
—, Margaret	1400-1408	–
—, Margaret, dau. of Thomas	1404-1428	–
Mord, William	1418	–
Morell, Robert	–	1440-1455
Morgan, John	1402	–
Nedham, John	1405-1410	–
Newman, Agnes	1400	–
—, Alice	–	1448-1458
—, John	–	1424-1458
—, Thomas	1403-1458	–
—, Thomas, of Warboys	1403	–
—, William	–	1458
Northbourgh, Henry	1400-1430	–
—, John	1400	–

NAME	1400-1425	1426-1458
Northbourgh, ?, son of Alice	1400	—
Nunne, Richard, of Warboys	1402-1403	—
Olyver, Robert	1400-1405	—
—, William	1400-1440	—
Oundell, Joan	—	1455-1458
—, John	—	1427-1428
—, Thomas	—	1427-1448
—, William	—	1427-1430
Owty, John, son of John sen.	—	1427-1428
—, Thomas	—	1427
Pannton', Chaplain, John	1400-1402	—
Papworth, John	1405	—
Pilgrim, Alice, dau. of John	1400-1404	—
—, Margaret, dau. of John	1400-1405	—
—, William, of Wodehirst	1400-1402	—
Plombe, Joan, of Houghton	1403	—
—, John	1403-1458	—
—, John sen.	—	1440-1455
—, John jun.	1400-1458	—
—, John, son of John	1412-1440	—
—, John, of Caldecote	1410-1412	—
—, John, medicus	—	1448
—, John, son of John sen.	—	1440
—, John, brother of John, son of John jun.	—	1440
—, John, in the Lane jun.	—	1440
—, Margaret	1424	—
—, Richard	1400-1448	—
—, Richard jun.	1400-1410	—
—, William	1423	—
—, William jun., carpenter	—	1455
Pury, William	—	1458
Purdy, William, of St. Ives	1424	—
Pyper, Agnes	—	1427
Ramsey, Thomas	—	1428
Randes, (Raundes), Thomas	—	1440
Randolf, Richard	—	1448
Raundes, Robert	1421	—
Raveley, Agnes	1410-1418	—
—, Alice	1423-1424	—
—, John	1400-1418	—
—, John sen.	1400	—
—, John, son of William	—	1448
—, Robert	1400-1424	—
—, William	—	1428-1455
Raven, John	1400-1411	—

NAME	1400-1425	1426-1458
Raven, John, of St. Ives	1400	–
—, John, of Needingworth	1402	–
—, Robert	–	1427
—, Thomas	–	1455
Rector,	1424	–
Rede, Thomas, of Wistow	–	1448
Robysson, Richard	–	1440
Rolf, John, son of Robert	1400-1404	–
Samson, Roger, of Colne	–	1448
—, William, of Colne	–	1448
Sand, Agnes	1410-1428	–
—, John	–	1428-1440
—, Richard	1410-1424	–
—, William	1410-1424	–
—, William & John, sons of John sen.	–	1458
Scotenyll, Matilda	1400	–
Scut, (Skutt), John	1400-1430	–
—, John, son of John sen.	–	1424-1455
—, John, son of John	–	1455-1458
—, William, son of John	–	1448-1458
Semar, Agnes	1400-1408	–
—, Emma, dau. of (Thomas)	1403-1405	–
—, John, son of Thomas	1400-1412	–
—, Thomas, son of William	1404-1418	–
Sewale, Thomas	–	1427
Shakestaff, John	1418-1434	–
—, William	1410-1434	–
Sharp, (Scharpe), Agnes	–	1458
—, John	–	1448-1458
—, William	1405-1440	–
Shepherd, John	–	1434-1458
—, Nicholas	1418	–
—, Richard	1402-1410	–
—, Roger	1410	–
—, Thomas	–	1448
Slough, (Slegh), Margaret	1424	–
—, Robert	–	1427-1455
Smart, Simon	1410	–
—, Simon, of Caldecote	1402-1410	–
—, William	1404-1418	–
Smythe, Agnes	1410-1440	–
—, Katherine	1421	–
—, Nicholas	1421	–
—, Richard	–	1423-1455
—, Roger	1405-1440	–

NAME	1400-1425	1426-1458
Smythe, Thomas	–	1428
—, Walter, of Wistow	–	1427
—, William	1405-1424	–
Sqwyer, William	1405	–
Strugge, William	1412-1440	–
Taylor, (Taillour), Agnes	–	1448
—, John	1418	–
Templere, Nicholas	1412	–
Thakker, John	–	1430
Thacher, Alice	–	1427
Thoday, Simon, of Wistow	–	1427
Turf, Richard	1405	–
Vicory, Thomas, son of Robert	1400	–
Walgate, John	–	1428
Walies, John	1421	–
Walsshe, John, shepherd of Broughton	1412	–
Webbester, Peter	1411	–
—, Thomas, (alias Fraunceys)	1403-1405	–
Wennington, John	1400	–
Whete, Alice	–	1427-1448
—, John	–	1427-1440
Wilkes, (Wylkes), John sen.	1400-1412	–
—, John jun.	1400-1440	–
—, Richard	1410-1428	–
—, Richard, son of John	–	1424-1440
—, Thomas	–	1440-1448
—, William	–	1448
Willimot, Joan	1400	–
Wittelsey, John	1410-1423	–
—, Robert	1421-1423	–
Wodehill, John	1402-1412	–
Wodewarde, Walter	–	1427
Wolle, John, son of John	–	1440-1458
Wolley, William	–	1428
Woode, (Wode), Agnes	–	1427
—, John	–	1427
Woodward, ( )	1411	–
Wright, (Wrghte), John	1412	–
—, John, of Wistow	–	1427
—, Richard, of Wistow	–	1427
—, Robert	1421	–
—, Thomas	1405	–
Wroo, Thomas	–	1448-1458
Wyllesson, Richard	–	1427-1449

Chapter III

SURVIVALS AND NEW ARRIVALS

GENERATIONS OVER TWO CENTURIES

While varied social involvements of the villagers has required their distinct identification in the court rolls, and thereby made the construction of Table I possible, survival of the family determined the chronological extensions of these data. The next logical step, therefore, is to break down the above table according to the continuity or discontinuity of families and individuals at Warboys over the whole of our period. For the present, families alone will be considered to the exclusion of isolated individuals. For the present, too, families are taken simply from the above table, that is as more than one individual grouped under a common surname. Also excluded from the following table are non-residents of the village, a group usually indicated in one way or another in the court rolls (cf. below Tables VII and VIII).

The length and chronological pacing of generations actually vary widely from family to family and are not adequately indicated by the broad categories 1290-1318, 1320-1347, etc. In the following table, therefore, generations are reconstructed prior to 1458 as the pattern emerges for specific families. From the 1251 extent, the account rolls in the 1250's, the Hundred Roll of 1279, various account rolls from 1288 to 1458, and the early-fifteenth-century Court Book further information is supplied to complement that of the court rolls. Three early Table I names—Bumbel, Folbe and Ellsworth—only clearly emerged as families in early fourteenth-century account rolls. More importantly, the survival of a good series of land rentals from the 1370's together with the Court Book from 1399 make possible the clearer framing of generations from that time. From Table II one can see where some member of a family has continued the central rôle of the family in the village even though his or her relationship to the parents has not been indicated. In addition, however, Table II demonstrates that a great number of individuals from more important families as well as the less important failed to enter the main stream of village life. In order to indicate as much as possible this peripheral involvement in the village, where the court entry is such as not necessarily to indicate residence (e.g. trespass), and especially when there is a considerable break in information for a number of years after this type of entry, a comma rather than a dash is employed between dates.

Surnames form an adequate base for tracing the history of most families. In turn, nearly all surnames derive from the readily discernible categories of place, occupation and christian name. More information will be given on place-name derivatives in the next chapter. Many of the christian names that evolved into surnames originate before our period. A few such surnames, that begin during a generation of our period, and are not traceable to other families, are assumed to be new families rather than subdivisions of other known families in the village. For lack of evidence to the contrary, it must also be assumed that many tradesmen were newcomers to the village. Of course some christian name surnames have been able to be related to main stem families, as with Godfrey. And some tradesmen also retain the family surname; especially is this apparent for aliases *ca* 1400. For the trades carpenter, carter, chapman, smith, miller, pigman, reeve, shepherd, skinner, cobbler, taylor, webster, satisfactory family relationships for more than one or two generations do not appear, although this problem lessens after the mid-fourteenth century.

Christian names are remarkably few, as may be seen in the following list. At the same time there is a considerable shift in the christian names employed over our period. This is indicated below by the decline in the variety of christian names employed by the fifteenth century as well as the change in relative frequency for several names.

CHRISTIAN NAMES
1290-1347

MALE	No.	FEMALE	No.
Adam	7	Agnes	39
Alan	9	Alice	50
Albinus	3	Allota	2
Alexander	11	Amitia	3
Andrew	6	Anabella	1
Bartholomew	2	Ascelin	1
Benedict	5	Beatrice	17
Edmund	3	Cassandra	1
Edward	3	Caterina	1
Gilbert	3	Cecilia	7
Godfrey	37	Constance	2
Goselyn	2	Cristina	19

MALE	No.	FEMALE	No.
Henry	22	Dionysia	2
Hugh	23	Dulc'	1
Ivo	1	Elena	4
John	172	Emma	26
Lawrence	7	Gratia	2
Luke	1	Hawysia	5
Martin	2	Henrietta	1
Maurice	2	Isabella	2
Michael	2	Joan	5
Nicholas	41	Juliana	17
Nigel	2	Katherine	2
Paul	1	Lillian	1
Peter	1	Mabel	2
Ralph	15	Margaret	19
Ranulph	1	Mariota	5
Reginald	17	Matilda	22
Richard	101	Pauline	1
Robert	81	Phillipa	3
Roger	21	Rosia	1
Sampson	1	Sarah	3
Simon	34		
Stephen	20		
Thomas	51		
Valentine	1		
Walter	5		
William	149		

CHRISTIAN NAMES
1349-1398

MALE	No.	FEMALE	No.
Adam	1	Agnes	33
Alan	5	Alice	23
Alexander	2	Amitia	1
Andrew	2	Beatrice	4
Baldewyn	1	Cristiana	3
Bartholomew	1	Emma	5
Benedict	1	Felicia	1
Bochardus	1	Isabella	1
Clemens	1	Katherine	2
Collon	1	Letitia	1
Edward	1	Lucy	2

MALE	No.	FEMALE	No.
Edwin	1	Joan	15
Gilbert	2	Juliana	1
Godfrey	6	Margaret	5
Henry	7	Mariota	3
Hugh	11	Matilda	3
John	159	Philippa	1
Lawrence	1	Rose	1
Nicholas	9	Sarah	1
Peter	1		
Ralph	4		
Richard	35		
Robert	59		
Roger	13		
Simon	7		
Stephen	4		
Thomas	42		
Walter	3		
William	66		

CHRISTIAN NAMES
1400-1458

MALE	No.	FEMALE	No.
Clemens	1	Agnes	21
Godfrey	3	Alice	17
Henry	2	Cristiana	1
Hugh	2	Emma	5
John	155	Joan	9
Lawrence	1	Juliana	1
Nicholas	6	Katherine	7
Peter	1	Margaret	9
Ralph	1	Matilda	3
Richard	31		
Robert	17		
Roger	5		
Simon	9		
Stephen	1		
Thomas	49		
Walter	3		
William	50		

In Warboys these christian names were supplemented by "junior" and "senior". Occasionally, when a "junior" is first introduced, the previous member of the family is not noted in the same year, or, not being in the same context, is not noted as senior. For the following table, however, the senior is assumed in such cases to be the older member of the family with the same christian name. In similiar fashion, when both the designations "junior" and "senior" are dropped, it is assumed that the senior member has died and the younger member survived. Since the junior and senior designations usually occur for the more important families of the village, in most cases it is clear when the junior member is first getting involved publicly in the village and only gradually assumes more responsibilities. In the following table, the designation "junior", "senior", son or daughter of, are only employed when these have been used in the records throughout most of the period. In a few cases the Christian names of large families became so involved that an effort was made to distinguish further the members with the same Christian names as of Caldecote or Warboys, although Caldecote was in no real sense a hamlet distinct from Warboys.

The number of generations are synopsized in Table III. It is important to stress here that these generations have been calculated in many instances from observable activities and not from direct information about family descent. As a result, the numbers of generations are minimal. Very likely another generation actually existed for many families between the 1250's and the 1290's. Often, too, a generation has not clearly emerged for some families because of fewer surviving records. Above all is this true for the decade after the Black Death and for the last decade of the fourteenth century. Certainly the active period for some of our people is almost impossibly long (Richard Benson, 1371-1449; Richard Berenger, 1386-1458). It has not been possible to trace the transformation of first name to surname, if this has actually occurred within the village, for the early part of the fourteenth century. On the other hand, it has usually been possible to ascertain family continuation with the addition of "son", which seemed to happen in the second half of the fourteenth century (Bonde—Bondesson, Colle—Collesson, Hiche—Hichesson, Reeve—Revisson, Robyn—Robinsson, Sande—Sandisson, Sarra—Sarrison and Thomas—Thomisson). The extension of the designation junior to others than those with the same first name, employed simply to designate a younger member of the family, would seem to have become common around and after 1400 and to have been infrequent one hundred years earlier. The question of aliases appearing in the fifteenth century posed no great problems of identification.

At the same time, the trend in numbers of families at Warboys is unmistakeable. This may be seen in Table IV. For 1251 the number of families that continued to the latter part of the century is quite small, but as may be seen by the figure in brackets for that year, the actual number of families in 1251 may not have differed greatly from that of 1300. Our more complete data for the end of the thirteenth century indicates a period of rising population. The first break in this rise occurs after the famine of the second decade of the fourteenth century. From that time there is a gradual falling off until the Great Plague. The decline from the plague is not as great as might have been expected from other evidence of this time, that is something in the order of 20% rather than over 30%. The recovery in the generation after the plague seems to have brought the population of 1370 back almost to the level of 1340. From that time, however, a steady and prolonged decline set in. This was most drastic after 1400, so that by the mid-fifteenth century the population would seem to have been less than one half of that one hundred and fifty years earlier.[1]

Table II

GENERATIONAL SCHEMA OF WARBOYS FAMILIES

1251-1458

AGATH	
First Noted:	Robert 1294-1320
Second Generation:	Richard (son of Robert) 1306-1313
ALAN	
First Noted:	William 1299
	Ralph, son of 1306-1313, 1343
Second Generation:?	Agnes 1334
	Richard 1343
	Robert 1320, 1333
ALBYN	
First Noted:	Albinus, of Caldecote 1279-1290
	Nicholas 1294-1301

[1] The above remarks are based upon trends as indicated by families, estimated on the basis of one family per generation to the surname. For more precise analysis about the actual size of families in relation to the population, see below, Chapters VII and VIII.

Second Generation:	Robert 1305-1325 (d)
	Alice, wife of Robert 1325 (heriot)
	Richard 1301-1334, 1350-1353
	Cristina, dau. of Albyn 1290
	Henry, son of Albyn 1290
	John, son of Albyn 1309-1339, 1349
	Robert, (son of Albyn, of Caldecote) 1320-1369
	Agnes 1348-1349
Third Generation:	Hugh, son of Robert 1322-1360
	Alice, dau. of Robert 1320
	Beatrice, dau. of Robert 1320-1322
	Cecilia 1320
	William 1326-1347
	Martin 1325-1347
	Matilda 1343-1347
	Ralph 1333
Fourth Generation:	Agnes 1382
	Emma 1382-1386
	Nicholas 1386-1405

ALOT
First Noted:	John 1322
	Robert 1333-1339
Second Generation:	Richard 1349-1353
Third Generation:	John 1382-1405
	Alice, wife of John 1382-1390
	?, dau. of John 1386-1388
	Richard 1360-1392
Fourth Generation:	Joan 1410
	Margaret, dau. of John 1410

ALTHEWORLD
First Noted:	Alice, wife of William 1428
	William 1403-1408

ASHWELL
First Noted:	Robert 1440-1455
	Margaret, wife of Robert (widow of Wm. Olyver) 1445
	William 1440-1449

ASPLOND
First Noted:	John 1369, 1413-1414, 1428
	Thomas 1401, 1421-1422
	Richard 1427

ATTEGATE
First Noted:	Stephen 1363
Second Generation:	John 1393-1455
	Robert 1386-1428

ATTEHILL

First Noted: Richard 1369
                                      William 1353-1386

Second Generation: Agnes 1371-1386
                                      John 1377-1400
                                      Robert 1384-1408

ATTEWODE

First Noted: Richard 1251-1279

Second Generation: Godfrey 1279

Third Generation: Adam 1301-1313
                                      Matilda 1306
                                      Richard 1306-1331
                                      Robert 1313-1322
                                      Roger 1306-1322

Fourth Generation: Agnes 1322-1347
                                      Alice 1330
                                      Joan 1347
                                      Phillipa 1329-1336
                                      William 1320-1347

Fifth Generation: John 1371-1408

Sixth Generation: William 1421-1422
                                      Catherine 1411-1449
                                      Simon 1424-1455
                                      Margaret, wife of Simon 1441
                                      John 1448
                                      John, *liber* 1405
                                      Emma 1408

AUGUSTYN

First Noted: John 1369
                                      Simon 1369

Second Generation: William 1384

BAROUN

First Noted: John 1322, 1331-1376 (1393)

Second Generation: Richard 1349-1422
                                      William 1349-1388

Third Generation: William 1386-1418

Fourth Generation: Thomas 1405-1458
                                      Agnes, wife of Thomas 1423
                                      John 1393-1458
                                      Alice 1442-1449
                                      Agnes, dau. of John 1401-1411
                                      Cristina, dau. of John 1401

70

BASELEY

First Noted:	Simon 1251
	Ralph (Basille) 1251
Second (third?) Generation:	Agnes 1294-1299
	Nicholas (Bas') 1313

BEADLE

First Noted:	Richard, son of Richard 1288-1289
	John, son of Thomas 1299-1306
	Thomas 1299
	Richard 1294
	Simon 1292
	Reginald 1313
Second Generation:	Godfrey 1325-1330

BELE

First Noted:	Alice 1360
	Thomas sen. 1384-1414
Second Appearance:	Thomas jun. 1407-1446
	Robert 1413-1422
Third Generation:	John 1442-1458
	Richard, son of Thomas 1446

BENET[1]

First Noted:	Thomas, son of Benedict 1251
Second Generation:	John, son of Thomas 1294
Third Generation:	Hugh 1294-1334
	Reginald 1305-1337
	Cecilia 1299-1313
	Roger 1327
Fourth Generation:	Hugh, jun., son of Hugh 1336-1347
	Beatrice, dau. of Hugh sen. 1336
	Beatrice, dau. of Reginald 1336
	Nicholas 1320
Fifth Generation:	John 1340, 1347-1349
	Richard 1343-1348
Sixth Generation:	John 1371-1410
	Robert 1375-1425

[1] The Benson or Bennesson family obviously derive their name from Benet (Benedict) and the first names of the Benson's are often similiar to those of the Benet's. However, the two families are clearly distinguished in property, etc. from the time of the first appearance of the name Benson after the Black Death. So we assume that the Benson family entered the village at this time.

Seventh Generation:	John 1418-1449
	Thomas 1404-1440
	Joan, wife of Thomas 1414
Eighth Generation:	William 1455
	Alice, dau. of Thomas 1446
	Joan, dau. of John 1450
	Juliana 1445

BENSON (BENNESSON)[1]

First Noted:	Richard 1360-1400
	Robert 1390
Second Generation:	Alice, dau. of Richard 1404-1405
	John 1402-1449
	Agnes, wife of John sen. 1440
	John, of Caldecote 1413-1421
	Matilda 1403-1418
	Nicholas 1424-1449 (son of Richard 1400)
	Emma, wife of Nicholas 1446
	Richard 1371-1449
	Joan, wife of Richard 1446
	William 1400-1428
	Agnes, wife of William 1440
Third Generation:	Richard, of Caldecote 1415-1444
	Thomas 1427-1458
	William 1423-1458
	Agnes, wife of William 1440
	Joan, dau. of John 1442
	Florence, dau. of John sen. 1440

BERENGER

First Noted:	Richard (Berengarius) 1251
	Nicholas 1254-1255
Second Generation:	John 1279, 1301-1309
Third Generation:	William 1290-1326
	William, son of John 1301
	Richard, son of John 1316-1342
	Robert 1313-1347 (d)
	Alice, wife of Robert 1320
	Roger 1322

[1] A John Bennesson senior alias Palfreyman came to Warboys from Ramsey in 1436 and was admitted to the village with his wife Agnes, sons William and Thomas and daughter Florence.

Fourth Generation:	William, jun. (son of William) 1333-1353
	Alice, dau. of (William) 1318-1319
	Juliana, dau. of William 1325-1326
	John, son of Robert 1332-1388
	Agnes, wife of (Richard?) 1339-1349
	Agnes, wife of John 1387-1388
	Robert 1350-1369 (d)
	Thomas 1353
	John, of Warboys 1360-1376

Fourth Generation:
William, jun. (son of William) 1333-1353
Alice, dau. of (William) 1318-1319
Juliana, dau. of William 1325-1326
John, son of Robert 1332-1388
Agnes, wife of (Richard?) 1339-1349
Agnes, wife of John 1387-1388
Robert 1350-1369 (d)
Thomas 1353
John, of Warboys 1360-1376

Fifth Generation:
Margaret 1360
Joan, dau. of Robert 1365-1369
Mariota 1371-1376
Richard 1386-1390, 1400-1458
Richard, of Caldecote 1387-1390
Agnes, wife of Richard 1384-1388
William 1386-1392, 1400-1440
Joan, wife of William sen. 1426

Sixth Generation:
Joan, dau. of William 1405-1428 (Joan 1406)
John, son of Richard 1418-1458
Catherine, dau. of Richard, of Caldecote 1402, 1405-1408
Margaret 1400
Thomas, jun., son of Richard 1418-1427
William, son of Richard 1418-1421

Seventh Generation:
John sen. 1424-1428
Juliana, wife of John 1425
John 1402-1458
Alice, wife of John 1410
John jun. 1423-1448
Thomas 1413-1440
Agnes, wife of Thomas 1413
Agnes, dau. of John 1421
Emma, dau. of John sen. 1416
William jun., son of John 1425-1441

Eighth Generation:
John, son of William 1448-1455
Richard, son of William 1458
Mariota, sister of Richard 1451
John, medicus 1440
John in the Lane 1448
John, of Hirst 1448
John, farmer 1455
John, of Caldecote 1440
Cristina, dau. of John 1440-1448
Joan 1455
Catherine, dau. of Richard 1455-1458
Thomas atte Townsende 1448

William, brother of Thomas atte Townsende 1440
Emma, wife of William 1441
Joan, dau. of John 1440-1458 (John jun. 1441)
Agnes, dau. of John jun. 1440
William 1458

BETTES
First Noted: Godfrey 1333-1343 (d)
                                        Agnes, wife of Godfrey 1343 (heriot)

Second Generation: William 1353, 1387-1388
                                        Joan 1386-1392

BIGGE
First Noted: John 1369
                                        William 1372-1373

BIRD (BIRT)
First Noted: Henry 1440-1458
                                        Helena, wife of Henry 1447

BISSOP (BISHOP)
First Noted: Robert 1288-1294 (d)
                                        Agnes, wife of Robert 1292-1320

Second Generation: Beatrice 1316
                                        Emma 1316-1331
                                        Sarra 1339

BOKELOND
First Noted: Henry 1339-1353
                                        John 1384-1386

Second Generation: Ralph 1409-1412

BOLBY
First Noted: Hugh 1318-1334
                                        Cristina 1331

BOLEYN
First Noted: John 1446 (alias Weber)
                                        Alice, wife of John 1446

BONDE[1]
First Noted: Simon 1251

Second Generation: Richard 1279, 1288-1316
                                        Martin 1290-1294
                                        Luke 1290-1301
                                        Juliana 1290-1316
                                        Robert 1299-1333
                                        Agnes 1325-1326 (heriot)

[1] In the later fourteenth century this name took on the various spellings of Boonde, Bounde and Bowde. A Joan and Robert Bowde taking up property after 1400 are not clearly related to the old Bonde family, but certainly over the late fourteenth century Bowde was just a variation of Bonde.

Third Generation:	Stephen, son of Richard 1305, 1316-1350
	Nicholas, son of Richard 1301
	Benedict, son of Richard 1313-1322
	Richard, son of Martin 1313
	John, son of Robert 1318, 1339
	William, son of Robert 1326
	William 1316-1363
	?, wife of William 1316-1320
	Ralph 1316-1339
	Joan, wife of Hugh 1322-1325
	Hugh?
	Alice 1331
	Maurice 1320
	Paul 1320-1322
	Matilda, wife of Paul 1320-1322
	Emma 1320
Fourth Generation:	Margaret, (daughter of Paul 1320), 1350
	Matilda 1339
	William 1353-1379
	John 1369-1393
	Andrew 1322, 1339-1379
	Agnes 1375-1376
Fifth Generation:	Stephen 1371
	Juliana 1382
	Robert 1384, 1400-1422
	Richard 1421-1422
	John, son of William 1424
Sixth Generation:	William 1400-1449
	Joan, wife of William 1424
	John 1429-1458
	Alice, wife of John 1435
BOST	
First Noted:	John 1294-1333
	Alice 1322-1353
Second Generation:	John 1363-1379
BOTILLER	
First Noted:	William 1375-1428
	Thomas 1423
Second Generation:	Hugh 1436-1449
BOYS	
First Noted:	John 1316, 1332-1337
	Richard 1343, 1369
	William 1331-1337
	Sarra 1349

| Second Generation: | Ralph 1365-1408, 1423 |
| | Alice 1382-1403 |

Third Generation:

John (son of Ralph) 1400-1449
Juliana, wife of John 1400
Margaret, dau. of Thomas 1403
(Thomas) 1440

Fourth Generation:

Richard 1448-1458

BRAMPTON
First Noted:

John 1411-1426
Robert 1371

BRANDON
First Noted:

Emma, wife of Richard 1251
Juliana, dau. of Edith 1303

Second Generation:

William 1301-1316

Third Generation:

John 1320-1331
Alice 1318-1334 (d)

BRONNING
First Noted:

Robert 1290, 1320
Simon 1288-1292

Second Generation:

Simon, son of Simon 1290
Godfrey 1309
Nicholas 1316-1339

Third Generation:

John 1326-1360
Joan 1343
Roger 1349-1350
Robert 1349
Cristina 1349

Fourth Generation:

John 1371-1412

Fifth Generation:

John, of Caldecote 1400-1402

Sixth Generation:

John (jun.) 1386-1424

Seventh Generation:

Agnes, dau. of John jun. 1405, 1418
Alice, dau. of John jun. 1418 (d)
Emma, dau. of John jun. 1418-1428
Margaret, dau. of John jun. 1418 (d)

BRONNOTE
First Noted:

John 1369-1384, 1404-1408
William 1391-1414

BRUN (Broun)
First Noted: William 1288-1290
                                    Alice, wife of William 1288-1290
                                    Lawrence 1292-1294
                                    Nicholas 1294, 1325
                                    Alice 1294-1336
                                    Thomas 1294-1326
                                    Richard 1294

Second Generation: Henry 1306-1349
                                    John 1325-1347
                                    Felicia 1353
                                    Cristina 1353
                                    Adam 1354-1369
                                    Philip(a) 1353

Third Generation: Alice 1382
                                    Godfrey 1372-1422
                                    Agnes, wife of Godfrey 1416
                                    John (jun.) 1369, 1387, 1400
                                    William 1365-1378

Fourth Generation: Richard 1382-1428
                                    Agnes 1427, 1442-1449
                                    Robert 1413-1422

Fifth Generation: John 1435-1449

BRYD
First Noted: Richard 1316-1339
                                    Emma, wife of Richard 1313-1343
                                    Godfrey 1322-1325
                                    Cristina 1331-1343

Second Generation: Simon, son of Richard 1324-1345 (fugitive)
                                    William 1337-1353
                                    Michael 1337

BUCKWORTH
First Noted: William 1369-1405
                                    Agnes 1390-1403

BUGGE
First Noted: William, son of Ralph 1294
                                    Richard 1294-1299
                                    Nicholas 1290-1316, 1337
                                    Amitia 1306-1322
                                    John 1299
                                    Godfrey 1299-1316
                                    Matilda 1301

BUK
First Noted: Richard 1251

Second (third?) Generation: Thomas 1294
                                                Agnes 1294
                                                Ralph 1306

Third Generation: Robert 1331-1333
                                                Simon 1347
                                                Richard 1332

BUNTYNG
First Noted: Thomas 1424-1455
                                                Isabella, wife of Thomas 1431
                                                William 1428

BURBRIGGE
First Noted: Joan 1350-1360
                                                Steven 1350

BRYNNEWATER
First Noted: John 1375-1422
                                                Alice 1400-1418

BURG
First Noted: John 1294
                                                Alice 1306
                                                Godfrey 1306
                                                John, son of Godfrey 1306

BYTHEWATER
First Noted: William 1423
                                                John 1386-1388, 1425
                                                Catherine, wife of John 1425

CARPENTER
First Noted: Simon 1251
                                                William, brother of Simon 1251

Second (third?) Generation: Roger 1294-1301
                                                Alice, wife of Robert 1301
                                                Reginald 1301
                                                Simon 1299

Third Generation: Richard 1292-1325
                                                John 1332

Second Appearance: Hamond 1425

CARTER
First Noted: John 1349-1378
                                                Joan 1371
                                                Simon 1387
                                                Nicholas 1347-1348

CATOUN
First Noted: Richard 1279, 1290-1313 (1322, 1333?)
                                                Cristina 1292-1294

Second Generation:	Hugh, son of Richard 1294-1301 John, son of Richard 1309, 1301-1326 Margaret, wife of John 1322-1326 (heriot) Hawysia 1292-1322 Beatrice 1306-1325 Alice 1301-1320
Third Generation:	John, son of John 1326-1370 Alice (wife of John?) 1320-1339 William 1349
Fourth Generation:	Emma 1373-1377 John 1370-1422, 1449 John, of Broughton 1363-1373 Thomas 1384 Joan, wife of John 1371-1405
Fifth Generation:	John (jun.) 1413, 1416, 1440-1458 Margaret 1413-1425

CECILIA

First Noted:	Cecilia 1292-1301
Second Generation:	Godfrey, son of Cecilia 1299-1326 Stephen, son of Cecilia 1301-1306 Agnes, dau. of Cecilia 1301, 1306 John, son of Cecilia 1316-1333
Third Generation:	Alice, dau. of Godfrey 1318-1319 Cristina, dau. of Godfrey 1329-1330 Letitia 1353 Richard 1332

CHAPMAN

First Noted:	Emma 1306 William 1306-1320
Second Generation:	Thomas 1347
Third Generation:	John 1363-1390
Fourth Generation:	John jun. 1386-1427 William 1424 Alice 1410-1418, 1435
Fifth Generation:	Catherine, wife of Simon 1435-1458 Simon, son of John 1427-1458

CHAUMON

First Noted:	Richard 1294-1306, 1322 Margaret, wife of Richard? 1306-1316 Goscelin 1294

Second Generation:	Agnes, wife of William (?) 1353, 1371
	Cristina 1313-1316
	John 1322, 1339, 1363, 1371
	Thomas 1347
	William 1320-1343, 1360

CHILD

First Noted:	Alice 1390-1394
	Thomas 1378

CHOSE

First Noted:	Roger 1305
	Robert 1305 (d)
	Godfrey, son of Robert 1305

CHYCHELEY

First Noted:	Stephen 1306
Second Generation:	Godfrey 1320
	John 1326-1334
	Cristina 1347-1348

CLERK

First Noted:	William 1251
Second Generation:	Godfrey 1279, 1290-1301
	Robert 1288-1305
	Alice 1292-1306
Third Generation:	Reginald, son of Godfrey 1313-1339
	Cristina, dau. of Robert 1294
	Dionysia 1306
	Simon 1316-1322
	Amitia, wife of Simon 1322
	John 1305-1349
	Margaret, wife of John 1320-1337
Fourth Generation:	William 1331-1347
	Gilbert 1331-1333, 1339
	Alice 1333-1353
Second Appearance:	Agnes, wife of John 1421
	John 1421

CLERVAUX

First Noted:	John 1318-1322
Second Generation:	William, son of John 1318-1326
	Michael 1334

COBBE

First Noted:	Emma, wife of John 1425
	John jun. 1427-1455
	John sen. 1425-1440

COLLE (COLLESSON)
First Noted: Roger 1333
                                      Richard 1347-1348
                                      Robert 1342-1388

Second Generation: Henry 1369
                                      William 1348, 1360-1363
                                      Thomas 1375-1376

Third Generation: Robert 1390-1414
                                      Richard 1410

Fourth Generation: John jun. 1404-1405

COLIER (COLLIER)
First Noted: William sen. 1339-1347
                                      John 1350-1353
                                      Alice 1348-1350

Second Generation: John 1349-1390
                                      Alice 1350-1392

COLEVILLE
First Noted: William 1390-1423
                                      John 1405-1412

Second Generation: William 1393-1455
                                      Alice, wife of William 1407
                                      Richard 1400-1449

CORBETT
First Noted: John 1441
                                      Robert 1441

COSYN
First Noted: Thomas 1333-1334
                                      John 1333-1337

COUS
First Noted: William 1322-1326
                                      Alice 1339

COWHERD
First Noted: Richard 1254-1255

Second (third?) Generation: Robert 1290-1316
                                      Nicholas 1294-1322
                                      Isabella, wife of Nicholas 1294
                                      Henry 1294
                                      Isabella, wife of Henry 1292
                                      Simon 1320
                                      Agnes, dau. of Ralph 1305-1309

Third Generation:	William 1316-1347
	Agnes, dau. of Simon 1322-1325
	Emma 1326
	Matilda 1322
	Richard 1333
Fourth Generation:	Juliana 1347
	Peter 1350

CROXTON

First Noted:	Joan, wife of John 1439
	John 1439

DALLY (DALLYNG)

First Noted:	John 1387-1422
	Thomas 1363
Second Generation:	John jun. 1404-1422
	Emma, wife of John jun. 1409

DERWARD

First Noted:	Richard 1294
	Alice 1306-1313
Second Generation:	John 1313-1320, 1348-1363
	Beatrice 1331
	Henry 1334-1343
Third Generation:	Hugh 1353-1405
Fourth Generation:	Gilbert 1372-1391
	Catherine 1382-1392
Fifth Generation:	William 1390-1427
	Joan, wife of William 1401
	Walter 1400

DIKE

First Noted:	Alice, wife of Godfrey 1322-1353
	Godfrey 1322-1347
	Simon 1325-1348
	John 1325-1326
Second Generation:	Richard 1353

DURAUNT

First Noted:	Duraunt' 1251
Second (third?) Generation:	Hugh 1299-1316, 1318
	Emma 1322-1326
	Cristina 1331

EDWARD

First Noted:	Henry 1369-1394 (d)
	Robert 1369
Second Generation:	John 1386-1414

| Third Generation: | Thomas, son of John 1398-1449 |
| Fourth Generation: | Alice, dau. of Thomas 1406 |

EDWYNE

| First Noted: | Robert, son of Edwin 1251 |
| | Ralph, brother of Robert, son of Edwin 1251 |

| Second (third?) Generation: | Robert 1305-1316 |
| | Robert, son of Ralph 1306 |

ELLIOT

First Noted:	John 1353, 1360
	Richard 1372
	Thomas 1369

ELLSWORTH

First Noted:	Simon of 1292, 1299, 1320
	John of 1320-1331
	Joan, wife of John of 1320
Second Generation:	Nicholas, son of John of 1334

ELY (ELYS)

| First Noted: | Richard of Ely 1413-1422 |
| | John 1428 |

EVERARD

| First Noted: | Alice, wife of John 1410 |
| | John 1410 |

EYR

| First Noted: | Thomas 1382-1423 |
| | Rose 1390-1392 |

| Second Generation: | Richard (alias Geffreyson) 1406-1422 |

Third Generation:	Alice, dau. of Thomas 1405-1448
	Joan, dau. of Richard 1423-1424
	Catherine, dau. of Richard 1423-1424

EYDON

First Noted:	Hugh 1292-1309
	Matilda, widow of Hugh 1318
	John, son of Hugh 1306-1320
	Stephen 1299

FABER (SMYTH)

First Noted:	William 1251
	Bartholomew, son of John 1251
	Walter 1251
	William, son of Ralph 1251

Second (third?) Generation:	William 1290-1294
	Agnes, wife of William 1289-1322
	Richard, son of Henry 1292-1301
	wife of Richard 1301
	Stephen, son of Henry 1290-1306
	Juliana, wife of Stephen 1294
	Hugh 1294
Third Generation:	William, son of William 1299, 1316-1350
	Emma, wife of William (jun.) 1339
	Matilda, wife of William (jun.) 1318
	Benedict, son of Thomas 1316-1339
	Richard, (son of Richard?) 1331-1347
	Stephen, (son of Stephen?) 1325-1343
	Mariota 1339-1343
	Sampson 1320-1326
	Simon 1320
Fourth Generation:	William 1363-1375
Fifth Generation:	William 1392-1455
	Agnes 1410-1440
	Catherine 1421
	Nicholas 1421
	Roger (alias Raven) 1404-1455
Sixth Generation:	Richard 1401-1455
	Catherine, wife of Richard 1401
	Thomas 1428
	Walter (alias Raven) 1421-1455
	Robert, son of Roger 1442-1449
	Juliana, wife of Robert 1445

FEKER

First Noted:	Walter 1251
Second (third?) Generation:	Thomas 1294
	Alan 1294-1299

FINE

First Noted:	Robert 1251
Second (third?) Generation:	William 1290-1325
	wife of William 1290
	mother of William 1313
	Margaret 1299-1325 (heriot)
	Agnes 1301
	Matilda 1306
	Emma 1306
	Ralph 1290-1325
	Richard, father of Richard 1316

84

Third Generation:	Richard, son of Ralph 1306-1334
	Alice, dau. of Ralph 1322-1325
	Cecilia 1325
Fourth Generation:	Alan, son of R(ichard?) 1334
	Phillipa 1347
	Agnes 1349
	John sen. 1334-1377
Fifth Generation:	John jun. 1353-1375

FISHER

First Noted:	John 1360
	Robert 1369-1392
	Simon 1363
Second Generation:	John 1440-1458
	John jun. (alias Bekwell) 1421
Third Generation:	Thomas 1450
	Catherine, wife of Thomas 1450

FLEMING

First Noted:	John 1347-1392
Second Generation:	John 1407-1430
	William 1375-1410
Third Generation:	Thomas, son of William 1403-1458
	John, son of William 1405-1411
	Thomas, son of John 1403

FOLYET

First Noted:	Simon 1251
Second (third?) Generation:	John 1279, 1289-1309
	Cristina, wife of John 1290-1294
	Richard 1301-1322
	Roger 1320
	William 1301

FORDYNGTON

First Noted:	Hugh 1413-1450
Second Generation:	Thomas, son of Hugh 1450-1458
	Joan, wife of Thomas 1450

FOT

First Noted:	Godfrey 1288-1301
Second Generation:	William, son of Godfrey 1294-1333
	Beatrice, wife of William 1305-1306, 1339
	Robert 1305-1326
Third Generation:	Hugh 1333-1375
	Alice 1343
	Richard 1343

FRAUNCEYS[1]
First Noted: Alice 1251
                                            John 1254-1255

Second (third?) Generation: William 1294, 1318
                                            John, son of John 1294
                                            William, son of John 1294
                                            Nicholas 1316

Second Appearance: Thomas 1400-1428

FREMAN
First Noted: Thomas 1418
                                            William 1418

Second Generation: Thomas, son of William, of Ramsey 1403-1421
                                            Alice 1418

GALEWAY
First Noted: Walter 1294-1322
                                            Thomas 1320

Second Generation: Beatrice, dau. of Walter 1318-1319

GARDENER
First Noted: Anabelle 1279

Second Generation: Godfrey, (son of Richard?) 1292-1302
                                            Ralph 1294
                                            Richard 1299
                                            Nicholas 1316
                                            Matilda 1322

GERNOUN
First Noted: John 1334
                                            Agnes 1332

GEROLD
First Noted: Richard 1251
                                            Cristina 1251

Second (third?) Generation: Richard sen. 1288-1290

Third Generation: Richard jun. 1292-1334
                                            Matilda, dau. of Richard 1303
                                            Simon 1288-1337
                                            William 1299-1326
                                            Agnes, wife of Simon 1316-1337
                                            Emma 1305-1306
                                            wife of William 1326

[1] The Thomas Webester alias Fraunceys noted in 1403/1405 may be the Thomas Fraunceys
of this generation, although the alias only appears for 1405.

86

Fourth Generation:	Agnes 1333-1353
	Godfrey 1306-1347
	John, son of Richard 1333
	Thomas 1333-1347
	Nicholas 1325-1326
	Cristina, dau. of Richard 1336
	Juliana, dau. of William 1318-1319
	Agnes, dau. of Simon 1324-1325

| Fifth Generation: | Richard 1347-1354 |
| | Godfrey jun. 1347 |

| Sixth Generation: | John 1349-1379 |

| Seventh Generation: | Emma, dau. of John 1403-1405 |
| | Robert 1377-1408 |

GODFREY (MOLT?)

First Noted:	Alice 1306-1331
	John 1313, 1333
	Roger 1301
	Hawysia, dau. of John, son of 1294
	Sarra 1313

GODWYNE

First Noted:	? Godfrey 1290
	Richard 1299-1313
	Matilda, wife of Richard 1306
Second Generation:	Andrew, son of Richard 1305-1306

GOOSELOWE

| First Noted: | John 1455-1458 |
| | Juliana 1455-1458 |

GOSSE

| First Noted: | Godfrey 1251 |

Second (third?) Generation:	Robert 1290-1313
	Simon 1292-1301
	Richard 1316-1319

Third Generation:	Emma, dau. of Richard 1306
	Alice, (wife of John) 1313-1347
	John 1320-1347
	Beatrice 1325

Fourth Generation:	Mariota 1370
	Thomas 1375-1379
	William 1382
	Agnes 1391-1392

GRENDALE

First Noted:	Alan 1299-1316
	Agnes 1299
	Richard 1305-1306

Second Generation:	Joan 1320-1339
	husband of Joan 1337-1339
GYLES	
First Noted:	Agnes 1427, 1431
	John 1428-1449
HALIDAY	
First Noted:	Benedict 1251-1255
Second Generation:	William 1279, 1290-1294
	Margaret, wife of William 1288-1299
Second Appearance:	John 1363
HARSINE	
First Noted:	William 1251
	Richard 1251
Second Generation:	Godfrey 1294-1320
	Robert, son of Richard 1294-1334
	Agnes, wife of Robert 1318
	Cristina 1331-1339 (d)
Third Generation:	William 1313, 1344-1346
	John, (son of Cristina) 1333-1379
Fourth Generation:	John 1369-1408
	Alice 1390
	William 1386-1394
	Agnes 1405
	Catherine 1400
HAUGATE	
First Noted:	Alan 1290-1322
	Alice 1313-1331
	mother of Roger 1299
	Margaret 1294
	Thomas 1299-1326
Second Generation:	John, brother of Roger, son of John 1294-1339
	John, son of Alice 1324-1325
	Roger, son of John 1294
Third Generation:	John 1372
	Margaret 1369
HAYWARD	
First Noted:	Richard 1251
Second (third?) Generation:	Alice 1313-1331
	William 1313
	Richard 1294
Third Generation:	William 1337-1340

HENRY[1]
First Noted: Robert 1251
                                      Thomas 1251
                                      John 1251

Second (third?) Generation: Stephen 1306
                                      Richard 1316
                                      William 1334

Third Generation: Robert (Herry) 1360

HERBERT
First Noted: Herbert, ad finem ville 1251
                                      Cecilia 1251
                                      Robert, son of 1251
                                      Robert 1251

Second (third?) Generation: Alice, wife of John 1301
                                      John 1299, 1318
                                      Godfrey 1288-1309
                                      William 1294-1313 (1326-1334?)

Third Generation: Reginald 1333
                                      Robert 1322-1344
                                      Agnes, wife of Robert 1344-1345 (heriot)

HERING
First Noted: Matilda 1288-1322
                                      husband of Matilda 1306-1322
                                      John 1290-1299
                                      Nicholas 1301

Second Appearance: John 1386-1410
                                      Alice 1390

Second Generation: John jun. 1390-1455

HERRESSONE
First Noted: John 1371-1392
                                      William 1372

Second Generation: John jun. 1390-1402

HERVEY
First Noted: John (sen.) 1369-1428
                                      Thomas 1386, 1400

---

[1] It is clear from various sources that this name re-appears in the third quarter of the fourteenth century and evolves into Herresson. However, since there is no linkage possible between the Henry family of the earlier part of the fourteenth century and that appearing almost a generation after the Black Death, it is assumed that these are different families. Property entries from the 1370's also make it clear that the Hervy and Herresson families are distinct.

Second Generation:	John jun. 1403-1428
	Richard 1423-1424
Third Generation:	William 1423-1441

HICHESSON (HICHE)[1]

First Noted:	Henry 1369
	Stephen 1369
	John 1348-1369
Second Generation:	John (son of Robert in 1375) 1363-1394
	Hugh 1387-1388
Third Generation:	Thomas 1401-1414
	John 1400-1427 (sen.)
Fourth Generation:	Agnes, dau. of Thomas 1418-1448
	Margaret, dau. of Thomas 1455-1458
	John jun. 1427

HIDE

First Noted:	Thomas 1413-1422
	William atte, of Bury 1407
	Catherine, wife of William atte 1407
Second Generation:	William 1442-1455

HOREWODE

First Noted:	Richard 1390-1428
	Joan 1400-1428
Second Generation:	John 1410-1458
Third Generation:	Agnes 1427-1448
	William 1427-1449

HUNTER

First Noted:	Emma 1316-1322
	G(om) 1325
Second Generation:	Thomas 1349-1405
	John 1375-1376
	Emma 1390-1421
Third Generation:	Robert 1382 (1440)
	Agnes, wife of Robert 1416
	William, son of Thomas 1386-1388
Fourth Generation:	Robert 1442-1458
	Thomas 1443

---

[1] From the second generation of this family Hiche and Hichesson alternate as the surname making it difficult to trace the generations, especially with respect to the first name John.

HYGH (HY, HEY)[1]

First Noted:
Emma 1301-1322
William 1305-1313
Isabella 1334

Second Generations:
Richard 1353, 1360-1408
John 1369-1390
Juliana 1371-1376

Third Generation:
John jun. 1382-1390, 1400-1423 (sen.)
Simon 1379-1422
Alice 1386-1388
William 1372-1373

Fourth Generation:
Agnes 1408
John 1404-1458
Catherine, wife of John 1408-1424
Thomas jun. 1421
John, of Wolney 1413-1422

Fifth Generation:
Alice 1448
Simon sen. 1406, 1423-1458
Simon jun. 1407-1455

HYGENEY

First Noted:
William 1279

Second Generation :
Amitia, widow of Robert 1290-1320
Cecilia, wife of Roger 1325
Roger 1294-1334
Cristina 1294-1301, 1326
John 1292-1316

Third Generation:
Allotta 1322
Alice 1325
Beatrice 1331-1347
Hugh 1320-1326
Matilda 1343
Richard 1332-1339
William 1325-1343

Fourth Generation:
William 1349-1382
Agnes 1350, 1360

Fifth Generation:
Alice 1407-1408

HYRST

First Noted:
Ivo 1251, 1279

---

[1] This name was difficult to distinguish from the short form for Hayward around 1300, as may be seen in col. 1. of Table I above.

Second (third?) Generation:	Ivo 1290-1313
	Simon 1292
Third Generation:	Roger, son of Ivo 1320-1350
	Robert, brother of Roger 1332
	William 1322
	Roger 1350, (1398-1402)

ISABEL

First Noted:	John 1290-1294
	Henry 1290-1320
Second Generation:	John, son of Henry 1322
	Richard, son of Henry 1313-1326
	William, son of Henry 1326
	Agnes 1331
	Matilda, wife of William 1347

JEKKISSON

First Noted:	Agnes, wife of John 1371-1379
	John 1343-1365

JOHN

First Noted:	Richard 1251
	William 1251
	Walter 1251
	Martin 1251
	Nicholas 1251
Second Generation:	Nicholas 1294-1309
Third Generation:	Gilbert 1325

JULIANA

First Noted:	Richard 1292-1299
	William 1299

KATHERINE

First Noted:	Katerina 1251
Second (third?) Generation:	Richard 1313
	William 1316

KAUNT (CAUNT)

First Noted:	Lawrence 1290-1320
	Henry 1292-1320, 1334
	Nicholas 1299-1316 (1343?)
	William 1292-1301
Second Generation:	Alice 1347
	Andrew, son of Nicholas 1306
	Juliana 1320-1331
	Richard 1306, 1322-1333
Second Appearance:	Thomas 1371-1405
	Agnes 1386-1392

KAYE
First Noted: Beatrice 1306, 1318-1319

Second Generation: Agnes 1333-1343
                                          Emma 1327
                                          Richard 1343-1379

Third Generation: John 1360

Fourth Generation: John 1410

LAMBEHIRDE
First Noted: Robert 1371-1377
                                          Walter 1390

LAWRENCE
First Noted: Simon 1322
                                          Benedict 1316-1339
                                          John 1325
                                          Richard 1326
                                          Andrew 1333

Second Appearance: William 1404
                                          John, of Stanton 1444

LENOT
First Noted: Robert 1301-1326
                                          Anabelle, wife of Robert 1309-1326
                                          Benedict 1309-1332
                                          John 1301

Second Generation: Allota 1320
                                          Alice 1333-1343
                                          Robert, (husband of Alice?) 1331-1339, 1350-1353
                                          John 1331-1349

Third Generation: William, son of Robert 1347
                                          Matilda 1349

Fourth Generation: John, of Caldecote 1350-1392
                                          Emma 1349-1379
                                          John, of Warboys 1353, 1371-1375
                                          Agnes, wife of John, of Warboys 1353
                                          Joan 1350
                                          Juliana 1373-1377
                                          John, fisher 1371-1372
                                          John jun. 1360, 1399-1408 (d)
                                          Joan, wife of John jun. 1399

Fifth Generation: Joan 1382-1392
                                          Gilbert 1391-1392
                                          John 1398-1422

LONDON
First Noted: William 1279, 1290-1294
                                          Emma, wife of William 1290-1301

Second Generation: Ralph, son of William 1290-1301
                                          William, son of William 1301, 1322-1343, 1360
                                          Stephen, son of William 1301
                                          Alan 1299

Third Generation: John 1322, 1353
                                          Robert 1339
                                          Rose 1322
                                          William, at Fenton 1326

Fourth Generation: Richard 1360

Fifth Generation: Robert 1425-1455

Sixth Generation: William 1421-1458

LONE
First Noted: Simon 1290-1316
                                          wife of Simon 1313
                                          Nicholas 1299-1305

Second Generation: Robert, son of Simon 1320-1322
                                          Hugh, son of? 1324-1327
                                          William 1339-1373
                                          Agnes, wife of William 1353
                                          Margaret 1347

Third Generation: John 1369
                                          Emma 1386
LONG
First Noted: William 1294-1343

Second Generation: Richard 1339
                                          Robert 1337-1347
LUCAS
First Noted: Lucas 1251

Second Generation: William 1279, 1290-1313
                                          John 1294

Third Generation: Alice, dau. of William 1306-1322
                                          Richard 1313-1326, 1334

Fourth Generation: Thomas 1347

MABLY
First Noted: Roger 1305
                                          Robert 1313-1316

MARGARETE
First Noted: Simon 1290-1301
                                    Matilda, wife of Simon 1306-1307 (heriot)
                                    Nicholas 1290

Second Generation: Richard, son of Nicholas 1299-1313
                                    Robert, son of Nicholas 1299, 1320-1347
                                    Richard, son of Simon 1313-1331
                                    William 1331

Second Appearance: Agnes, dau. of Richard 1404, 1427-1455
                                    John 1410-1414

MARTYN
First Noted: John 1292-1294, 1316

Second Generation: Henry 1320-1339
                                    Agnes 1339-1373
                                    husband (Richard?) of Agnes 1339-1343
                                    Richard 1307, 1320-1347

Third Generation: John 1347
                                    John 1391, 1403-1405
                                    John, chaplain 1427

MERCATOR
First Noted: Henry 1290-1294
                                    wife of Henry 1288-1290

Second Generation: Emma, dau. of Henry 1292
                                    William, son of Henry 1294-1309

MICE
First Noted: William 1339
                                    John 1347
                                    Agnes 1334

MILLER
First Noted: Ralph 1290-1305
                                    wife of Ralph 1301
                                    Richard 1292
                                    Robert 1301
                                    Roger 1292
                                    Hugh 1294

Second Generation: Elena, dau. of Robert 1301
                                    ?, sister of Elena 1301
                                    Emma, dau. of Ralph 1294
                                    Godfrey 1333, 1347
                                    William 1326, 1347
                                    Nicholas 1305-1331
                                    Walter 1313

95

MILNER (MILLER)
First Noted: Ralph 1350-1353
                                      John 1369, 1372-1373
                                      John jun. 1369
                                      Alan 1371
                                      Collon 1382

Second Generation: Richard 1424
                                      John 1400-1448
MOKE
First Noted: John 1326-1339
                                      Richard 1334
                                      Matilda, servant of John 1339

MOLT[1]
First Noted: Godfrey 1325-1377
                                      Alan 1326
                                      William 1326-1345 (d)
                                      Agnes, widow of William 1345-1349

Second Generation: Reginald, son of Godfrey 1325-1334
                                      Simon, son of Godfrey 1331-1347
                                      John, son of Godfrey 1333-1379
                                      Richard, son of Godfrey 1337-1388
                                      Alice, wife of John 1350

Third Generation: John jun. 1378-1392
                                      Thomas 1386-1388

Fourth Generation: John 1402-1455
                                      Agnes, dau. of Thomas 1404
                                      Alice, dau. of Thomas 1404-1428
                                      Margaret, dau. of Thomas 1404-1428
                                      Agnes, dau. of John 1403, 1408
                                      Alice, dau. of John 1405
                                      Margaret 1400-1408

Fifth Generation: Alice 1448

MORY
First Noted: Robert 1306-1333
Second Generation: William 1347
Third Generation: Robert 1377

[1] The second generation of this family seems to be made up of four sons of Godfrey and bears no identifiable relationship with the Godfrey family that disappeared after the first generation of the fourteenth century. Identification remains difficult, however, because the father (Godfrey) lived a long life so that his sons became frequently known as 'sons of Godfrey' only rather than 'of Godfrey Molt'. There are no distinctions between John Molt jun. and John Molt sen. in the fifteenth century, so very likely there was another John in the fifth generation.

NEL
First Noted: Richard sen. 1294-1313

Second Generation: Richard 1301-1316
                                      Agnes, wife of Richard 1316

Third Generation: John 1316, 1325-1347
                                      Juliana 1343
NEWELL
First Noted: Joan 1369
                                      John 1371

NEWMAN
First Noted: Thomas 1369
                                      William 1369
                                      Agnes 1400 (d)
                                      Emma, wife of Thomas 1424

Second Generation: Thomas 1403-1449
                                      Alice 1448-1458
                                      John 1424-1458

Third Generation: William 1458
                                      Thomas jun. 1442-1458
                                      Alice, wife of Thomas jun. 1439

NICHOLAS
First Noted: John 1309, 1331-1337
                                      Matilda 1316-1320
                                      Godfrey, son of Matilda 1316

Second Generation: Richard, son of 1326-1343
                                      Robert, son of 1337, 1347-1349
                                      Joan 1334-1337
                                      Nicholas, son of 1343

NOBLE
First Noted: Richard 1251
                                      William, brother of Richard 1251
Second (third?) Generation: Richard 1290-1320

Third Generation: Richard, son of Richard 1306-1334
                                      Simon, brother of Godfrey 1320-1334
                                      Godfrey 1318-1337
                                      Alice, wife of Godfrey 1322 (1347)
                                      Richard, son of Godfrey 1320
                                      Agnes 1322
                                      John 1324-1325

NORREYS
First Noted: Alice 1313-1337

Second Generation: Sarra 1350

Third Generation: John 1373-1379

NORTHBOURGH

First Noted: Hugh 1371-1422
Henry 1398-1449

Second Generation: John 1400-1405

NUNNE

First Noted: William 1299-1325 (d)
Dionysia (wife of William) 1316-1325

Second Generation: William 1325-1347
Richard, brother of William 1325-1326 (1350)
Robert 1313-1326

Third Generation: Nicholas, son of William 1347
Richard 1350-1394
William 1372-1373

Fourth Generation: Richard 1401-1422
Richard, of Warboys 1402-1403
Richard jun. 1378-1408

ODE

First Noted: John 1426
Anna, wife of John 1426

OLIVER

First Noted: Agnes 1360
Henry 1371-1388

Second Generation: Robert 1363, 1377-1408

Third Generation: William (1360) 1371-1433
Margaret, widow of William 1445

Fourth Generation: William 1450

ONTY

First Noted: John Oty 1251

Second Generation: Cristina 1294-1299
Emma 1294
Richard 1299

Third Generation: John 1326, 1333, 1369

ORDEMAR

First Noted: John 1415
Joan, wife of John 1415

OUNDELL

First Noted: John 1427-1428

98

Second Generation:	Thomas 1427-1448
	William 1423-1455
	Cristina, wife of William 1423
	Joan 1455-1458

PAGE (PEGE)

First Noted:	John 1369
	William 1353-1371

PAKEREL

First Noted:	William 1251

Second Generation:	Alice 1288-1294
	William 1290-1299
	Lawrence 1290
	Richard 1290-1316

Third Generation:	William (son of William?) 1316-1347
	Benedict, son of Lawrence 1320-1345
	Richard, son of Lawrence 1309
	Alice, dau. of Lawrence 1290
	Cristina, dau. of Richard 1294
	Gratia, dau. of Richard 1305-1306
	Hugh 1294, 1306-1308
	Henry 1306-1343
	Matilda 1306
	Nicholas 1322

Fourth Generation:	Robert 1353
	John 1365-1379
	Alice 1373-1378
	Juliana 1371
	Joan?

PALMER

First Noted:	John 1325-1350, 1371
	Agnes 1337-1343
	Thomas 1326
	William 1334
	Richard 1347
	Adam 1332

PELLAGE

First Noted:	Thomas 1334
	Simon 1332

PERSON

First Noted:	Thomas 1387-1388
	William 1363-1390

Second Generation:	John 1442-1449

PIGMAN
First Noted:

Robert 1294
Joan, dau. of Reginald 1294
John, son of Benedict 1313

Second Generation:

Reginald 1337
William 1322
Roger 1363

PILCHE
First Noted:

Ralph 1251
William 1251

Second (third?) Generation:

Godfrey 1301-1305
Alice, dau. of William 1292-1325
Matilda, dau. of William 1299-1331
Robert, son of William 1301
Emma 1292-1334
Sarra 1309
Hugh 1299
Richard 1299-1313, 1337-1343
Bartholomew 1292-1294

Third Generation:

John, son of Godfrey 1333-1347
William, son of Godfrey 1320-1325
Nicholas, son of Margaret 1303, 1320, 1325
Simon 1331
Agnes 1326-1343
Margaret 1339

Fourth Generation:

Beatrice 1347-1348
John, son of Simon 1347

PILGRIM
First Noted:

Ralph 1251
William 1251-1255

Second (third?) Generation:

Alice 1290
William 1289-1290, 1326

Third Generation:

Agnes, dau. of William 1292-1299
Cristina, sister of Agnes 1292-1301
Hawysia, sister of Agnes 1299-1301
Richard 1299-1339
Stephen 1313-1339

Fourth Generation:

Alice 1347
Agnes 1339-1347
John 1339-1363
Matilda 1331-1343
Nicholas 1339-1347, 1360-1379
Robert 1331-1333

Fifth Generation:	Alice, dau. of John 1360-1404 (d)
	William 1387-1404
	Margaret, dau. of John 1400-1405

PLUMBE

First Noted:	Alan 1251
	Simon 1251, 1279
Second (third?) Generation:	Nicholas 1294-1339 (d)
	Alice, wife of Nicholas 1339
	Richard 1306-1309, 1347
Third Generation:	Simon 1339, 1343
	John 1343-1347
	John jun. 1347
	William 1326
Fourth Generation:	John 1371-1422
	John (jun.) 1347-1398
	Joan 1375-1376
	Beatrice 1360
	Richard 1365-1410
Fifth Generation:	Thomas 1386-1388
	John, of Caldecote 1410-1412
Sixth Generation:	John 1393-1458
	John jun. 1400-1458
	John, son of John, of Caldecote 1412-1440
	Margaret 1424
	Richard jun. 1400-1449
	William 1423
Seventh Generation:	John sen. 1400-1455
	John medicus 1448
	John, son of John sen. 1440
	John, brother of John sen. 1440
	John in the Lane jun. 1440
	William jun., carpenter 1455
	Thomas, son of John 1448

PONDER

First Noted:	William 1254-1255
Second (third?) Generation:	John 1288-1313
	Margaret 1294
Third Generation:	Alice, dau. of John 1305

PRESTECOSYN

First Noted:	Henry 1378-1409
	John 1378-1408

PUTTOCK
First Noted: Alexander 1251

Second (third?) Generation: Simon 1290-1309, 1313
                                       Henry 1288-1289
                                       Richard 1299-1320
Third Generation: Beatrice 1299-1320, 1339
                                       Thomas 1320-1343

RANDOLF
First Noted: John 1369

Second Generation: Richard 1448

RAVELEY
First Noted: John 1363-1408

Second Generation: William 1401-1425
                                       Robert 1390-1424
                                       Agnes 1410-1418 (1416 wife of Robert)
                                       Alice 1423-1424
                                       John 1400-1418

Third Generation: Joan, wife of William jun. 1446
                                       Margaret, dau. of Robert 1445
                                       William (jun. 1424), 1428-1449

Fourth Generation: John, son of William 1448
                                       Juliana, dau. of William 1442

RAVEN
First Noted: Robert 1251

Second (third?) Generation: Thomas 1294-1335
                                       William 1305

Third Generation: Thomas (jun.), son of Thomas 1325-1371
                                       Agnes, dau. of Thomas 1303
                                       Nicholas, stepson of Thomas 1316
                                       Robert, brother of Thomas 1326-1347
                                       Roger 1322-1347
                                       Alice 1322-1349
                                       William 1322-1379
                                       Joan 1331
                                       Mariota 1333-1339
                                       John 1325-1333
                                       Katherine 1343, 1349
                                       Thomas, son of Hugh 1347, 1360
                                       John, son of Ralph 1350
                                       John, son of Alice 1350
                                       William, son of Alice 1350

Fourth Generation:	Thomas (jun.) 1365-1382
	John 1360-1390
	Robert, son of Thomas 1360
	Richard 1363-1392
	Godfrey 1363-1372
Fifth Generation:	John 1400-1411
	Robert 1411-1449
	Emma, wife of Robert 1426
	William 1411
Sixth Generation:	Thomas 1455

REDE

First Noted:	John 1306-1339
	Juliana (wife of John?) 1333-1339
Second Generation:	Agnes 1333
	Dulciora, wife of 'M' 1334
	Richard 1343-1347
Third Generation:	Robert 1369-1373
Fourth Generation:	John 1378-1405
	Amitia, wife of John 1378-1394

REEVE

First Noted:	Richard, son of Ralph 1251
Second (third?) Generation:	William 1290-1334
	Albinus 1290
	Hugh 1292-1299
	Mabel, widow of Godfrey 1290
	Thomas 1316
Third Generation:	Mable, dau. of Godfrey 1290

REGINALD

First Noted:	William 1309-1339
	Richard 1306-1337
Second Generation:	John? 1353

REVISSON[1]

First Noted:	Richard 1369
	Robert 1390
Second Generation:	Richard 1442-1455

[1] There is a considerable time break between the appearance of this family and the disappearance of the Reeve family, and nothing to suggest that they are related.

RICHARD
First Noted: William, son of 1299
                                      Godfrey 1306-1337

Second Generation: Dionysia, dau. of Godfrey 1329-1330
                                      ?, son of Godfrey 1325
                                      Simon 1325
                                      John, son of 1339, 1353-1360

ROBYN (ROBERT)
First Noted: Walter, son of Robert 1251
                                      Thomas, son of Robert 1251

Second (third?) Generation: Richard, son of Robert 1290-1301
                                      William, son of Robert 1292
                                      Thomas, son of Robert 1299-1313
                                      Simon, son of Robert 1301
                                      Beatrice, wife of Simon 1313-1333
                                      Maurice, son of Robert 1301

Third Generation: Hugh, son of Thomas 1333-1347
                                      Robert, son of Thomas 1332-1347
                                      Margaret 1347-1369
                                      William, husband of Margaret 1349
Fourth Generation: John 1369

ROGER
First Noted: Godfrey 1251

Second (third?) Generation: Cristina 1309
                                      Simon 1299

Third Generation: (?), son of Simon 1318-1319
                                      Nicholas 1334

ROLF
First Noted: William 1305-1325
                                      Cassandra, wife of William 1309, 1320-1339

Second Generation: Robert, son of William 1320-1369
                                      Isabella, wife of Robert 1350-1360
                                      Agnes, wife of Robert 1371
                                      Agnes, wife of John 1339, 1369
                                      Hugh 1343-1360
                                      Mariota 1334
                                      Matilda, wife of Hugh 1353
                                      John, son of William 1326-1369

Third Generation: Alice 1363
                                      Joan 1360
                                      William 1365
                                      John, son of Robert 1400-1404
                                      Beatrice, dau. of Hugh 1400

ROPERE
First Noted: John 1391-1392
                                         Robert 1379

SANDE[1]
First Generation: John 1371-1390
                                         Agnes 1372-1392
                                         William 1372-1373, 1410-1424

Second Generation: Richard 1410-1424
                                         John, son of William 1424-1449
                                         Agnes 1428-1440
                                         Emma, dau. of William 1416

Third Generation: William, son of John sen. 1458
                                         John, son of John sen. 1458

SARRISON
First Noted: Ralph, son of Sarra 1363-1373
                                         John 1372-1373
Second Generation: Isabella, dau. of Ralph 1375-1376

SAWERE
First Noted: Robert 1322, 1334
                                         William 1322
Second Appearance: John 1387-1388

SCULLE
First Noted: Richard 1251

Second (third?) Generation: William 1294-1306
                                         Robert 1294-1299
Third Generation: Alice, dau. of Juliana 1305-1306
                                         Beatrice 1320

SCUT
First Noted: John 1290-1294 (1325-1333?)
                                         Elena 1292-1294
                                         Godfrey 1290-1306 (1331-1333?)
                                         Ralph 1288-1322
                                         Henry 1288-1316
                                         Agnes 1318 (heriot) – 1326
                                         Robert 1301

Second Generation: John jun. 1333-1382
                                         William, son of Godfrey 1299-1316
                                         Thomas 1322-1379
                                         Sarra 1335-1336 (heriot)

---

[1] John Sandisson 1353, 1371, may have been the same John Sande noted in 1371-1390 when
he was a junior, but there is no clear proof of this, and if the same person his active life would
have been extraordinarily long.

Margaret 1325-1326 (1333)
Richard 1333-1392
Agnes 1349, 1371-1377

Third Generation:

Ralph 1372-1373
Thomas jun. 1360-1392

Fourth Generation:

John 1400-1430

Fifth Generation:

John, son of John sen. 1421-1455 (d)

Sixth Generation:

John, son of John 1455-1458
William, son of John 1438-1458
Emma, dau. of John 1432

SEGELEY
First Noted:

Albinus 1290-1301
John 1288-1313, 1333
William 1306-1322
Benedict, brother of William 1322

Second Generation:

Alice, dau. of John 1306-1313
Mariota 1322
Robert 1316-1326
Richard 1313-1347

Third Generation:

William, son of Richard 1347

SEMAR
First Noted:

Godfrey 1251
Martin 1251

Second (third?) Generation:

Albinus 1290-1306 (1313)
Cecilia, wife of Albinus 1292-1305
Henry 1290-1322
Juliana 1292

Third Generation:

William, son of Albinus 1306, 1325-1350
Richard 1320-1353
Reginald 1313-1342
Robert 1313-1337
Martin 1318-1339
Juliana 1343
John 1333-1334
Roger 1327

Fourth Generation:

William 1360-1375
Agnes, wife of William 1369-1372
Thomas 1349-1378, 1386
Reginald 1371-1394
Richard 1360-1398

Fifth Generation:	John, son of Thomas 1400-1412 Agnes 1400-1408 Emma, dau. of Thomas 1403-1405 Thomas, son of William 1404-1418 Roger 1404-1408

SEWYNE

First Noted:	Richard 1305, 1316 Thomas 1316, 1363

SHAKESTAFF

First Noted:	John 1413-1455 William 1407-1449

SHARPE (SCHARPE)

First Noted:	William 1405-1455 Agnes, wife of William 1414
Second Generation:	John, son of William 1441-1458 Agnes 1458 Agnes, wife of John 1447

SHEPHERD

First Noted:	Stephen 1251
Second (third?) Generation:	Robert 1294-1333 Roger 1299-1322 Phillipa, wife of Roger 1316 John 1313-1332 Emma, wife of John 1322-1332
Third Generation:	Alice, dau. of John 1331 Henry 1313, 1339 Richard 1334, 1360 Thomas 1325 William 1322-1331
Fourth Generation:	Roger 1360-1422 John 1371-1379 Clemens 1390 Hugh 1386-1388 Nicholas 1390, 1422
Fifth Generation:	John 1434-1458 Richard 1402-1410 William 1421-1422
Sixth Generation:	Joan, wife of Thomas (Catelyn) 1434 Thomas 1448
Seventh Generation:	Walter, son of Thomas 1434

SIST'NE
First Noted: Richard 1407-1408
                                    Robert 1404-1405
                                    Roger 1371-1408

Second Generation: Beatrice, wife of Richard 1419
                                    Richard, son of Robert 1419

SKYNNER
First Noted: Osbert (Skyny) 1251

Second (third?) Generation: Alice 1288-1289
                                    Elena 1301-1313

Third Generation: John 1322-1343
                                    Agnes 1333
                                    husband of Agnes 1333
                                    Agnes 1369
                                    Alice 1369
                                    Joan 1360
                                    John 1365

SLOUGH (SLEGH)
First Noted: Margaret 1424

Second Generation: Robert 1427-1455

SMART
First Noted: Robert 1290-1350

Second Generation: William, son of Robert 1320-1347
                                    Alice 1349
Third Generation: Richard 1347

Fourth Generation: Simon 1371-1408

Fifth Generation: Simon, of Caldecote 1402-1410
                                    William 1400-1449

SON
First Noted: John 1371-1378
                                    Robert 1371-1379
                                    Thomas 1377

Second Generation: Richard ?

SOPER
First Noted: Emma 1294-1305
                                    father of Emma 1294
                                    Constance 1294
                                    William 1294-1313

SPARHAWK
First Noted: William 1292-1322
                                      Alice, wife of William 1316

SPERNER
First Noted: Ralph (Sperver) 1251
                                      Hugh (Sperver) 1251

Second (third?) Generation: Cristina 1290-1294
                                      Juliana 1294
                                      Margaret 1294-1301
                                      Bartholomew 1294-1320
                                      Lawrence 1299-1316
                                      Richard 1294-1322
                                      Robert 1292-1294
                                      Phillipa 1306-1316

Third Generation: Matilda 1322
                                      Stephen 1320-1334
                                      Richard 1349-1369

Fourth Generation: John 1375-1390

STRUGGE
First Noted: William 1412-1449
                                      Margaret, wife of William 1425

SQWYER
First Noted: John 1413-1422

Second Generation: William 1407-1440

SUTOR
First Noted: Robert (Souter) 1251

Second (third?) Generation: Alexander 1295-1325
                                      Henry 1294
                                      Reginald 1299

Third Generation: Hugh 1339-1375
                                      John 1326
                                      John, son of John 1326
                                      Agnes 1350, 1360, 1371

SUTTON
First Noted: Reginald 1292-1294
                                      Juliana 1316
                                      Godfrey 1299
                                      master Lawrence 1316
Second Generation: Margaret, dau. of Reginald 1301
                                      William 1343

SWAN
First Noted: Robert 1294

Second Generation: John, son of Robert 1294-1299, 1334
                                                Thomas, son of Richard 1294, 1320-1353
                                                Reginald 1334
                                                Richard 1347
                                                Sarra (dau. of Hawysia?) 1306-1307

Third Generation: Bartholomew 1349-1394
                                                Robert 1353, 1372-1373
                                                Alice, wife of Robert 1353
                                                John 1365-1394

Fourth Generation: John jun. 1382
                                                Agnes 1371

TAYLOR (TAILLOUR)
First Noted: Richard 1320
                                                Godfrey 1332
                                                Nicholas 1320, 1322-1333
                                                Joan 1320

Second Generation: Agnes, dau. of Nicholas 1339
                                                Robert 1334
                                                Roger 1347
                                                Henry 1347

Third Generation: Godfrey 1371-1379

Fourth Generation: Beatrice 1387-1388
                                                Richard 1390-1422
                                                Robert 1391-1405
                                                John 1418

Fifth Generation: Agnes 1448
                                                Reginald 1441-1449

TASKER
First Noted: John 1382-1390
                                                Emma 1384-1388

THACHER
First Noted: Alice, wife of John 1375-1427
                                                John 1371

Second Generation: Elena, wife of John 1444
                                                John 1444

THOMISSON
First Noted: John 1369-1376
                                                William 1369-1375

THRESHER
First Noted: Thomas 1360
                                      William 1360
                                      John 1386

THURBERNE
First Noted: Ralph 1288-1290

Second Generation: Walter, son of Ralph 1290
                                      William, son of Ralph 1303

Third Generation: Robert, son of William 1303
                                      Simon, son of Godfrey 1325-1326

THURKYLD
First Noted: John, son of William 1307-1316
                                      wife of John 1316

TONYNGTON
First Noted: John 1423
                                      Richard 1423
                                      Mariota, wife of Richard 1423

TOP
First Noted: William 1290-1294
                                      Valentine 1294
                                      Godfrey, brother of Valentine 1294

Second Generation: Alice 1337
                                      Agnes 1329-1343
                                      Cristina 1320
                                      John 1334
                                      Thomas 1347
                                      William (1339), 1347
                                      John (Tappe) 1353

TORTORIN
First Noted: Alexander 1289-1313

Second Generation: John, son of 1301

TYMME
First Noted: John 1320-1347
                                      Nicholas 1339
                                      Hawysia 1343

UNFREY
First Noted: heirs of William 1251

Second (third?) Generation: John 1299-1333
                                      William 1320-1322
                                      Alice 1332

VERNON
First Noted: John 1363
                                      Richard 1363-1364

VICORY
First Noted: William 1329-1347
                                                      Richard 1326

Second Generation: Robert 1372-1390
                                                      Alice 1390

Third Generation: Thomas, son of Robert 1400

WALSH
First Noted: Godfrey (Walse) 1251

Second (third?) Generation: Godfrey 1294

Third Generation: Nicholas 1318
                                                      Reginald 1318-1332
                                                      Richard 1316-1322
Fourth Generation: Thomas 1331-1347

Fifth Generation: Agnes, wife of John 1372-1382
                                                      John 1350-1382

Second Appearance: Agnes, wife of John 1416
                                                      John 1416-1422

WALTER
First Noted: Simon 1251
                                                      Herbert 1251

Second (third?) Generation: Nicholas 1290-1320
                                                      John 1290-1313
                                                      Godfrey, son of Simon 1299
                                                      Alice 1316

Third Generation: William, 1320-1345
                                                      Agnes 1327
                                                      Emma, wife of William 1318-1339
                                                      Margaret, dau. of Nicholas 1318-1319
                                                      Thomas 1331
                                                      Juliana 1347
                                                      Simon 1334

Fourth Generation: John 1360-1379

WALTHAM
First Noted: Robert, carpenter 1451
                                                      Agnes, wife of Robert 1451

WARREN
First Noted: William, 1372-1405
                                Emma, wife of William 1378-1405

Second Generation: John 1407-1408

WEBESTER
First Noted: Hugh 1316-1347
                                John, son of Richard 1320
                                John 1332

Second Generation: Robert 1331-1337
                                Walter 1334-1347
                                William 1339
                                Agnes, dau. of Alexander 1343

Third Generation: Agnes, wife of Thomas 1391-1392
                                Hugh 1377-1394
                                Edwin 1387-1388
                                John 1382
                                William (of Bury) 1407-1422
                                William 1382-1392
                                Henry 1393-1394
                                Robert 1371-1374

Fourth Generation: Thomas 1403-1405
                                Peter 1411
                                John 1413
                                Agnes, wife of John 1413

WENNINGTON
First Noted: Robert 1294-1332
                                Richard 1313

Second Generation: John, son of Robert 1316-1339
                                Ralph 1339
                                William 1333

Third Generation: John 1369-1400
                                Thomas 1377-1379

WETHE
First Noted: Hugh 1390's.?

Second Generation: William 1400
                                Joan, wife of William 1400

WHETE
First Noted: Alice 1427-1448
                                John 1427-1455

WILKES
First Noted:

William 1299
Richard 1320-1337
Juliana, wife of Richard 1320-1353
Agnes 1331-1339
Reginald 1331
Roger 1333
Henry 1339
Joan 1343

Second Generation:

Hugh, son of Richard 1320-1331
William 1334, 1350-1379
Richard 1350-1373, 1386

Third Generation:

John (sen.) 1365-1412

Fourth Generation:

Agnes, wife of John 1428
John jun. (son of William 1375-1376), 1384-1428
John, in the Lane 1384
Beatrice 1382

Fifth Generation:

Richard 1410-1428
Richard, son of John 1424-1446 (d)
Alice, widow of Richard, son of John 1446
Thomas 1438-1449
William 1448
John 1429-1449

WILLIAM
First Noted:

John 1251
Simon 1251

Second (third?) Generation:

John 1299
Thomas 1294-1314

Second Appearance:

John, son of 1369
Alexander, son of 1371

WILLIMOT
First Noted:

Joan 1371-1392, 1400
John 1371-1394
Thomas 1360-1369

WITTESLEY
First Noted:

John 1410-1423
Robert 1421-1423

WODEHILL
First Noted:

John 1402-1412
Elena, wife of John 1406

WODEKOC
First Noted: Cristina 1251
Henry 1251

Second Generation: William 1290-1313
Richard 1290-1305
Hawysia, wife of Richard 1290-1294
(Richard), son of Henry 1290

Third Generation: John, son of William 1301-1339
Godfrey 1301-1331
Emma 1309-1322

Fourth Generation: John jun. 1339-1347
Alice, widow of John 1347-1348 (heriot)
William 1331-1353
Richard 1331-1333

Second Appearance: William 1401

WOODWARD
First Noted: Alexander 1288-1290
Richard 1294
Lawrence 1313-1316
Simon 1334

Second Appearance: Walter 1413-1455

WOLLE
First Noted: William (Webester) 1413-1422

Second Generation: John 1408, 1442-1455
Agnes, wife of John 1408

Third Generation: John, son of John 1440-1458

WOLNEY
First Noted: Henry 1371-1394
Elena, wife of Henry 1371-1379

WOODE (WODE)
First Noted: Agnes 1427

Second Generation: John 1427, 1442-1455

WRIGHT
First Noted: Agnes 1382-1388
John 1375-1376, 1413-1422
Robert 1379-1408, 1421
Thomas 1405

Table III

SUMMARY

Families in Warboys from
1251 to 1458

NAME	NUMBER OF GENERATIONS	YEARS
AGATH	II	1294-1320
ALAN	II	1299-1343
ALBYN	IV	1279-1405
ALOT	IV	1322-1410
ALTHEWORLD	I	1403-1428
ASHWELL	I	1440-1455
ASPLOND	I	1413-1428
ATTEGATE	II	1363-1455
ATTEHILL	II	1353-1408
ATTEWODE	VI	1251-1455
AUGUSTYN	II	1369-1384
BAROUN	IV	1322-1458
BASELEY	II	1251-1313
BEADLE	II	1288-1330
BELE	III	1360-1458
BENET	VIII	1251-1455
BENSON (BENNESSON)	III	1360-1458
BERENGER	VIII	1251-1458
BETTES	II	1333-1392
BIGGE	I	1369-1373
BIRD (BIRT)	I	1440-1458
BISSOP	I	1288-1339
BOKELOND	I, I	1339-1353, 1410-1412
BOLBY	I	1318-1334
BOLEYN	I	1446
BONDE	VI	1251-1458
BOST	II	1294-1379
BOTILLER	II	1375-1449
BOYS	IV	1316-1458
BRAMPTON	I	1371-1426
BRANDON	III	1251-1334
BRONNING	VII	1288-1428
BRONNOTE	I	1369-1414
BRUN	V	1288-1449
BRYD	II	1313-1353
BUCKWORTH	I	1369-1403
BUGG	I	1290-1337

NAME	NUMBER OF GENERATIONS	YEARS
BUK	III	1251-1347
BUNTYNG	I	1424-1455
BURG	I	1294-1306
BURBRIGGE	I	1350-1360
BRYNNEWATER	I	1375-1422
BYTHEWATER	I	1386-1425
CARPENTER	III, I	1251-1325, 1425
CARTER	I	1347-1387
CATOUN	V	1279-1458
CECILIA	III	1292-1353
CHAPMAN	V	1306-1458
CHAUMON	II	1294-1371
CHILD	I	1378-1394
CHOSE	I	1305
CHYCHELEY	II	1306-1348
CLERK	IV, I	1251-1353, 1421
CLERVAUX	II	1318-1334
COBBE	I	1425-1455
COLEVILLE	II	1390-1455
COLLIER	II	1339-1392
COLLE (COLLESSON)	IV	1333-1405
CORBETT	I	1441
COSYN	I	1333-1337
COUS	I	1322-1339
COWHERD	IV	1254-1450
CROXTON	I	1439
DALLY	II	1387-1422
DERWORTH (DERWARD)	V	1294-1427
DIKE	II	1322-1353
DURAUNT	II	1251-1331
EDWARD	IV	1369-1449
EDWYNE	II	1251-1316
ELLIOT	I	1353-1372
ELLSWORTH	II	1292-1334
ELY	I	1413-1428
EVERARD	I	1410
EYDON	II	1292-1320
EYR	III	1382-1448
FABER (SMYTH)	VI	1251-1455
FEKER	II	1251-1299
FINE	V	1251-1377
FISHER	III	1360-1458
FLEMYNG	III	1347-1458
FOLYET	II	1251-1322

NAME	NUMBER OF GENERATIONS	YEARS
FORDYNGTON	II	1413-1458
FOT	III	1288-1375
FRAUNCEYS	II, I	1251-1316, 1400-1428
FREMAN	II	1403-1421
GALEWAY	II	1294-1322
GARDNER	II	1279-1322
GERNOUN	I	1332-1334
GEROLD	VII	1251-1408
GODFREY	I	1294-1333
GODWYNE	II	1290-1313
GOOSELOWE	I	1455-1458
GOSSE	IV	1251-1392
GRENDALE	II	1299-1339
GYLES	I	1427-1449
HALIDAY	II, I	1251-1299, 1363
HARSINE	IV	1251-1408
HAUGATE	III	1290-1372
HAYWARD	III	1251-1340
HENRY	III	1251-1334, 1360
HERBERT	III	1251-1345
HERING	I, II	1288-1322, 1386-1455
HERRESSON	II	1371-1402
HERVY	III	1369-1441
HICHESSON (HICHE)	IV	1348-1458
HIDE	II	1407-1455
HOREWODE	III	1390-1458
HUNTER	IV	1316-1458
HYGENEYE	V	1279-1408
HYGH (HY, HEY)	IV	1301-1458
HYRST	III	1251-1350
ISABEL	II	1290-1347
JEKISSON	I	1343-1379
JOHN	III	1251-1325
JULIANA	I	1292-1299
KATHERINE	II	1251-1316
KAUNT	II, I	1290-1347, 1371-1405
KAYE	IV	1306-1410
LAMBEHIRDE	I	1371-1390
LAWRENCE	I, I	1316-1339, 1404-1444
LENOT	V	1301-1422
LONDON	VI	1279-1458
LONE	III	1290-1386
LONG	II	1294-1347
LUCAS	IV	1251-1347

NAME	NUMBER OF GENERATIONS	YEARS
MABLY	I	1305-1316
MARGARETTE	II, I	1290-1347, 1404-1455
MARTYN	IV	1292-1427
MERCATOR	II	1288-1309
MICE	I	1334-1347
MILLER	II	1290-1347
MILNER	II	1350-1448
MOKE	I	1326-1339
MOLT (MOLD)	V	1325-1455
MORY	III	1306-1377
NEL	III	1294-1347
NEWELL	I	1369-1371
NEWMAN	III	1369-1458
NICHOLAS	II	1309-1349
NOBLE	III	1251-1347
NORREYS	III	1313-1379
NORTHBOURGH	II	1371-1449
NUNNE	IV	1299-1422
ODE	I	1426
OLYVER	IV	1360-1450
ONTY	III	1251-1369
ORDEMAR	I	1415
OUNDELL	II	1423-1455
PAGE	I	1353-1371
PAKERELL	IV	1251-1379
PALMER	I	1325-1371
PELLAGE	I	1332-1334
PERSON	I, I	1363-1390, 1442-1449
PIGMAN	II	1294-1363
PILCHE	IV	1251-1348
PILGRIM	V	1251-1405
PLUMBE	VII	1251-1455
PONDER	III	1254-1313
PRESTECOSYN	I	1378-1409
PUTTOCK	III	1251-1343
RANDOLF	I, I	1369, 1448
RAVELEY	IV	1363-1449
RAVEN	VI	1251-1455
REDE	IV	1306-1405
REEVE	III	1251-1316
REGINALD	II	1306-1353
REVISSON	I, I	1369-1390, 1442-1455
RICHARD	II	1299-1360
ROBYN	IV	1251-1369

NAME	NUMBER OF GENERATIONS	YEARS
ROGER	III	1251-1334
ROLF	III	1305-1404
ROPERE	I	1379-1392
SAND	III	1371-1458
SARRISSON	II	1363-1376
SAWERE	I, I	1322-1334, 1387-1388
SCULLE	III	1251-1320
SCUT	VI	1290-1458
SEGELEY	III	1288-1347
SEMAR	V	1251-1418
SEWYNE	I	1305-1316
SHAKESTAFF	I	1407-1455
SHARPE	II	1405-1458
SHEPHERD	VII	1251-1458
SIST'NE	II	1371-1419
SKYNNER	III	1251-1369
SLOUGH	II	1424-1455
SON	II	1371-1379
SMART	V	1290-1449
SOPER	I	1294-1313
SPARHAWK	I	1292-1322
SPERNER	IV	1251-1390
SQWYER	II	1407-1440
STRUGGE	I	1412-1449
SUTOR	III	1251-1375
SUTTON	II	1292-1343
SWAN	IV	1294-1394
TAYLOR	V	1320-1449
TASKER	I	1382-1390
THACHER	II	1371-1444
THOMISSON	I	1369-1376
THRESHER	I, I	1360, 1386
THURBERNE	III	1288-1326
THURKYLD	I	1307-1316
TONYNGTON	I	1423
TOP	II	1290-1353
TORTORIN	II	1289-1313
TYMME	I	1320-1347
UNFREY	II	1251-1333
VERNON	I	1363-1364
VICORY	III	1326-1400
WALSH	V, I	1251-1382, 1416-1422
WALTER	IV	1251-1379
WALTHAM	I	1451

NAME	NUMBER OF GENERATIONS	YEARS
WARREN	II	1372-1408
WEBESTER	IV	1316-1422
WENNINGTON	III	1294-1400
WETHE	II	1390's-1400
WHETE	I	1427-1455
WILKES	V	1299-1449
WILLIAM	II, I	1251-1314, 1369-1371
WILLIMOT	I	1360-1400
WITTESLEY	I	1410-1423
WODEHILL	I	1402-1412
WODEKOC	IV, I	1251-1353, 1401
WOLLE (WELLE)	I, I	1413, 1458
WOLNEY	I	1371-1394
WOODE (WODE)	II	1427-1455
WOODWARD	I, I	1288-1334, 1413-1455
WRIGHT	I	1375-1422

Table IV

SUMMARY

Number of Families in Warboys by Decades
1251 to 1458

YEAR	NUMBER	YEAR	NUMBER
1251	50 (95)	1400	80
1290	(71)	1410	71
1300	101	1420	71
1310	111	1430	61
1320	109	1440	62
1330	107	1450	51
1340	93		
1350	79		
1360	80		
1370	89		
1380	86		
1390	89		

Another category of people discovered on the court rolls were those isolated individuals, not seemingly related to any family, yet clearly involved in the village in more than a temporary capacity. Perhaps these too were one-generation persons, but our information does not usually suggest many years of residence in the village. Table (V) lists those isolated villagers and, along with the years of their appearance on the court rolls, the entries that suggest at least temporary residence in the village.

The existence of these isolated individuals, as well as rarely mentioned members of some families, indicate that by the nature of their survival, our court rolls may not net all villagers over this period. Furthermore, identifiable individuals vary from one document to another. From the account rolls, for instance, one can discover several individuals not mentioned in the court rolls: Agnes Baldewyne, tenant in 1342-1343; Cristina Chycheley, tenant in 1347-1348; Alice Geffrey, daughter of John, 1288-1289 (perhaps Alice Godfrey in the court rolls from 1306); Benedict Lawesson, tenant in 1344-1345 (likely son of Laurence of court rolls). Account rolls also reveal various officials of the lord who have escaped the court rolls such as Master John Bulloc, 1342-1343. Other series of documents also reveal new names of Warboys people, as in the following two lists from the tax rolls in the early fourteenth century: (1327)[1] Roger Beneyt, Hugh Lone, Emma Kaye, Roger Semar, Hugh Bully, Agnes Walter, Matilda Person; (1332)[2] Richard Buk, Richard Cecilia, William Choo (   ), John Carpenter, Agnes Gernoun, Agnes Gilberd, John Nrook, Simon Pellage, Matilda Person, Adam Palmer, Alice Unfrey.

Again, however, one must keep in mind that in Warboys we are dealing with a living and changing society, rather than a static list of villagers. Even for some of the tenants noted in the above tax records one must question whether several were not freemen and perhaps non-resident in the village. And certainly a good number of the new names in the tax rolls are those of women, a much smaller percentage of whom appear on the court rolls. More generally, however, for a good number of persons mentioned in the court rolls as well as the account rolls, it is difficult to establish any certain relationship with the village. For the most part these were tradesmen and officials of the lord—a carpenter, beadle, gardener, miller, ponder, pigman, reeve, soper, shepherd, taylor,

[1] E 179/122/4.
[2] E 179/122/7.

webester, woodward. Some of these names that appeared just incidentally in the court rolls and account rolls are as listed below:

Bailiff, John Couper	1344
—, Thomas servant of	1334
Couper, Richard the	1309
—, Robert the	1309
Constable	1332, 1334
Custodian of the wood of	
Warboys, John, of Cranfield	1290
Butcher, Andrew Brumeswater	1347
—, John Tabard	1309
—, Ralph Tra	1322
Hundreder, Alan the,	
of Gilbert of Kirkeby	1294
Infirmarian, Hayward of *Parson*[1]	1294
Ploughman of lord, William Howell	1324-1325
Sowing Offcials?, Hauley	1342-1343
Wardale	1342-1343

Table V

Isolated villagers
1290-1347

NAME	DATE	ENTRY
Arnold, Thomas	1294	sells land
Balentyne, Simon	1301	e. dec.
Ben', Lawrence	1333	jur.
Bereshers, Nicholas	1316	malefactor
Beuge, John	1334	e. dec.
Bewford, William	1347	e. dec.
Blosme, Juliana	1301	pregnant
Bulloc, Robert	1316	pledge
Buntyng, John	1331, 1339	tr.
Cam (Kam of Long Stanton), John of	1320	default; land
Chatteris, Agnes of	1301	plea
—, Alice of	1299-1316	assize of ale
—, Juliana of	1316	gl. m.
Cook, Amitia, wife of Ralph	1320	assize of ale
Dalebrok (Delbrok), Andrew	1320	thief; e. dec.

[1] See Chapter IX, p. 248.

NAME	DATE	ENTRY
Decoun, Mabel	1337	adult.
Dourdonn	1331	gl. m.
Drake, Cecilia	1320	fals. pl.
Draper, John the	1337	e. dec.
Drayton, Cristina of, and husband	1299	theft
Duton, William	1290	tr.
Dyt', Nicholas	1309	rec. outsiders
Everard, Agnes, dau. of Ralph	1294	assize of ale
Fabian, Edmund	1322	fals. pl.
Fabion, Edward	1333	tr.
Fabyn, William	1316	defamed
Faconn (Facin), John	1320, 1334	assault; pledge
Fannel (Fennel), John	1343	attached
Fenreve, Simon the	1313	pledge (2)
Fikeis, John	1322-1334, 1353	e. dec.; tr.; pledge; etc.
Freman, Catherine	1332-1334	assize of ale; gl. m.
Frost, William	1299	land bought
Gagon, Stephen	1306	malefactor
Galyon, Thomas	1316	malefactor
Gille, Roger	1301	e. dec.
Godrych, Robert, of Woodhurst	1326	tr.; debt; worked badly
Gouler, Margaret, dau. of Stephen	1299, 1301	pregnant
Hamemaker, Margaret the	1301	assize of ale
Hawys, Richard	1339, 1347	worked badly
Homificii, William	1322	pledge
Jewel, Juliana	1339, 1343	assize of ale
Keston, Matilda of, and husband	1333	tr.; pledge
Kocis, Robert of	1322	essoin
Longe Curte, Roger	1294	hue
Lyrtebrok, William	1339-1347	tr.
Mabel, Robert, son of, of Caldecote	1301	sold land
Malitraz, Agnes	1313	malefactor
Mariot, Cristina	1292	assize of ale
Palfreour, William the	1294, 1299	pledge
Paulyn, Margaret	1339	gl. m.
Peres, Robert	1299-1306	e. d.
Powel, Margaret	1320	pregnant
Ralph, Robert, son of	1309-1316	tr.
Ramsey, Nigel of	1325	e. dec.
Ramsey, Nigel Ailward, of	1326	e. dec.
Roper, Beatrice	1318	hue
Roper, William	1316	hue
Sarra, Emma, dau. of	1294	married
Selome, Alexander	1309	malefactor
Seuster, John, son of Alice	1339	gl. m.

NAME	DATE	ENTRY
Simon, William servant of	1332	hue
Smult, Emma	1294	pregnant
Stratford, Robert of	1309, 1313	assault; malefactor
Temat, Ascelin	1325	e. dec.
Temesford, John of	1305, 1322-1325	tr.; essoin; default
Thacher, Alexander	1322	debt
—, Thomas the	1334	e. dec.
Therngg', Quena of	1294	assize of ale
—, Reginald of	1305	tr.
Thresher, ?	1347	e. dec.
—, (Threche), William	1334	hue
Thomas, John, son of	1306-1316	e. d.
Toperhyl, Thomas	1306	tr.
Trille, Juliana	1332	pregnant
Trobe, Adam	1320	tr.
Uphele, Hugh	1331, 1334	hue; e. dec.
Waleboy, Thomas	1334	tr.
—, William	1313, 1316	overstocked pasture; tr.
Walsoken, Margaret of	1301	hue; theft
Warboys, John of	1316	pledge
—, (Boys), John of	1332-1337	tr.; default
—, Richard of	1343	tr.
—, Richard (Ebe) of	1292	tr.
—, William of	1331, 1337	concord; tr.
Wrek, Ralph	1294-1306	e. d.
Wycher, Godfrey	1294-1313	e. d.
Wymar, Agnes	1299	defamation
Wymark, Alice	1306	assize of ale
Wyne, John	1337, 1339	hue
Wynt', Gratia	1306-1313	assault; forn.; pregnant
Wynton, Alice, dau. of Stephen	1299	assault

Table V

Isolated Villagers
1349-1458

NAME	DATE	ENTRY
Alexander, John, son of	1369-1371	tr; + property
Attehill, John, Richard servant of	1386	d.

NAME	DATE	ENTRY
Asshewode, John	1458	e. dec.
Attetownsende, Thomas	1440	pl; tr.
Attewell, ( )	1369	tr. lambs; wood
Barbat, Thomas	1400-1405	default; pl.
Barford, John	1448	waste
Bachelor, Ralph	1371	sell m.; ed.; tr.
Balde, Robert	1376	pledge (2)
Birgate, Agnes atte	1350	assis.
Blackwell, Thomas	1427	op. (wood)
Bocher, Nicholas	1423	overloaded med. sheep
Bokkison, John	1353	tr; pledge
Bolle, John	1407-1408	had property
Breustr, Beatrice	1390	tast. pres.
Briesson, John	1375-1382	waste build.
Broughton, William, of Bury	1371-1379	had property
Bunte, Thomas	1391-1392	waste land Caldecote
By, Simon	1387	butcher
Byrere, Richard	1410	op.
Caldecote, Thomas	1424	noc. n.
Catelyn, John	1371-1455	had property
Cooke, Agnes	1379	had property
Coole, Robert, chaplain	1404-1408	had property
Couper, Adam	1407-1408	had property
Cost'ne, Richard	1407-1408	had property
Cott, Thomas	1363	jur.
Cotalio', Godfrey	1353	e. dec.
Cristyne, John	1413-1414	100/= debt.
Delboys, John	1410	jur.
Demar, John	1379	had property
Dicoun, Thomas	1371-1379	had property
Done, Nicholas, chaplain	1391-1392	d.
Elmesle, John	1427	op. (wood)
Euge, (Eugene), John	1353-1365	pl. of John Bercar
Farendon, ( )	1369	withdrew service for ten.
Faron, John, shepherd of Richard	1369	tr.
Ferour, William	1349	op.
Flexhower, Nicholas	1371	pledge
Forester, John	1372-1412	jur; op; + property
Free, Agnes	1390	contra stat.
Gandissen, Thomas	1365	op.
Gaze, Robert	1371-1379	had property
George, Katherine	1421	blood; r. hue m.
Gildesowe, Robert	1365	d.
Gouler, Benedict	1369	jur.
Hacon, John	1407-1408	had property

NAME	DATE	ENTRY
(H)arewode, Richard	1390	waste buildings
Hawkyn, John	1369, 1458	default
Hawkinnsson, ( )	1369	tr.
Hawys, Richard	1349	tr. (pigs)
Henene, Margaret	1386	op.
Herrow, Nicholas	1369	jur; op.
Hoberd, William	1400-1422	tr; jur.
Hyd, John	1411	jur.
Janne, Agnes	1360	gl. m.
Khisson, John	1369	horses
Lambard, Godfrey	1455-1458	tr; waste
Lawshill, John	1379-1405	tr; blood; op; pl; d; hamsok; + property
Laveyn, Richard	1442-1449	had property
Leheir (Theheir), Thomas	1378-1379	had property
Lirtebrook, William	1353-1378	tr; sell reeds m. + property
Lowe, William	1372	waste buildings
Make A Mayden, Alice	1386-1388	tr. m.
Make, John, chaplain	1427	holds one cokrode in woods
March, (Merch), John of Bury	1393-1405	had property
Merton, Agnes	1369-1372	tr.; assis.
—, Lawrence	1434	tr. (12 pigs)
Miles, John	1369	pledge
Mord, William	1418	pledge
Morell, Robert	1449-1455	elect. cust.; tr. + property
Nedham, John	1378-1410	elect. cust. aut.; jur; tr.; op.; cond as poor; + property
Ordemar, John	1413-1422	had property
Orewell, John	1365-1369	fals. d.; pl.; tr.
Othehiche, Thomas	1382	default
Pannton', John, chaplain	1400-1402	d-.; conc. re. d.
Papworth, John	1405	waste
Payne, William	1369	pledge; tr.
Peny, Robert	1369	op.
Phobe, Richard	1371	jur.
Pikeler, Matilda	1369	op.
Pury, William	1458	e. dec.
Ramsey, Thomas	1428	op; did not go hunting in woods
Renale, Agnes	1382	gl. m.
Rewale, John	1369	contra. wodeward pres. rebel
Rising, William	1371-1379	sell reeds; + property

NAME	DATE	ENTRY
Robysson, Richard	1440	ten. waste m. d.
Ronale, Baldwyn	1387-1390	tr.; pl.
Roger, Cristina	1372	assis.
Rooleg, Walter	1382-1384	waste; def; e. dec.
Sabyn, Richard	1374-1379	had property
Sadelar, William	1375-1376	fals. cl.; pl.; tr.
Sandisson, John	1353-1371	op; tr.
Scotenyll, Matilda	1400	op. m.
Segrave, Alan	1363, 1371	toll excess; tr.
Sewester, Joan	1386	tr. wood
Simon, John, son of Simon	1353	op.
Stryng'e, John	1387-1388	not in dec.
Stratton, Nicholas, chaplain	1379	had property
Sywell, John	1393-1405	had property
Thakker, John	1430	op.
Walgate, John	1428	op; did not go hunting in the woods
Wolley, William	1428	e. dec.
Wynde, John	1407-1408	had property
Wroo, Thomas	1448-1458	waste; def.; + property
Wrangil, William	1404-1405	had property
Wyllesson, Richard	1427-1449	op.; pledge
Wyne, Mary	1413-1422	had property

NOTE:
Since there was a rapid turnover in small holdings over the early fifteenth century, many isolated people are missed because of gaps in the surviving account rolls and court rolls. The Court Book makes it possible to identify these small people taking up property: William Dand, 1439; John Dunde, 1334; Robert Henyt, 1438; Walter Hert, 1405; Robert Hill, 1406; Richard Laneyn, 1440; John Payne, 1408; John Peverell, pre-1400; Hugh Pulter, pre-1443; Robert Russell, 1435; Robert Rabyn, pre-1445; Roger Wethirle, 1409 and Roger White jr., 1408.

Explanation of short forms for Table V

jur.	= juror
tast.	= taster
assis.	= breaking of assize of ale by wrong brewing, selling etc.
d.	= debt owed
d-	= one to whom debt owed
op.	= work and service owed
noc. n.	= harm done to neighbor or neighbors by road, meadow, stubble etc.
tr. n.	= trespass on other villagers, by road, meadow, etc.
noc. or tr. (without n.)	= harm or trespass to lord by road, meadow, stubble etc.
rec.	= wrongly receiving someone else
rec' d.	= the one wrongly received
e. dec.	= out of tithing
e. d.	= out of demesne or fee of lord
conc.	= concord
plea. def.	= defendant in plea
pl.	= plea
fals. pl. (or fals. cl.)	= false plea or claim
default	= default, i.e. failure to appear in court on a charge
r. hue	= the one raising a hue and cry
r. hue m.	= the one raising a hue and cry wrongly
hue-	= the one on whom the charge has been raised by hue and cry
defam.	= the one who has defamed another
defam.-	= the one defamed
gl. m.	= gleaned wrongly to harm of lord and villagers
assault	= physical harm, blood, etc.
hamsok.	= hamsoken, i.e. breaking and entering
theft	= stealing
forn.	= fornication
adult.	= adultery
capit.	= fined in chapter (usually for fornication or adultery)
exch. l	= exchange land
l+	= bought land
l—	= sold land

Chapter IV

MIGRATION OF VILLAGERS

Section 1

NORMAL ACTIVITIES WITH NEIGHBOURING VILLAGES

In the final analysis, the inability of the court rolls to supply more complete data for identification of the traditional categories of demographic information stems from the fact that court roll entries are indices of individual behaviour. At the same time the wide spectrum of individual behaviour represented by court roll data makes possible the identification of several common patterns of individual behaviour. Foremost among these is geographical mobility. The first category of such mobility is that of daily tasks usually reflected in court roll entries by trespass (and occasionally by debt, assault, etc.) of a villager from Warboys upon neighbouring vills, or of neighbouring villagers upon Warboys. As will be seen below, the following three tables are really indicators of the degree to which the operative economy of the villagers was wider than the area of Warboys. Since court rolls are not extant for every year, and the following entries usually occur because of violations only, in number these entries can be no more than a token measure of the actual mobility of ordinary villagers. The following table lists individuals, clearly coming from established Warboys families, that were cited in the court of the neighbouring villages of Wistow and Broughton over the first half of the fourteenth century. As might be expected, references to Warboys villagers were much less frequent upon the court rolls of more distant villages. Nevertheless, at King's Ripton there was mention of the following Warboys names: Baroun, Arnold, Dike, Durant, Martin, Norreys, Palmer, Smart and Unfrey. With completion of the index of all names for the district to be found in court rolls, it is to be hoped that this pattern of mobility will be able to be traced more fully.

Table VI

Warboys people appearing in the court of Wistow

NAME	DATE	ENTRY
Albyn, John, of Caldecote	1326	tr.
Brandon, Alice	1318	tr.

NAME	DATE	ENTRY
Brandon, John, de Warboys	1320	fl. cl. as executor of William Caldecote
—, William, de Warboys	1301	tr.
Broughton, John of	1294	pledge for two Warboys men
Bugge, Nicholas	1316	tr.
Bolby, Hugh	1318	tr.
Catoun, Richard, son of Howis	1307, 1309, 1316, 1339, 1342, 1347	tr.
Caunt, Henry	1334	tr.
Chaplain, de Warboys, Robert	1320	tr.
Clerk, Gilbert	1339	hue
Duraunt, Emma	1325	tr.
—, Hugh	1318	tr.
Egaze, Robert	1320	tr.
Faber, Agnes de Warboys	1318	tr.
—, Sampson, of Warboys	1320	tr.
—, William, of Warboys	1307	tr.
Fraunceys, William	1318	tr.
Galeway, Walter	1318	tr.
Gerold, Godfrey	1316, 1318	tr.
Gerold, Simon	1294	harm to another villager's land with beasts
Godfrey, Alice	1325	tr; cond.
—, John, of Warboys	1333	tr.
—, Sarra, of Warboys	1313	tr. –; distrained
Gosse, Robert	1294	harm to another villager's land with beasts
Hau (Gate?), Alice	1308	blood
Herbert, Godfrey	1294, 1297	harm to another villager's land with beasts; warren
Herbert, John	1318	tr.
—, Robert	1331	tr.
Lucas, Richard	1313, 1326, 1334	tr. (3)
Nicole, Matilda	1316	tr.
Palmer, John, of Warboys	1326	tr.
Puttok, Simon	1313	tr.
Rede, John le, of Warboys	1326	pl; tr.
Rolf, John de, of Warboys	1334	tr.
Rolf, William	1313	pl.
Scut, Ralph	1307	damaged a hedge
Semar, Richard	1326	tr.
Smart, Robert	1313	pl. of Adam Miller

NAME	DATE	ENTRY
Soper, William le	1294	harm to another villager's land with beasts
Sperwe, Stephen	1334	tr.
Tymme, John	1347	tr.
Unfrey, John	1307, 1318	tr; pl.
Vaccarius, Ralph, of Warboys	1301	tr.
Walsh, Thomas	1339, 1347	tr.
Wodekoc, Emma	1318	tr.

Table VI

Warboys people appearing in the court of Bronghton

NAME	DATE	ENTRY
Alot, John	1322	debt*
Baroun, John	1322	debt (2)*
Beadle, Godfrey the, of Warboys	1320	tr. with cows
Beneyt, John	1340	debt
Bonde, Andrew	1322, 1339	tr. woods*
Bouk' (Bugge), Nicholas	1337	tr. woods
Caunt, (Kaunt), Richard	1306	assault*
Chycheley, Godfrey, of Caldecote	1320	tr.*
Dike, Godfrey	1339	tr.
Emma, of Caldecote	1331	tr.
Hayward, William	1340	tr. woods
Lenot, Robert, son of John	1307, 1316	debt. plea
Maister, Nicholas	1332, 1334	tr. grain
Martyn, John	1316	debt; false plea
—, Richard	1307	esples
Mice, Agnes	1334	gleaned m.*
Pakerel, Henry	1308	assault (2)
—, Hugh	1308	assault
Rolf, Mariota	1334	tr.*
Smart, Robert, of Caldecote	1301	tr.
Segeley', Albinus	1301	tr.
Simon, Matilda, wife of, of Caldecote	1297	debt
Unfrey, John, of Warboys	1322	tr.
Warboys, John of	1314	default
—, William	1334	gleaned m.
William, Thomas, son of	1314	fl. plea

* All common Warboy's names, although not appearing in the Warboys list.

The following table (VII) lists clearly designated outsiders who were fined in the court of Warboys. Most of these were from villages contiguous to Warboys, and can be easily identified where court rolls have been studied for such neighbouring villages. This casual intercourse among villages must have lead to the easy assumption that the provenance of the outsiders was known to all the court. Hence a good number of persons fined in Warboys court were probably outsiders, but not so indicated in the court record. Table VIII lists such individuals, with their possible provenance from our knowledge of neighbouring families.

Table VII

Outsiders presented at the court of Warboys
1290 to 1350

NAME	DATE	PLACE
Balde, John	1333	Broughton
Balde, John	1333	Fenton
Balle, (Allan)	1350	Pidley
Ballard, John	1294	Broughton
Bateman, Robert	1347	Pidley
—, Richard	1347	Barnwell
Barnwell, John	1334	Barnwell
Bodyngton, John	1339	Bodington
Botelar, John	1334	Broughton
Boty't, Richard	1305	Fenton
Brancaster, Alan	1301	Brancaster
Bronnote, Robert	1299, 1316	Wistow
Brownote, Adam	1349	Wistow
Broughton, community of	1334	Broughton
Broughton, 2 men of	1333	Broughton
Broughton, parson	1333	Broughton
Burg, John	1294	Peterborough
—, Alice	1306	Peterborongh
—, Godfrey	1306	Peterborough
—, John, son of Godfrey	1306	Peterborough
Canne, William	1343	Woldhurst
Catelin, Richard	1332	Broughton
Chamberlain, Alexander	1316	Wistow
Collier, Simon	1316	Woodhurst
Curteys, Robert	1316	Wistow
Ecclesiam, William	1299	Wistow

NAME	DATE	PLACE
Edward, Roger	1316	Woodhurst
Elington, Alice	1347	Ellington
Ellesworth, Simon	1292	Ellsworth
Ely, John	1331	Ely
Est, William	1337	Fenton
Faber, Godfrey	1316	Wistow
Fenton, John, son of Edward	1333	Fenton
—, John	1334	Fenton
—, William, son of John	1294	Fenton
Fersonator, Stephen	1294	Fersonator?
Godfrey, son of Gocelyne	1299	Little Raveley
Godrych, Robert	1316	Woodhurst
Gore, John	1313	Broughton
—, Thomas	1347	Broughton
Gray, Robert	1305-1306	Niddingworth
Hobbe, William	1305	Broughton
Justice, Katherine	1292	Broughton
—, John	1334	Broughton
—, Adam	1334, 1343	Broughton
Lacey, Roger	1313	Houghton
Lanerok, Thomas	1316	Wistow
Long, Richard	1299	Little Raveley
Martin, Thomas, son of Benedict	1299	Little Raveley
Nel, Simon	1334	Broughton
Oky, Robert	1316	Woodhurst
Odyham, Stephen	1299, 1301	Odyham
Prepositus, Adam	1316	Wistow
—, Stephen	1316	Wistow
—, John	1316	Wistow
—, Nicholas	1316	Woodhurst
Pidley, Richard	1306	Pidley
Ramsey, Robert, the Glover	1333	Ramsey
Ravele, William	1331	Raveley
Raven, John	1347	Woldhurst (Old Hurst)
Russell, John	1313	Broughton
—, Thomas	1334	Broughton
—, Alan	1334	Broughton
Sewyne, Thomas	1316	Woodhurst
—, William	1316	Woodhurst
Somersham, John, servant of forester	1332	Somersham
—, cowherd of	1320	Somersham
—, John, son of John, of	1325	Somersham
—, John	1337	Somersham
—, Margaret	1322	Somersham
Sudbury, William	1353	Sudbury

NAME	DATE	PLACE
Sutton, Juliana	1316	Sutton
—, master Lawrence	1316	Sutton
—, Andrew	1316	Sutton
—, Godfrey	1299	Sutton
—, Reginald	1292	Sutton
—, Margaret, daughter of Reginald	1301	Sutton
—, William	1343	Sutton
Swan, Thomas	1337	Wistow
Stukeley, Nicholas	1350	Stukeley
Upwood, Hugh	1292	Upwood
Ulf, William	1316	Woodhurst
Warin, John	1326	Wistow
Warwyk, Thomas	1299	Broughton
Wolney, Edmond	1320	Wolney
Wistow, Agnes	1339	Wistow
Wolfeye, Reginald, servant of farmer, of	1331	Wolfeye
—, farmer of	1306	Wolfeye

Table VII

Outsiders presented at court of Warboys
1349-1458

NAME	DATE	PLACE
Alderne, Simon	1386	Woodhurst
Almer, John	1391-92	Wistow
—, Thomas	1424	Hemingford Abbots
Andrew, John jun.	1424	King's Ripton
—, John	1448	Somersham
Attegate, Stephen	1440	Wistow
Austin, John	1448	Bluntisham
—, Thomas	1448	Bluntisham
Baker, John	1424	Huntington
—, Richard	1448	Wistow
Badburgh, Robert	1353	Badburgh
Bercar, John	1389	Wistow
—, Richard	1427	Wistow
Bone, Thomas	1448-1455	Wistow
Brgge, Robert	1448	Wistow

NAME	DATE	PLACE
Catoun, John	1363-1373	Broughton
Clynt, John	1418	Brech?
Cristyne, John	1418	Brech?
Dallyng, Simon, parson	1424	Holywell
Ellington, Alice	1349	Ellington
Fenton, Nicholas	1363	Fenton
Freman, Thomas, son of William	1403-1421	Ramsey
Frere, John	1427-1448	Wistow
Gernoun, John	1369	Wistow
—, Richard	1387	Wistow
Goderke, Clemens	1448-1458	Wistow
Godfrey, Nicholas	1360	Niddingworth
Gore, Thomas	1365	Broughton
Haulond, William	1365-1376	Broughton
Hry, ? son of Thomas	1403	Broughton
Horne, John	1423	Broughton
Hunne, Godfrey	1428-1448	Wistow
Hyche, Robert	1427	Wistow
—, William	1427-1428	Wistow
Maddyngle, John	1424	Hertford
Papworth, Alice	1391-1392	Papworth
—, John	1386-1388	Papworth
Pilgrim, William	1400-1402	Woodhurst
Plombe, Joan	1403	Houghton
Prat, John	1375-1376	Broughton
Purdy, William	1424	St. Ives
Roger, Edward, son of	1365	Fenton
Raven, John	1390	St. Ives
—, John	1390	Holywell
—, John	1402	Needingworth
Raundes, Robert	1421	Raundes
—, Thomas	1440	Raundes
Rede, Robert	1382	Wistow
—, Thomas	1448	Wistow
Samson, Roger	1448	Colne
—, William	1448	Colne
Sceme, Robert	1386-1388	Fenton
Shephird, John	1390	Broughton
Smythe, Walter	1427	Wistow
Thoday, Simon	1427	Wistow
Top, Richard	1386-1388	Somersham
Walshe, John	1412	Broughton
Wright, John	1427	Wistow
—, Richard	1427	Wistow

Table VIII

Apparent outsiders and their possible provenance
1290-1347

NAME	DATE	ENTRY	PLACE
Above the Town, Henry	1326	d.	?
Ailmer, Adam	1326	tr. marsh	Wistow
Akerman, Stephen	1316	tr.	Wistow
Ande, John	1306	tr.	Wistow
Aspelon, John	1334	tr. marsh	Wistow or Upwood
Asshebech, Beatrice	1339	tr.	?
—, John	1347	tr.	?
Ategate, John	1334	tr. marsh	?
—, William	1334	tr. marsh	?
Ate Hall, William, servant of Thomas	1316	plea	?
Atewold, John	1334	tr. marsh	?
Badburgh, Robert	1353	tr.	?
Balde, Thomas	1334	tr. marsh	Broughton
Balle, Stephen, forester	1306	forestall	Upwood, Abbots Rip.
Baroun, Elena	1313	prohibited	Wistow
Barre, William	1333	hue-	?
Begger, Robert	1334	hamsok	Upwood
Beste, Henry of the	1326	tr. marsh	Wistow
Bigge, John	1334	tr. marsh	Upwood
Blosme, John	1334	tr. marsh	Broughton
Bok' (Buckworth), William	1292	plea	Upwood
Bon, John	1334	tr. marsh	Broughton
Brgge, John at the	1334	tr. marsh	Broughton
Bus', William, son of William	1313	gl. m.	?
Bynethetun, Richard	1301	fals. cl.	?
Cappe, Edward	1316	tr. wood	?
Chechely, John	1326-1334	gl. m.	?
Chop, William	1294	tr.	?
Chychely, Stephen	1305	fals. pl.	?
Cobe, (William)	1343	fals. cl-.	?
Crane, ( )	1334	tr. marsh	?
—, William	1322-1334	tr. marsh	Broughton, Upwood, Wistow
—, Mariota	1322	r. hue	?
Cros, Thomas ate	1334	tr. marsh	Abbots Ripton
Dam, Simon ate	1334	tr. marsh	Broughton
Dekne, Simon le	1306	plea	?
Dille, William	1343	reeds	?
Drewes, William	1331	hue-	Upwood
Duncepere, John	1337	tr.	?

NAME	DATE	ENTRY	PLACE
Dunheved, Edmund	1337	default	Wistow
Edmund, William son	1320	contra aut.	?
Edward, Juliana, and two sons	1326	marsh	Broughton Upwood
—, Nicholas	1305	reeds	Upwood, Broughton
—, Roger	1305	reeds	Upwood, Broughton
—, Robert, son of Robert	1305	reeds	Upwood, Broughton
—, William son	1333	tr.	?
Eliot, William	1325	d-.	Wistow
Emma, Richard son	1301	tr.	?
Encrord, John	1333	tr.	?
Engyne, John	1334	hue. m-	?
Everard, John	1334	tr. marsh	Upwood or Broughton
Eugene, John	1353	fals. cl.	?
Frere, John, son of Alexander	1337	conc.	Wistow
Freyl, John	1333	hue-	?
Gerneys, William	1306	d-.	Abbots Ripton
Gernoun, John	1334	tr. marsh	Broughton, Upwood
Goscelyn, Stephen	1325	pledge	?
Goselin, Thomas	1333	plea	Abbots Ripton
Grobbe, Joan	1306	r. hue; assault	Wistow
Henry, William	1334	tr. marsh	Broughton
Herny, Custancia	1294	gl. m.	?
Hiche, Emma	1322	gl. m.	?
Hill, John of the	1331	d-.	?
—, William of ye	1353	tr.	?
Hobbe, John	1333	hue-	Wistow
Horseman, John	1320	hue-	Broughton
Hugh, William, son of	1322	conc.	Abbots Ripton, Broughton
Hugh, (G), son of	1334	tr. marsh	Abbots Ripton, Broughton, Upwood
Hunne, Gilbert	1313	rescue	Wistow
Jordon, Beatrice	1299	reeds	Abbots Ripton
Ingram, Richard	1309	forn-.	?
Lane, Emma in the	1339	tr.	?
Lanerok, Thomas	1316	pledge	Wistow
Lauwe, John	1326	tr. marsh	Wistow
Lerhert, John	1337	tr. marsh	?
Little John	1333	tr.	Abbots Ripton
Lomb, William	1337	tr.	Broughton
Lonik, Richard	1334	tr. marsh	?
Lord, Emma le	1331	hue-; blood	Wistow
Lytemold, Robert	1305	tr.	?
Malyn, Alice	1333	hue	?

NAME	DATE	ENTRY	PLACE
March, William	1337	hue-	Abbots Ripton
Mice, John	1347	tr. ditch	Broughton
Mise, William	1339	hue-	Broughton
Mohaut, Thomas	1334	tr. marsh	Broughton
Mousichet, John, servant of John	1325	r. hue. m.	?
Mowyn, William	1325	noc. n.	Wistow
Neweman, Robert le	1316	tr.	Upwood
Norton, John of	1339	blood noc.	Abbots Ripton
Onty, William	1334	tr. marsh	Broughton
Othehill, Richard	1334	tr. marsh	?
Parewe, Stephen	1334	blood	?
Patrick, Margaret	1334	gl. m.	?
—, Alice, sister of Margaret	1334	gl. m.	?
Pellage, Thomas	1334	tr. marsh	Broughton
Peny, Henry	1313, 1325	gl. m.	Upwood
Phiche, Nicholas	1337	tr.	?
Potter, William	1306	forestall-	?
Proudhele, John	1332	forestall	?
Querdunmyng, William	1299	plea-	?
Reginald, John, son of	1334	tr. marsh	Broughton
Rewleg, William	1347	hue	?
Reynoke, Alice	1331	gl. m.	?
Roger, Nicholas	1334	tr. marsh	Broughton
Rooleg, Walter	1347	tr-.	?
Rougetunte, Richard	1294	hue	Ramsey
Salbe, William	1294	tr.	?
Sawere, William	1322	r. hue; blood	?
—, Robert	1322, 1334	hue-; blood	?
Sbnger, Joan	1343	gl. m.	?
Sewar, William	1331	tr. marsh	?
Stilke, John	1333	hue	?
Sudbury, John of	1333	tr.	Upwood
Syneker, Nicholas	1322	hue	?
Tannator, John	1306	d-.	?
Wake, Thomas	1322	r. hue	Abbots Ripton
Welle, William	1343	hue-	?
Weston, Thomas, servant of John	1334	hue m-.	Upwood
Will (Mot), William	1334	tr. marsh	Broughton
Wilmot, William	1347	tr.	Broughton
Woyne, John	1339	tr.	?
Wright, Thomas	1347	d-.	?
Writte, William	1322	tr.	Abbots Ripton
Wulle, John of	1332	r. hue	?

NAME	DATE	ENTRY	PLACE
Wyri, Nicholas	1294	tr. wood	?
Wyttawere, Thomas	1331	hue	?
Ychener, Nicholas	1325	d.	?

Table VIII

Apparent outsiders and their possible provenance
1349-1458

NAME	YEAR	ENTRY	PLACE
Abbot, William	1363	tr.	Broughton
Adam, William	1360	pl. d.	Abbots Ripton
Alcok, John	1360	blood	Upwood
—, Richard	1353	tr.	Upwood?
—, William	1369	tr.	Upwood
Attecrouch, Thomas	1375-1376	tr.	Broughton
Aubus, ( )	1369	tr.	Upwood?
Balle, Andrew	1365	tr.	King's Ripton
—, John	1369	cust. aut.	Upwood
Bare, Richard	1350	tr.	?
Barker, Richard	1448	tr.	?
Barre, William	1349	conc. re. d.	?
Barnwell, John	1382	tr.	Broughton
Bene, Thomas	1424	tr.	?
Bochild, Godfrey	1350	hue-	?
Bodeseye, William	1391-1392	tr.	?
Botild, Joan	1360	blood; hue	?
—, John	1360	tr.	?
Bouller, Thomas	1423	tr. ditch; marsh	?
Bowes, John	1421	tr. wood	?
Brayn, John	1384	tr.	?
—, Roger	1363	tr.	?
Braseer, Thomas	1440	tr.	?
Braban, Lucy	1390	tr.	?
Bym, ( ), Thomas	1369	tr.	?
By the Water, William	1423	tr.	?
Canter, Simon	1365	pl. tr.	?
Channtely, John	1384	tr.	?
Chiple, John	1448	tr.	?
Coppynghall, ( )	1458	waste	?
Corner, John jun.	1424	r. hue m.	?
Croxton, John	1363	tr.	?
Dalby, John	1410	tr. marsh byelaw	?
Dallyng, John	1421	tr.	Holywell?

NAME	DATE	ENTRY	PLACE
Edham, John	1405	pledge	?
—, Robert	1405	pledge	?
Flexman, William	1369	tr.	Wistow
Fox, John	1369	tr.	Upwood
—, Roger	1386-1388	tr.	Upwood?
Freeston, Agnes	1428	tr.	?
Grubbe, John	1372-1373	tr.	?
Harpour, Thomas	1458	tr.	?
Herbin, Thomas	1369	tr.	?
Hird, John	1428	tr.	?
—, Thomas	1421-1424	tr. (2)	?
Hethe, Roger of the	1405	tr.	?
Heven, Margaret	1384	tr.	?
Hewe, Thomas	1458	tr.	?
Hobbe, Richard	1371-1372	pl; d; d.	Wistow
Hugh, Thomas, son of Hugh	1363	tr.	?
Hsethe, Agnes	1403	tr.	?
Hythe, John of the	1386-1388	tr.	?
Juesson, John	1363	tr.	Wistow
Kilpesham, John	1387-1388	blood; hue	?
Kirkeley, Thomas	1372-1373	tr.	?
Ladde, John	1369	pl.	Abbots Ripton
Lavell, Richard	1455	tr.	?
Leffen, John	1412	assault-	?
Lyvedon, Robert	1349	blood	?
May, Alan	1365	pl. d.	Holywell?
Mons, Walter	1390	tr.	?
Morgan, John	1402	d-.	?
Niddingworth, Nicholas	1360	tr.	?
Oky, John	1369	woodward pres.	?
Olneye, Henry	1372	tr.	?
Oryn'e, Mariota	1369	tr.	?
Percan', John	1369	tr.	?
Perrot, William	1350	tr.	?
Pike, William	1371	tr.	?
Pontislure, Richard	1363	tr.	?
Pook, son of John	1369	tr. n.	?
Poulyn's, Amitia	1369	woodward pres.	?
Pyper, Agnes	1427	pl. def. conc.	?
Redhoved, John	1369	tr.	?
Saundra', John	1371	tr.	?
Say, Robert	1371-1376	blood	?
Skite, John	1363	tr.	?
Stukeley, Nicholas	1350	default	?
Stotenill, Godfrey	1363	tr.	?

NAME	DATE	ENTRY	PLACE
Suron, John	1369	tr.	?
Swafham, Edward	1365	pl. tr.	?
Sudbury, Roger	1349	pledge	Upwood?
—, William	1353-1365	tr.	Upwood?
Symond, William	1369	tr.	Upwood?
Tame, John	1360	hue	?
Templere, Nicholas	1412	d-.	?
Tinemew, Roger	1350	tr.	?
Walies, John	1421	tr.	?
White, Roger	1375-1376	tr.	?
Wilynsson, Alexander	1371	tr.	Wistow
Willis, ( )	1363	tr.	?
Wyngood, Thomas	1375-1376	tr.	?

It was mentioned at the end of the previous chapter that it was impossible to determine whether some important freemen holding property in Warboys were actually ever resident in the village, and certainly the lords' administrators did not reside in the village. Another method of measuring the periphery of this part-time interest in Warboys or the people of Warboys, is through the list of witnesses to land charters. About one dozen charters survive for Warboys over the five or six decades prior to 1350. As the following list shows, most of the witnesses were from Warboys itself or the neighbouring villages of Broughton, Woodhurst (and Oldhurst), Pidley, Fenton and Ramsey.

List of witnesses to Warboys charters
Ca. 1290 to 1350

Atehale, Thomas, of Woodhurst	1330
Attedam, John, of Broughton	1330
Aula, Stephen de	1303
Beranger, John	1352
Berenger, Robert	1341, 1342
Baron, John	1334
Boys, John of	1331
Broughton, William (son of John of Broughton)	1330
Broughton, William of	1324, 1325, 1328, 1334
Broughton, Thomas of, clerk	1324, 1325, 1328 (2), 1330
Broughton, John of	1300, 1303, 1318
Broughton, John of, son of Thomas Clerk	1330
Broughton, Richard of, clerk	1290
Campronn, Hugh the	1300

Catoun, John, of Warboys	1330, 1334, 1342, 1352
Chamberlain, Benedict, of Woodhurst	1324, 1325, 1328 (2), 1330, 1331
Chaode, William, of Ramsey	1330
Claxton, John of	1328
Clervaux, Ralph	1328
Clervaux, Ranulph, of	1290
Cook, Thomas, of Wistow	1290
Cotenham, Hugh of	1300
Couherde, William	1341, 1342
Deen, Walter of	1303
Deen, John, Lord of	1328
Eydon, Hugh of	1293, 1300
Forester, Godfrey the, of Woodhurst	1330, 1331
Forester, Godfrey the, of Pidley	1324, 1325
Fulchet, John	1293
Gocelyn, John, of Broughton	1303
Grendale, Alan of	1300
Grendale, Richard of, in Fenton	1318
Gryndale, Roger of	1293
Higney, William	1290, 1352
Higney, Hugh of, of Warboys	1324, 1325
Higney, John of, of Warboys	1293, 1303, 1318
Hale, Robert of, clerk	1290
Hirst, Ivo of	1300
Hirst, Roger of	1318, 1324, 1325, 1341, 1342, 1352
(Hyrst), Thomas of	1290
Houghton, Gilbert of	1328, 1330
Hrien, Reginald, of Elton	1300
Leyr, Henry, of Woodhurst	1342
London, William of	1290, 1293
Milner, Nicholas le	1331
Morton, Richard de, of Heightmangrove	1330
Mowyn, William, of Oldhurst	1324, 1325, 1318, 1328 (2), 1330, 1331, 1334
Letchworth, John of, of Ramsey	1330
Moigne, William le	1290, 1318, 1328 (2)
Norreys, Ralph	1300, 1303
Raveley, John of	1328 (2)
Rideman, Thomas le, of Heightmangrove	1350
Ramesholt, Richard	1352
Ralph, William son of, of Broughton	1290
Stukeley, Nicholas of	1334
Stivintone, James of	1290
Swynelond, William of	1290
Unfrey, John	1303
Unfrey, William, of Warboys	1318
Wassingle, William of, steward	1293
Wistow, John of	1293

LONG TERM MOVEMENTS

A second general category of mobility is that of more long-term movement from the village as indicated by entries for those off the demesne
both with and without licence (Table IX) as well as by the place-name
origin of Warboys people (Table X). For those leaving with or without
license there were two main periods of activities, around 1300 and after
1400. In the former period no great concern was expressed in the village
court about the return of these villagers,[1] and in fact there is little or no
evidence that villagers did return. For this reason, undoubtedly, absent
villagers frequently did not have their whereabouts traced. It is interesting too that, as the accompanying map indicates,[2] Warboys people who
went abroad in the early fourteenth century most often went to another
village of their lord. Surprisingly,[3] there is little evidence for movement
of Warboys people from the village after the Black Death. Over the
next half-century only William, son of William Bonde, was noted to be
absent without licence at Heightmangrove (1353), and Agnes Albyn
was at Fenton without licence (1382). Away from the village with licence
were William Bettis (1353), William Pege (1360-1371) and Richard
Allot (1360-1392).

From 1400 the movement of villagers revived again but with a pattern
differing from that in the early fourteenth century. Most villagers now
were leaving without permission and, while there is no evidence that the
lord succeeded in recovering these persons, an effort was made to trace
them. For this reason we have fairly complete information about the
whereabouts of most villagers even though these now were obviously
not governed in their movements by the lord's economy. As the accompanying map indicates,[4] villagers moved farther afield in the early
fifteenth century, and it is frequently noted that they moved in response
to the new industrial attractions of the time.

There was little indication in the extent of 1251 for the place-name
origin of Warboys people. Surnames were only employed by places
Brandon, Brehill (Brill, Berks.), Grafham, Higney and Seaborough

---

[1] *Tenure and Mobility*, pp. 141-142.

[2] Below, p. 26.4

[3] Though, perhaps not surprisingly in view of rapid refilling of vacant tenancies. cf. *Estates*,
p. 252.

[4] Below, p. 265.

(Dorset), although some names may have indicated more remote place origins, as with Walse (Walsh, Welsh). By the time of the court rolls, however, obvious place-names that have become mentioned in Warboys records were many. The following table indicates 42 place names over 1290-1353 and 46 over 1360-1458. Some of these had become residents, as may be seen in family names of Table II above. But the majority were more casual visitors to Warboys. In either case, such names provide another picture of the geographical range of those entering into the life of one village over this period.

Table IX

Warboys people who emigrated between 1290-1347[1]

NAME	DATE	PLACE
Agath, Richard	1306-1313 (L)	Huntingdon (Hunts.)
Attewode, Robert	1322	Heitmangrove (Nr. Ramsey)
Alot, Robert	1333-1339 (L)	?
Bartholomew, Simon, son of	1305-1306	Elsworth (Cambs.)
Baseley, Agnes	1294-1299	Ramsey (Hunts.)
Beadle, John, son of Thomas	1299-1306 (L)	?
Bonde, Luke	1290-1301 (L)	Weston (Hunts.)
—, Benedict, son of Richard	1313-1322	?
Brun, Lawrence	1292-1294 (L)	Pidley (m) (Hunts.)
—, Nicholas	1294	Ramsey (Hunts.)
—, Richard	1294	Ramsey (Hunts.)
Bugge, Richard	1294-1299	Benwick (Cambs.)
—, Godfrey	1299-1316	?
—, William, son of Ralph	1294	Brampton (Hunts.)
Bumbel, William	1331-1339 (L)	?
Catoun, Hugh, son of Richard	1294-1301	?
Clerk, Reginald, son of Godfrey	1322-1326 (L)	Bluntisham (Hunts.)
—, Alice	1333 (m)	?
—, William	1331-1334 (L)	freehold (local?)
Cowherd, Robert	1294	?
Edwyne, Robert	1306 (L)	Ramsey (Hunts.)
Faber, Richard, son of Henry	1292-1294 (L)	? (Ramsey) (Hunts.)
—, Benedict	1316-1339 (L from 1325)	Somersham (Hunts.)
—, Hugh	1294 (L)	Hilton (Hunts.)
—, Stephen, son of Henry	1301-1306	Wistow (1305) (Hunts.)
Feker, Alan	1294-1299	Ramsey (Hunts.)

[1] L = licence;   m = marriage;   d = dead.

NAME	DATE	PLACE
Fot, William	1294	?
Fraunceys, William	1294	Huntingdon (Hunts.)
—, John, son of John	1294	?
—, William, son of John	1294	?
Gardener, Godfrey	1292-1294 (L)	Ramsey (Hunts.)
Gerold, Emma	1305-1306 (m)	Fenton (Hunts.)
—, Simon	1294-1301	Kent
Godfrey, Reginald, son of	1325-1334 (L)	?
Gosse, Emma	1306 (m)	Ely (Cambs.)
Harsine, Robert	1326-1334 (L)	?
Herbert, William	1294-1313 (L)	?
Henry, Stephen, son of	1306	?
Hering, John	1294-1299	?
Isabel, Richard	1313-1326	Holywell (Hunts.)
—, John	1322	?
Juliana, Richard, son of	1294-1299	Modney (Norfolk)
Kaunt, Henry	1292-1294 (L)	?
London, Ralph	1290	?
Lucas, William	1292	?
Mably, Robert	1313-1316	?
Margarette, Richard	1313-1331	Fenton (Hunts.)
Nel, Richard	1294-1313 (L)	Ramsey (Hunts.)
Noble, Richard, son of Richard	1316-1334 (L)	?
Nunne, Robert	1313	?
Onty, Cristina	1294-1299	Ramsey (Hunts.)
—, Emma	1294	Ramsey (Hunts.)
—, Richard	1299	?
Peres, Robert	1299-1306	Ramsey (Hunts.)
Pilche, Hugh	1299	Hemington (Northants.)
—, Richard	1299-1313 (L)	Bury (Hunts.)
—, Robert, son of William	1301	Kent
Pilgrim, Stephen	1313-1339 (L)	Somersham (Hunts.)
—, Hawysia	1299-1301 (m)	Fenton (Hunts.)
—, Agnes	1299	Pidley (Hunts.)
Richard, William, son of	1299	?
Robyn, Hugh	1333-1334 (L)	?
Sculle, Robert	1294-1299	Ramsey (Hunts.)
—, William	1294-1306	Ramsey (Hunts.)
Scut, Godfrey	1290-1299	Kent
—, William, son of Godfrey	1299	?
Semar, William	1331-1334, 1339	?
Sperner, Robert	1292-1294	Waresley (Hunts.)
—, Bartholomew	1294-1320 (L)	Colne (Hunts.)
—, Lawrence	1299-1316 (L)	Reach (Cambs.)
—. ( )	1292	Ramsey (Hunts.)

NAME	DATE	PLACE
Swan, John	1294 (L)	?
—, Thomas	1294	?
Thomas, John, son of	1306-1316 (L)	?
Top, Valentine	1294	Chatteris (Cambs.)
—, Godfrey	1294	?
Walter, Godfrey, son of Simon	1299	Ramsey (Hunts.)
Wennington, John	1316-1339 (L)	?
William, Thomas, son of	1294-1313 (L)	Pidley (Hunts.)
Wrek, Ralph	1294-1306 (L)	Benwick (Cambs.)
Wych, Godfrey	1294-1313 (L)	?

Table IX

Warboys people who emigrated between 1400 and 1458

NAME	DATE	PLACE	TRADE
Albyn, Nicholas	1404-1405	?	–
Baron, John	1455-1458	London	–
Berenger, John, son of Richard	1421-1455, 1458 (d)	Ramsey (L)	–
—, John, son of Richard, of Caldecote	1440-1455	?	–
—, son of John jun.	1440-1446	at School (L)	
	1454-1455	London (d)	–
—, John	1448	Lavenham	–
	1458	Little Stukeley	–
—, John jun.	1448	Earith	–
	1440	Ramsey	–
—, John, son of William	1448	Old Hurst	–
	1455-1458	Lincolnshire	–
—, John, son of Richard, of Caldecote	1454-1455	Little Stukeley	carpenter
—, Joan, dau. of William	1405-1412	Slepe	
	1418-1423	Cambridge	
	1424-1428	King's Lynn	
—, Joan, dau. of John jun.	1440	London (m)	–
—, Joan, dau. of John	1455-1458	Kent	–
—, Cristina, dau. of John jun.	1440 (49)	London	–
—, Cristina, dau. of John	1448	St. Ives (m)	–
—, Katherine, dau. of Richard	1455-1458	Potton	–
—, Richard, son of William	1458	Lincolnshire	–
—, Richard	1440-1458	Lavenham	–

NAME	DATE	PLACE	TRADE
Berenger, Richard, son of John	1447-1455	Ramsey (L)	–
—, Thomas	1448	?	–
Bennesson, William	1404-1405	Walton	–
	1410-1428	Brigstock	–
Benson, John	1446-1447	Stamford (d)	palfreyman of the lord
(Boys), Margaret	1403	?	–
Bronnyng, John jun.	1418-1424	Godmanchester	–
—, Emma, dau. of John jun.	1418-1428	Ramsey (m)	–
—, Agnes, dau. of John jun.	1418	Stamford	–
—, Alice, dau. of John jun.	1418	Stamford (d)	–
—, Margaret, dau. of John jun.	1418	Oundell (d)	–
Cobbe, John	1440	Ramsey	–
Eyr, Alice, dau. of Thomas	1405-1411	Ramsey (m)	–
	1412	Wistow	–
	1418-1448	Ramsey	–
—, Joan, dau. of Richard	1423-1424	St. Ives	–
—, Katherine, dau. of Richard	1423-1424	St. Ives	–
—, (?), son of Thomas	1404	Ramsey	–
—, (?), son of Thomas	1404	Slepe	–
Flemyng, Thomas, son of William	1403-1304, 1421	Colne	–
	1423	Chlarle	–
	1424-1458	?	–
—, John, son of William	1405	Colne	–
—, Thomas, son of John	1403	?	–
—, John	1410-1411	?	–
Freman, Thomas, son of William, of Ramsey	1403-1421, 1442	St. Ives (d)	tanner
—, William	1418	(L)	–
—, son and dau. of William	1442-1446	Godmanchester (m)	–
	1447-1449	Hemingford	
	1454-1455	Godmanchester	–
—, Alice	1446	Ramsey (m)	–
	1447-1449	Ramsey (widow)	–
Gerold, Emma, dau. of John	1403-1405	Pidley (m)	–
Hichesson, Agnes, dau. of Thomas	1440	King's Ripton (m)	–
—, Margaret, dau. of Thomas	1455-1458	King's Ripton (m)	–
Hyche, Agnes, dau. of Thomas	1418-1448	King's Ripton (m)	–
Margaret, Agnes, dau. of Richard	1427	?	–
	1448-1455	Earith	–
Molt, Alice, dau. of Thomas	1404	Godmanchester	–
	1405	Upton	–
	1410-1428	Godmanchester	–

NAME	DATE	PLACE	TRADE
Molt, Agnes, dau. of John	1403-1405	Slepe	–
—, Agnes, dau. of Thomas	1404	?	–
Molt, Margaret, dau. of Thomas	1404	Slepe	–
	1405-1412	Upton (m)	–
	1418-1448	Huntingdon	–
—, Alice, dau. of John	1405	Willingham	–
—, Alice	1448	?	–
Pilgrim, Margaret, dau. of John	1400-1405	Ely (m)	–
—, Alice, dau. of John	1400-1404	Wisbech (d)	–
Plombe, William jun.	1455	Peterborough	carpenter
—, John, son of John	1412, 1440	?	–
—, John	1440, 1455	?	–
—, John sen.	1448	Lavenham	–
—, John, son of John sen.	1440-1455	Whittlesey	–
—, John, brother of John sen.	1440-1455	Whittlesey	–
—, John	1448	?	medicus
Raven, John	1400-1411	St. Ives (L)	tanner
Raveley, William	1440-1448	Ramsey (L)	–
—, John	1403	?	–
—, John, son of William	1448	Ramsey	–
Rolf, John, son of Robert	1400	?	–
Sand, Richard	1421-1427	Ramsey (L)	–
—, William, son of John jun.	1458	Hemingford Abbots	–
—, John, brother of William, son of John jun.	1458	Hemingford Abbots	–
Scut, John	1455-1458	Oakington (L) (d)	–
—, John, son of John sen.	1421-1423	Huntingdon (L)	–
—, William jun., son of John	1455	?	–
—, John, son of John	1424-1448	overseas	–
	1455	Oakington (d)	–
—, William, son of John	1448	Oakington (L)	–
—, William	1458	London	–
—, William, son of William	1442-1446	?	–
	1447-1449	Oakington (d)	–
(Schon), William, son of John	1458	London	–
Semar, Thomas, son of William	1418	Tynwell	–
—, Thomas, son of (?)	1404	(Pid')	–
—, John, son of Thomas	1400-1405	Pidwell, nr. Stamford	
—, Emma, dau. of (Thomas)	1403-1405	Upwood	–
—, John	1410-1418	Tynwell, nr. Stamford	
Smart, William	1404	?	–
—, William	1405	Wrestlingworth	–
	1410-1412	Ramsey	–
—, Simon	1410	Woodhurst (L)	–

NAME	DATE	PLACE	TRADE
Vicory, Thomas, son of Robert	1400	Woodhurst	–
Wilkes, Richard, son of John	1404-1412, 1418-1428	Hartford ?	carpenter –
—, William	1448	?	–

Table X

Surnames indicating village of origin
1290 to 1353

SURNAME	PLACE NAME	COUNTY
Bernewell	Barnwell	Northants.
Bewford	Beauford	Cambs.
Bokeland	Buckland	Herts.
Bodyngton	Boddington	Northants.
Bokworth	Buckworth	Hunts.
Brancaster	Brancaster	Norfolk
Brandon	Brandon	Cambs.
Broughton	Broughton	Hunts.
Cam	Cam	Cambs.
Chatteris	Chatteris	Cambs.
Chycheley	Chicheley	Bucks.
Cranfield	Cranfield	Beds.
Drayton	Fen Drayton	Cambs.
Duton	(Dunton)	Beds.
Ellington	Ellington	Hunts.
Ellsworth	Elsworth	Cambs.
Ely	Ely	Cambs.
Eydon	Eydon	Northants.
Fenton	Fenton	Hunts.
Hygeney	Higney	Hunts.
Hockley	Hockley	Warks.
Hyrst	Hyrst (Oldhurst)	Hunts.
Keston	Keyston	Hunts.
London	London	London
March	March	Cambs.
Norton	Norton	Northants.
Pidley	Pidley	Hunts.
Ramsey	Ramsey	Hunts.
Raveley	Raveley	Hunts.
Somersham	Somersham	Hunts.

SURNAME	PLACE NAME	COUNTY
Stowe	Stowe	Northants.
Stratford	Stratford	Beds.
Sudbury	Sudbury	Beds.
Sutton	Sutton	Beds.
Temesford	Tempsford	Beds.
Therngg' (Thyring)	Finedon	Northants.
Walsoken	Walsoken	Norfolk
Warwyk	Warwick	Warks.
Wennington	Wennington	Hunts.
Weston	Weston	Northants.
Wistow	Wistow	Hunts.
Woodhurst	Woodhurst	Hunts.
Wynton	Wynton	Hunts.

Table X

Surnames indicating village of origin
1360 to 1458

SURNAME	PLACE NAME	COUNTY
Badburgh	Bady	Northants.
Barford	Barford	Northants.
Barnwell	Barnwell	Northants.
Bokelond	Buckland	Herts.
Brampton	Brampton	Hunts.
Bukworth	Buckworth	Hunts.
Burbrigge	Burbidge	Wilts.
Caldecote	Caldecote	Hunts.
Chiple	Chibley	Beds.
Colleville	Colevill	Cambs.
Coppynghalle	Coppinghall	Northants.
Croxton	Croxton	Norfolk
Dallyng	Dalling	Norfolk
Edham	Edenham	Leics.
Elington	Ellington	Hunts.
Elys	Ely	Cambs.
Fenton	Fenton	Hunts.
Farendon	Faringdon	Berks.
Freston	Freeston	Suffolk
Fordyngton	Fordington	Lincs.
Hirst	Hirst (Oldhurst)	Hunts.

SURNAME	PLACE NAME	COUNTY
Herrow	Harrow	Middx.
Higeneye	Higney	Hunts.
Horewode	Harrold	Beds.
Kilpesham	Clipsham	Rutland
Kirkeley	Kirkley	Northants.
Lawshill	Lawshall	Suffolk
Lyvedon	Livedon (Aldwinkle)	Northants.
London	London	London
Maddyngle	Maddingley	Cambs.
Merton	Merton	Cambs.
Nedham	Needham	Cambs.
Niddingworth	Niddingworth	Hunts.
Northbourgh	Northborough	Hunts.
Olneye	Olney	Northants.
Oundell	Oundell	Northants.
Orewell	Orwell	Oxford
Papworth	Papworth	Cambs.
Ramsey	Ramsey	Hunts.
Raundes	Raundes	Northants.
Raveley	Raveley	Hunts.
Segrave	Seagrave	Leics.
Slough	Slough	Bucks.
Sudbury	Sudbury	Beds.
Swafham	Swaffham	Norfolk
Wennington	Wennington	Hunts.
Wittelsey	Whittlesey	Cambs.

PART III

VILLAGE RESOURCES IN LAND AND LABOUR

Chapter V

THE VILLAGERS' PROPERTY

I

THE FIRST HUNDRED YEARS

Exactly what economic resources were available to inhabitants of Warboys around 1300 is not easily ascertained. The modern village of Warboys comprises some 8,435 acres, but as much as one-half (one league by one-half league in Domesday Book) of this acreage could have been non-arable fenland in the thirteenth century, and even with respect to the use of this Warboys fen as pasture several neighbouring villages held rights to common. Presumably the official manorial land unit count around 1300 would be somewhat the same as that in the 1251 extent, that is 144 tenements. Since only 130 individuals were recorded as tenants in 1251, and there is no evidence for a tenurial revolution during succeeding generations, very likely about the same number of individuals would be recorded as tenants were an extent drawn for the early fourteenth century. In short, one would expect that the greater number of those adults listed in the court rolls (Table I, Chapter II, above) had no direct relation to land in so far as manorial records were concerned.

Even for the mid-thirteenth-century Warboys extent, however, one must be cautious about describing a tenement as normal, either in terms of services owed or as obviously adequate for sustenance. The actual service—bearing units were given as the virgate (37 units), semi-virgate (14 units), a combination of messuage and croft (33 units), and the manse (10 units). The virgate was a classical villein unit; the semi-virgate was an official service-bearing unit; the messuage and croft (or *coterellus* of the Hundred Rolls) was strictly a labour-supply unit; the manse largely rent-bearing. However, the actual population recorded in the extent was not equated with types of tenements. Of the 37 virgate units only 13 were held entirely by one individual, 16 were held by two individuals, 7 by three, and 1 by four. In addition, undoubtedly each major tenurial unit included the lesser, that is to say the messuage and croft units must have also held a living abode or manse, while the virgate and semi-virgate units would have required both a messuage and manse. Indeed, some virgate units would have required several residential units.

If the resident population were to be equated with this smallest common denominator of service-bearing unit, then the total village population in 1251 could well have approached that indicated by the court rolls of around 1300. Nevertheless such concentration in the extent is only identified for a two-virgate freehold unit (10 acres + 10 acres + 10 acres + 1 messuage + 1 messuage + 1 messuage + 1 messuage + 1 messuage + 1 messuage + 1 "bordellum" + 1 "bordellum"). Nothing is told of the residents on the 2 virgates and messuage and one-half acre of the parson and the freeholds of William, the son of Hunfridus (1 virgate), Robert Raven (1½ virgate), Hugh the Vicar (½ virgate). Despite the great variations in size, the names of tenants are restricted to the four regular service-bearing units. Irregular combination of properties, that is, those not included in the regular units above are rare: one-half virgate under semi-work bearing land is held one-half free and one-half for work, 2 one-croft units and 3 one-half croft units were held separate from messuage, 5 rods of arable in 4 places were held by the tenant of one messuage and one croft unit, two semi-virgaters also held pieces of meadow, and one tenant was said to live on one acre although this was not described as a manse.

The Hundred Roll of 1279 is for the most part merely a compressed version of the 1251 extent. Main categories of land in 1279 appear much the same as earlier despite variations in nomenclature. In part variations in 1279 from the extent of 1251 may be explained by problems of nomenclature and by the lack of concern for precision at the later date. The 1279 picture, then, may be summarized as follows:

36 × 1 virgate units (Albinus of Caldecote and 35 others) (virgate = 30 acres)

14 × ½ virgate units (Simon Plumbe; Godfrey Clericus and 6 other with maltmanlands; William Lucas and 5 others with akermanlands); 34 × 1 messuage + 1 croft of 1 acre (*coterellus*) (Godfrey Attewode and 33 others)

5 messuage and croft units of 2 acres

4 messuage and curtilage units of ½ rod

6 other small units of varied sizes

10 varied freehold units.

These Hundred Roll land units are slightly fewer than those of the 1251 extent. In the latter document there would appear to be 37 one-virgate units, 15 one-half virgate units, 34½ croft units and some ten assorted small-holdings. The difference very likely comes from some slight increase in freehold or at least land held for money rents by 1279. However, the difference is not great and for the sake of a rough estimation of acreage the Hundred Roll gives more precise acreage data. Taking the virgate as 30 acres, as claimed in the extent, the total non-demesne acreage for Warboys indicated by the Hundred Rolls is 1,334 in regular units plus 258 acres in small units of varied sizes along with the ten freehold units.

Evidence from the account rolls indicates that the regular village land units remained over the hundred years after 1251. As given in the first list below, some of these conveyances were noted in the ordinary course of reporting the entry fine (*gersuma*). Other conveyances were noted when widows succeeded to their late husbands' lands and paid the heriot. A third list of tenancies has been obtained from entries pertaining to those unable to perform services for their land owing to illness (Table XI).

CONVEYANCES

TENANT ENTERING	FORMER TENANT	PROPERTY	FINE	YEAR
Son of Godfrey Herbert	Godfrey Herbert	?	5s.	1288-1289
Ralph Scut	?	?	16s.8d.	1288-1289
Nicholas, son of Margaret Pilche	Herbert Gerard	½ croft	?	1303
William, son of Ralph Thurberne	Ralph Thurberne	1 v.	66s.8d.	1303
Robert, son of William Thurberne	William Thurberne	¼ land	10s.	1303
William Segeley	father of William	1 v.	66s.8d.	1306-1307
Ralph Buk	Henry le Soper	1 croft	13s.4d.	1306-1307
William, son of Albinus	Albinus Semar	1 mess. ½ rod	3s.4d.	1306-1307
Godfrey Gerold	his father	½ v.	40s.	1306-1307
Sarra Swan	Hawysia Swan	1 cottage	12d.	1306-1307
Godfrey, son of Bartholomew	Bartholomew	½ v.	40s.	1306-1307
John, son of William Thurkyld	Nicholas Albyn	1 cotland	4s.	1306-1307
John de Rede	Richard Wodecok	½ v.	40s.	1306-1307
Martin Semar	William Skut	1 monday croft	2s.	1318-1319
Hugh Beneyt	(Nicholas Lewyne)	1 monday croft	2s.	1318-1319
(Godfrey), son of Richard le Noble	Richard le Noble	1 v.	40s.	1318-1319

TENANT ENTERING	FORMER TENANT	PROPERTY	FINE	YEAR
Richard Gosse	( ) de Sutton	1 monday croft	2s.	1318-1319
Simon Bryd	?	1 monday croft	3s.4d.	1324-1325
Hugh Lone	his father	½ v.	30s.	1324-1325
Alice Brandon	in lord's hands	¼ land	4s.	1324-1325
John le Noble	?	1 monday croft	2s.	1324-1325
John, son of Alice Hawegate	?	1 monday croft	5s.	1324-1325
Robert Raven	?	?	20s.	1324-1325
?	? London	?	13s.4d.	1324-1325
Nicholas Gerold	William Rolf	1 v.	20s.	1325-1326
John le Palmer	William le Reve	½ v.	40s.	1325-1326
Simon, son of Godfrey Thurberne	William Walter	½ v.	6s.8d.	1325-1326
John, son of John Bronning	Robert Rolf	¼ land	10s.	1325-1326
William Smart	his father	?	5s.	1329-1330
William Vicory	Robert Godrich	?	5s.	1329-1330
Hugh Beneyt jun.	Hugh Beneyt sen.	½ v.	26s.8d.	1335-1336

HERIOTS

TENANT ENTERING	FORMER TENANT	PROPERTY	FINE	YEAR
Matilda, widow of Simon Margaret	Simon Margaret	?	5s.	1306-1307
Agnes Skut	her husband	¼ land	15d.	1318-1319
Alice, widow of Robert Albyn	Robert Albyn	?	5s.	1324-1325
Margaret Fine	husband	?	2s.6d.	1325-1326
Agnes le Bonde	husband	?	15d.	1325-1326
Sarra Skut	husband	¼ land	15d.	1335-1336
Agnes Bettes	husband	?	2s.6d.	1342-1343
widow of Robert Herberd	Robert Herberd	½ v.	2s.6d.	1344-1345
Agnes, widow of William Mold	William Mold	½ v.	2s.6d.	1344-1345
Alice Wodecok	husband	?	2s.6d.	1347-1348

Table XI

Period of illness among Warboys landholders over the fourteenth century

NAME	SIZE OF HOLDING	PERIOD OF ILLNESS	DATE
Godfrey Bettis	½ v.	4 wks. (winter, died)	1342-43
Henry Brown	½ v.	8 wks. (winter)	,,
Robert Collesson	1 v.	2 wks. (winter)	,,
Agnes Baldewyn	mondaycroft	6 wks. (winter)	,,
Simon Dyke	1 v.	15 days summer + all autumn	,,
John Wodekoc	maltmanland	all post autumn	,,
Richard Berenger	¼ land	2 days (post autumn)	,,
William Mold	½ v.	4 days (winter, died)	1344-45
Agnes Herberd	½ v. (heriot)	winter	,,
Andrew Bonde	¼ v.	9 wks. (winter)	,,
Benedict Pakerel	(1 v.)	4 wks. (summer)	,,
William Walter	mondaymanland	4 wks. (summer) 5 wks. (autumn)	,,
Roger Raven	(1 v.)	3 wks. (autumn)	,,
Benedict Lawesson	1 v.	4 wks. (autumn)	,,
Godfrey Gerold	½ v.	9 wks. (winter)	1346-47
Ralph Aleyn	1 mondaymanland	26 wks. (winter)	,,
Robert Smart	1 v.	2 wks. (winter)	,,
John Tymme	½ v.	2 wks. (winter) 2 wks. (autumn)	,,
Robert Albyn	1 v.	28 wks., 4 days (whole winter) whole summer	,,
John Albyn	½ v.	28 wks., 4 days (whole winter) whole summer	,,
John Wodekoc	½ v.	whole autumn	,,
Richard Collesson	1 v.	all post autumn	,,
Richard Collesson	1 v.	all winter, summer and autumn	1347-48
William Vicory	1 v.	4 wks., 1 day (winter)	,,
William Colier sen.	1 v.	15 days (winter)	,,
Robert Margaret	1 v.	15 days (winter)	,,
John, son of Godfrey	1 v.	15 days in winter and 4 wks. in summer	,,
Robert Berenger	¼ land	1 wk. (winter)	,,
Godfrey Gerold	½ v.	1 wk. (winter)	,,
John Wodekoc	maltmanland	3 wks. (winter, died)	,,
William Lone	½ v.	2 wks. (summer)	,,
Nicholas Carter	cotland 2 mondaymanlands	8 wks., 3 days (all autumn and post autumn)	,,

159

NAME	SIZE OF HOLDING	PERIOD OF ILLNESS	DATE
Cristina Chicheley	I v.	4 wks. (autumn)	1347-48
Thomas Scut	½ v.	4 wks. (autumn + post autumn)	,,
Beatrice Pilche	mondaymanland	5 wks., 3 days (autumn)	,,
Benedict Lawesson	I v.	2 wks. (post autumn)	,,
Richard Smythe	¼ land	all post autumn	,,
Agnes Attewode	mondaymanland	all post autumn	,,
Benedict Lawesson	I v.	5 wks. (winter)	1348-49
John Flemyng	½ v.	4 wks. (winter)	,,
Simon Dyke	I v.	4 wks. (winter)	,,
Godfrey Molt	I v.	4 wks. (summer)	,,
John Gerold	maltmanland	3 wks. (summer)	,,
John Flemyng	I v.	3 wks. (summer)	,,
John Derworth	mondaymanland	9 wks. (summer)	,,
Agnes Molt	I v.	9 wks. (summer)	,,
Thomas Raven	1½ v.	3 wks. (summer)	,,
William Raven	mondaymanland + ¼ v.	4 wks. (summer)	,,
William Simon	I v.	3 wks. (summer)	,,
William Colle	I v.	4 wks. (summer)	,,
Richard Benet	maltmanland	2 wks. (summer)	,,
Stephen Bonde	¼ v.	3 wks. (summer)	,,
John Clerk	maltmanland + mond.	2 wks. (summer)	,,
Roger Brownyng	I v.	3 wks. (summer)	,,
Agnes Albyn	I v.	3 wks. (summer)	,,
Robert Smart	I v.	8 wks. (summer)	,,
John, son of Godfrey	I v.	4 wks. (summer)	,,
Robert Nicholson	I v.	8 wks. (summer)	,,
Henry Brown	¾ v.	2 wks. (summer)	,,
John Plumbe	maltmanland	I wk. (summer)	,,
John Hichesson	I v.	6 wks. (summer)	,,
John Harsene	I v.	4 wks. (summer)	,,
Alice Colier	I v.	4 wks. (summer)	,,
William Bryd	I v.	5 days (autumn)	,,
Robert Albyn	? (I v.)	3 wks. (winter) 7 wks. (summer)	1353-54
John Berenger	½ v.	3 wks. (autumn)	,,
Richard Gerold	¾ v.	4 wks. (autumn)	,,
Richard Alot	?	I wk. (autumn)	1359-60
John Jekkison	I v.	5 wks. (autumn)	1360-61
John Derworth	2 mondaymanlands	10 wks. (winter)	1362-63
Richard Scut	2 mondaymanlands	6 wks. (winter)	,,
William Bonde	1 mondaymanland	4 wks. (winter)	,,
John Colier	I v.	I month (winter)	,,
William Colle	I v.	6 wks. (winter; died in summer)	1363-64

NAME	SIZE OF HOLDING	PERIOD OF ILLNESS	DATE
Thomas Semar	½ v.	1 month (summer)	1363-64
Robert Berenger	1¼ v.	5 wks. (autumn)	„
Richard Nunne	1 v.	5 wks. (winter)	1365-67
Richard Nunne	1 v.	1 wk. (autumn + 2 wks. post autumn)	1375-76
Thomas Raven	1 v.	24 wks. (winter)	1377-78
Henry Edward	½ v.	3 wks. (autumn)	„
John Foster	½ v.	3 wks. (winter)	1378-79
John Molt	½ v.	3 wks. (autumn)	„
John Foster	½ v.	6 wks. (summer)	1393-94
Richard Nunne	1¼ v.	2 wks. (autumn)	„
Henry Edward	½ v.	whole winter, summer and autumn and died	„
John Bonde	¼ v.	16 wks. (died, winter)	„
John Othehill (Attehill)	½ v.	14 wks. (winter)	„
Richard Berenger	½ v.	5 wks. (summer)	1404-05
John Plumbe	maltmanland	4 wks. (summer)	„
John Brownyng	1 v.	2 wks. (autumn)	1407-08

Since the Warboys court rolls did not serve as a record for entry fines, or other routine payments such as heriots, it was only as a lawsuit or legal enquiry that tenurial questions come to the attention of the court. On the whole references to land in the court rolls are remarkably few in light of the large number of people involved and the array of entries. There were only seven references to what have been termed above "regular" entries:

Ralph Fine sold a grange barn from ½ v.	1294
4 men hold for Robert, son of Mabel, away without licence, 1 v.	1301
In the lord's hands from Alice Brandon, dead, 1 cottage	1334
John, son and next heir by blood to Robert Berenger, dead, 1 messuage, ¼ land, perch of meadow	1347
Alice, widow of Nicholas Plumbe, ½ v.	1339
son of Cristina Harsine, dead, ½ v.	1339
William Hayward, disrepair on 1 cotland	1339

The tenemental units found listed in the extent of 1251, and various other references to these units that we have been able to discover for the next hundred years, were employed to indicate the rent and the service assessment on the land. The actual productive deployment of Warboys land was quite different. In the extent of 1251 it was stated that the lord's demesne consisted of a number of *culturae*, and 37 of these cultivated furlongs were listed. The compilers of the extent could not commit themselves to estimating the number of acres in these furlongs, but contented themselves with the remark that this demesne of the lord could be cultivated with four ploughs, customary services and two boon works.

From the good series of Warboys charters available for later in the thirteenth century, it is clear that compilers of the extent did not elaborate upon acreage in each *cultura* because the actual units of cultivated land pertaining to each virgate were scattered in small parcels throughout the furlong. This description of land is illustrated below from several charters. These charters also identify the units by neighbouring tenants and it can be seen from these names that the charter information is not exceptionable but covers a wide cross section of the people of Warboys.

1) *18a. (Ca. 1290):*[1]

½a. on Longe Flexlond next Simon Lone
2r. at Middilgrove Yerdes next William Brandon
½a. at Alwolddisrodis next William Faber
½a. on Hayforlang next Richard Wodekoc
½a. on Clavehil next Robert Gose
½a. at Toncroft next Simon Lone
½a. at Seccetuppeforlang next Simon Lone
½a. on Waterforenes next Robert Gose
½a. on Estlong next Walter Galeways
½a. at Scor'croft next Walter Galeways
2r. on Calonhyl next Walter Galeways
1r. at Demildisbrigge next Richard Wodecok
1r. at Heyecros next Simon Lone
½a. at Onenestede next Robert Gose
½a. at C'newelle next Robert Gose
½r. on Calonhyl next Simon Lone
½a. at Brounbrigge next Simon Lone
½r. at Brounbrigge next William Prepositus
½a. on Brocforlong next Walter Galeways
1r. on Brocforlong next Richard Wodecok
½a. on Brocforlong next William Brandon
½a. on Blakelond next Walter Galeways
½a. below the same next Simon Lone

[1] Additional Charter 34176.

162

1r. on Brocforlong next Robert Gose
½a. on None Acars next Simon Lone
1r. on None Acars next Hugh of Eydon
½a. on Middilforlong next Walter Galeways
1r. at Brerehelsladis next William Wodecok
1r. on Hollond next Simon Lone
1r. on Langscet next Hugh Beneyt
1r. on Suorn'lond next Ralph Scut
1r. on Suorn'lond next William Wodecok
1r. on Longewold next Richard Wodecok
1r. on Chortewold next Robert Bonde
½a. on Longewold next Bartholomew Faber
½a. on Chortewold next William Prepositus
3 butts on Chortewold next Richard Ne(dham)
1r. on Walton next Simon Lone
2r. on Walton next Thomas Raven
1r. at Littelstok next William Brandon
½r. at Madecroft next Walter Galeways
1r. at Middilgrove next Simon Lone

2) *8a. (1293):*[1]

½a. on Longewold between Rector of the Church and Richard Gerold jun.
2r. on Watercroft between Hugh of Eydon and Godfrey
2r. on Thyrethorn between Hugh of Eydon and William Lucas
½a. on Bywelond between William, son of Walter and Simon Larke
½a. running to Bronconebrok between Hugh Benyt and Richard Wodekoc
1r. on Blakelond between Richard Gerold jun. and formerly Ralph Edwyn
½a. on Kranewell between Richard Gerold jun. and Richard Wodekoc
1a. on Longhortherd between Abbot of Ramsey and William of London
½a. on Walton between Godfrey Walsh and Stephen LeGuler
3r. on Lambecotestede between William, son of Robert and Martin Le Bonde
½a. on (Sc)urecroft between Richard Gerold jun. and William Faber
1r. on Toft called Hawedlond between Abbot of Ramsey and William Lucas
1r. next Custwell between Hugh Beneyt and Richard Gerold jun.
½a. next Byrywyere between Richard Le Bonde and formerly Simon Plumbe
½a. on Launnemer between Godfrey Walsh and Therild
2r. in the corner in Thonecroft between Richard Le Bonde and Richard Puttok

3) *10a. (Ca. 1324):*[2]

½a. on Alwoldesrodes next Agnes Le Smyth
½a. on Hayfurlong next John Le Rede
1r. on Lonnemer' next Henry Broun
1½r. below Clanehil next Henry Broun

[1] P. R. O. ancient deed A. 5156.
[2] Additional Charter 34177.

163

½a. at Seccecuppefurlong next Hugh Lone
½a. at Scorecroft next Walter Galeways
1r. at Denuldisbergg next John le Rede
1r. at Heyecros next Hugh Lone
½a. at Onenestede next Henry Broun
½a. at Cranewelle next Henry Broun
½r. on Calewehill next Hugh Lone
½r. at Bronnebrigge next William Prepositus
½a. on Brokfurlong next Walter Galeways
1r. on Brokfurlong next John Le Rede
½a. on Brokfurlong next Alice Brandon
½a. beneath Blakelond next Hugh Lone
1r. on Brokfurlong next John Le Rede
½a. on Nineacres next Hugh Lone
1r. on (Nineacres) next John of Clervaux
1r. on (Ha)lslades next Emma Wodekoc
1r. on Langsket next Hugh (   )
(1)r. on (Veme)lond next Thomas Scut
1r. on Longewold next John (   )
( ). on Shortewold next Robert Bonde
3 butts on Shortewold next John (   )
½r. at Madecroft next Walter Galeways
1r. at Middilgrove next Hugh Lone
½a. at Toncroft next Hugh Lone
½a. on Estlong next Walter Galeways

4) 7a. (Ca. 1325):[1]

½a. on Flexlond next Hugh Lone
1r. on Flexlond next Roger De Hyrst
1r. on Longflexlond next Hugh Lone
½a. on Clavehil next Henry Broun
2r. at Middilgroveyerdes next Alice Brandon
2r. on Claewehil next Walter Galeways
½a. on Waterforewes next Henry Broun
½a. at Bronnebrigge next Hugh Lone
½a. on Blakelond next Walter Galeways
½a. on Middilfurlong next Walter Galeways
½a. on Longewold next Godfrey, son of Bartholomew
1r. on Walton next Hugh Lone
2r. on Walton next Thomas Raven sen.
1r. at Littlestok mext Alice Brandon
1r. at Hollond next Hugh Lone
½a. on Shortewold next William Prepositus
1r. on Swornelond next Emma Wodekoc

[1] Additional Charter 34182.

5) *8a.* (*1328*):[1]

½a. between (Ratous) of Warboys and Richard Gerold
2r. on Whatcroft between Hugh of Eydon and Godfrey Clerk
2r. at Thenethorn between Hugh of Eydon and William Lucas
½a. on Rinelond between William, the son of Walter and Simon Larke
½a. towards Broughton broke between Hugh Beneyt and Richard Wodekoc
1r. on Blakelonde next Richard Gerold jun.
½a. on Brakenewell next Richard Gerold jun. on one side and Richard Wodekoc on the other
1a. at Longehurchard between Lord Abbot of Ramsey and William of London
½a. on Walton
3r. between Lambecotestede
½a. on Sacrecroft next Richard Gerold
1r. on Le Tofte called Hawedlond
1r. next Toftk(elk) next Richard Gerold sen.
½a. next Biriweye next formerly Simon Plumbe
½a. on Lammemerei next Godfrey of Walshe
2r. in the corner of Tonescroft next Richard le Bonde
1r. of meadow lying beneath the woods of the Lord of Ramsey between the meadow of Hugh formerly of Eydon and the meadow formerly of Benedict Prepositus

The court roll evidence reflects this scattering of many small units of land. Queries about the proper enfeoffment of freehold suggest that there was an extensive market in small units of land. In 1294 Ivo of Hirst bought one messuage and 13 acres from Cristina de Higney, in the same year (Sperner?) purchased eight acres from Ralph the gardener, and Roger Carpenter purchased one-half acre from Cristina de Higney. Charters were also involved in the 1313 purchase of two acre units of land by Thomas de Elington and John de Temesford respectively from Roger de Norreys. Thomas Raven jun., also had to show a charter for the one messuage and three acres of freehold received with his wife in free *maritagium* in 1325. In 1326 there was noted two small purchases of freehold from Robert the Chaplain, Margaret the wide of John Catoun and her son Robert having purchased one acre, and John, son of John Catoun and Agnes Pilche, having bought the other acre. In 1320 John de Kam of Long Stanton bought from Roger, son of Ivo of Hirst, the substantial property of one messuage and 24 acres. In the same year William, the son of John Clervaux, showed his charter for a messuage and two acres bought from John son of Hugh de Eydon in 1318. It is not always clear whether charters were involved. For example, when

[1] Additional Charter 34183.
These charters illustrate the variety of means employed to describe the location of lands as well as the variety of spellings for furlongs, crofts and other means of local identification.

Henry Semar purchased a piece of meadow in 1294, and rendered two chickens in recognition to the lord, this payment might have served as enrollment in place of a charter.

Customary law, too, as well as concern for enfeoffing, brought land transactions to the attention of the court. By acknowledging the prior rights of the widow over the customary tenement at the death of her husband, customary law at Warboys gave a certain priority to the whole family over the heir. That is to say, the widow would ensure that all her children had maintenance from the tenement. Stephen Smythe found that these family maintenance arrangements received the full support of the village courts when in 1334 he was forced to return the family property to his mother because he had not supported her as he had agreed to. Support of members of the family could also be managed by dispersal of property. Small pieces of land were purchased to supply daughters with a *maritagium*, as was noted for the wife of Thomas Raven jun., in the preceeding paragraph. And apparently an un-married daughter, like the sister of Nicholas Osbern, could be supported in the same fashion. We find out about this arrangement in 1313 when Nicholas Osbern recovered a land called sixpennyworth land given by his father to his sister. Nicholas apparently recovered this land because his sister had given it to Richard Godwyne. Furthermore, chattels could be bequeathed to various members of the family. Perhaps because this was an area of jurisdiction for the ecclesiastical court, we unfortunately know very little about the dispersion of chattels by will. But apparently wills were encouraged for Ramsey villagers, and beyond those chattels required for direct exploitation of the property, varied items of domestic value were passed on for support of members of the family.[1]

As with feudal services on a higher level of society, an effort was made to ensure the identity of the one responsible for villein services by strict control of subletting. For the longer-term subletting, the lessee assumed responsibility of obligations to the lord. An example of this may be seen in the agreement between William Cowherd and Thomas Gerold in 1347:

> It was established through evidence from the examination of neighbours that William Cowherd surrendered a messuage and nine acres to be held by Thomas Gerold at services, under these conditions, that the same William and his wife have for life a part of the messuage bounded by hedges and two acres of arable from the above land,

[1] Cf. *Tenure & Mobility*, chapter 3 for further examples of customary conveyances at Warboys and neighbouring villages.

and will pay two shillings to the same Thomas every year at Michaelmas. And the above Thomas will plough and cultivate those two acres every year at the proper time as often and in the same way as other like land is ploughed. And if the same Thomas should be unwilling to plough the two acres at the proper time William and his wife may keep the annual two shillings payment and provide for the ploughing of the two acres by someone else. It was also agreed by the same villagers that the above part of the messuage was not designated in length and breadth by feet but as bounded by the hedges. And they would find in the *gersuma* roll the length and breadth were not by common measure but by estimation.

No doubt at Warboys, as at other villages in the district, subletting of units of arable was allowed for a year or two without licence. We find examples of this when the regulations had been violated by subletting to a freeman. So William Frost was charged in 1299 with enfeoffing the crop of one sellion of wheat to Ralph Miller. And in 1333 William Semar had sublet one rod sown with peas to a freeman without licence. This short-term subletting must have provided a remarkable resource for the seasonal consumer needs of needy individuals and families. Quite simply because of its flexibility it is not surprising that little evidence exists of abuse of the system. One example, taken from the court roll for November 1306, may serve to illustrate the working of the local subletting custom:

> Godfrey Scut came and acknowledged that he had broken an agreement with Amicia Bugge about one sellion of land that he rented to the same Amicia for four years in part payment for one cow. And since it is established that no customary is able to sublet any part of his land in this fashion or to rent it to anyone except for a term of two years, such being the custom of the manor, it is ordered that the above sellion of land be taken into the lord's hands until, etc. (another entry in this court that is cancelled for the sake of the more complete above entry concludes: and it is ordered that the said Amicia may have that land for two crops).

Subletting of non-arable parts of the customary tenements seem to have been allowed under a variety of conditions so long as licence was received for the agreement. John Isabelle was charged in 1292 with letting of a part of a messuage to Cecilia the Brewer without licence. Isabella recovered this property seized by the lord in 1294. William Lucas had a part of a messuage and one-half rod and a crop sublet to Ralph Wrench and a part of messuage subret to John Ponder in 1290 seized by the lord. In 1294 the court roll announced that John Ponder now held a one-half messuage (alternatively described as a house) for three years from William Lucas at a rent of 8d., having paid an 8d. fine to the lord, and paying one chicken a year to the lord. By the same time

Ralph Wrench also had a licence to hold his one cottage of William Lucas, paying annually to the lord one chicken. In 1294 Margaret de Hawgate sublet part of her messuage to Richard Deward who was to build a smithy on the property, Richard agreeing to pay her 3d. rent a year. Towards the mid-century the same general arrangements pertained, since in 1347 the part of a servile messuage sublet by Ralph Aleyn to William Higney a freeman was seized because a licence had not been received.

The more obvious reasons for the lord obtaining control over movements of property were not immediately financial but rather the maintenance of the basic capital of the village. For this reason, by bringing freemen as well as the villeins under the court, much pressure could be brought to bear to avoid waste. In 1313 Richard Godwyne, a freeman, who held one cottage of the lord and let this go to waste, had the property seized by the lord. This regulation obviously protected the rights of fellow villagers as well as those of the lord, as was seen when John de Higney was assessed 12d. damage to be paid to Reginald de Sutton because John had failed to fulfill his agreement about a house. Usually, indictments on the court roll about buildings do not indicate who will gain from improvement to the property. Following are a list of some of these indictments found in the court rolls: 1333, William le Smythe built a *camera* on the common to the harm of others; 1325, the fine assessed on William Chaumon was condoned for his promise to re-build a house; in 1320 Nicholas le Milner was fined for having demolished some buildings and having sold timber that he had received (presumably from the common wood) for repair of these buildings; in 1299 Margaret Haliday had her land seized because she sold the grange off the property; in 1320 William Fine was reported to have failed to repair his buildings, not to have used timber allowed him for that purpose, and having taken timber from the collapsed buildings for use on his freehold; in 3 Ed. III it was reported that Godfrey Mold had not repaired his bridge according to the agreement he had made with the village. In 1326 Benedict Lenot escaped fine for having failed to maintain his buildings because of his poverty.

It is impossible to estimate the number of persons living directly off the land of Warboys because of the piecemeal nature of the above data from account and court rolls. But from the many avenues of access to property it would not be surprising if the actual units of property numbered several times those of the 1251 extent account. In short, the many individuals of Table I in the previous chapter could still largely be a propertied if not a landed people. It is even less possible to relate the social structure of Warboys to tenure of land. Obviously important freemen of the region like members of the Norreys family are involved in many freehold transactions, and the larger customary conveyances involved the more important villeins of Warboys. However, beyond the evidence for the spread of land in all classes, apparent villeins like Thomas Raven and William Fine would have freehold, freemen like William Higney might settle on a small customary unit, isolated individuals like Nicholas Osbern and special occupations like those of the hayward and smythe might supplement their revenues by small units ------ little more can be said.

The villagers of Warboys had access to a great many resources beyond the arable of the village, but information about the use of these resources is lamentably meagre. Fishing has been a great source of food for fenland people down through recorded history, yet in all the court rolls only a couple of entries can be found referring to fishing. In 1299 it was recorded that Richard Pakerel had been fined in the court of Broughton for interfering with the equipment and fishing in the waters of others. In 1320 William Fine was indicted for receiving one Andrew Dalebrook who had interfered with the fishing nets of others and taken their fish.

The marsh of Warboys is brought more clearly to our attention, again not because of information about the villagers own use of the marsh, but from the commercial value of the reeds. The court of 1292 ordained that the "bailiff should allow no one to sell or carry reeds beyond the village". However, the marsh proved difficult to administer. In 1305 William Hobbe of Broughton and Richard Pakerel and others were fined for breaking the ordinance. By the second quarter of the century the pressure on marsh resources had increased. In 1326 William of London, living at Fenton and twelve others had cut bearded reeds and taken two cart loads to Fenton. For this reason the ordinance was repeated more regularly from this time and with more detail. Nevertheless many fines became common in the ensueing court rolls, such as those of 1331 and 1334, and in 1343 the statute had to be reiterated again.[1] A slight glimpse of this vast fen resource can only be obtained from the indictments. The court of December 14, 1299, may be taken as an example:

> It was presented in the last court that Ivo of Hurst caused damage in the marsh by cutting reeds and digging turf to be carried to his home at Hurst. The bailiffs are ordered not to allow this Ivo nor anyone else not having his house or residence in

[1] Cf. further below, Ch. VII, p. 222 ff., for byelaws.

Warboys to be given, sold or permitted to carry in such things. And for Nicholas Plumbe claiming from Henry Scut, Richard Godwin and associates 600 reeds which at least contained 30 bundles, 3d., pledge William the reeve. And for Richard Catoun who wrongly claimed 130 bundles from the above Henry and associates... And for Henry Semar who wrongly claimed 100 bundles from the above Henry and associates... And for John, son of Walter wrongly claimed 200 bundles from the above Henry and associates... And for Thomas son of Robert who wrongly claimed 60 bundles from the above Henry and associates... And Richard Long of Little Raveley who wrongly claimed 400 reeds from the above Henry and associates... Richard Godwyn, Henry Scut and Richard Sperner acknowledged that they received from Hugh Duraunt of Warboys 200 reeds worth 6d., and from Jocelyn, son of Godfrey of Little Raveley 400 reeds worth 12d., and from Thomas, son of Benedict Martyn of Little Raveley 600 reeds worth 18d., and from Robert Brunnote of Wistow 800 reeds worth 2/—, and from William ad Ecclesiam of Wistow 800 reeds worth 2/—. And by the jurors they were convicted from taking from Richard Plumbe 600 (reeds) beyond the 30 bundles... and from Richard Catoun 600 reeds worth 18d., and from Henry Semar 400 reeds worth 12d., and from John, son of Walter 300 reeds worth 9d., and from Thomas, son of Robert 250 reeds worth 2½d., and from Richard Long 200 reeds worth 6d., and from Beatrice Jordan 500 reeds worth 15d. ...

The minor place of assarts in the tenure of Warboys indicates that clearing was virtually complete by the late thirteenth century. Assart units of six acres, three acres, three acres and twopence worth of *incrementum* remain on the rent roll of Warboys over the first half of the fourteenth century. Very likely, of course, substantial wood survived at Warboys where the core of an ancient forest still remains. But the forester's tasks did not seem pressing. There is only mention that Henry Forester raised the hue on Alan de Grendale for cutting wood in his bailiwick in 1301, and the woodward's hall was broken into and a pledge taken in 1306. There were only occasional suits because wood was being expropriated for commercial purposes; Ralph, son of William of London, had taken wood illegally in 1290; and enquiry was made about the sale of wood in 1294; William Carter was fined for selling two cart loads of bark to Thomas Raven in 1333; Richard Pilche, while servant of John Temesford custodian of the wood, sold and delivered wood illegally to Thomas, son of Robert. Likely we may assume that the villagers of Warboys, like other villages in the region, had access to the wood for basic needs of housing, fencing and repair. However, the extent only specifies "the villeins (*villani*) by the view and permission of the bailiff, may take sticks from the woods at a suitable season for repair of their ploughs".[1]

[1] *Carts.*, I, 307.

In the final analysis there is absolutely no information available from account roll or court roll about the villagers' use of the common for their own purpose. The 1251 extent states explicitly that "in this marsh both free and villein may cut (reeds and fen grass) and dig (turf)", yet how extensively this right was exploited we do not know. In similar fashion we must assume that all villagers had fishing rights since no fines were levied for abuse of fishing or licensing the fishing that clearly took place. And, as has been seen, wood was likely accessible to all to some degree.

The ability of the villagers of Warboys to pay for their tenements and to have the capital resources to assure themselves of the ability to exploit their lands, were also important needs in the village economy. On the whole the court rolls do not give much more information about the economic activity of Warboys than one might expect from courts of any reasonably well developed economy. The largest category of entries is that of lawsuits for indebtedness. As one can see in the following sample list, these suits usually cover the more formal legal problems of wills and debts owed to or from outsiders:

LAWSUITS FOR INDEBTEDNESS

OWED BY	OWED TO	NATURE OF DEBT	YEAR
Robert Cowherd	John Robert of Broughton	4s. 3d. for malt purchased	?
Emma le Soper	to executors of Robert Chose (of Fenton?)	4s. 10d.	1305
Thomas Raven senior	executors	debt	1326
John, son of Cecily	Nicholas Milner		1326
Robery Goderich	executors of Alice Albyn		1326
Robert Goderich	Hugh Albyn		1326
Thomas Puttock	Richard Puttock	part of messuage and corn	1320
Richard Cissor	William Bumbel	6d. per yr - 3 yrs	1320
Godfrey le Noble	his brother Simon	1/3 of furnace of their fathers	?
Robert Bissop	Alice Woodward	15d. for 1 acre of meadow	1290
Richard Bonde	Alice Woodward	15d. for 1 acre of meadow	1290

It was of special concern to the lord to maintain the capital of the village, and under customary law he attempted to assert an ultimate ownership over the chattels as well as the persons of these villeins. The following were charged with removing their chattels from the village when they departed: in 1292 Robert Sperner, in the same year Henry Kaunt, in 1313 William Harsine, in 1316 Richard le Noble, and in 1325 Benedict Faber. However, there is no evidence that any of these chattels were recovered. There is only the one entry with respect to the lord's effort to assert control over plough capital, this is the charge in the court of 1322 that William Segeley sold an ox cheaper to an outsider than he would to the lord's bailiff. In the court of 1325 villagers with handmills were threatened with a fine of 2/— although there is no evidence for the actual imposition of this fine.

One of the ways in which the villagers had to struggle to maintain their own capital was against the perennial problem of theft. In the court of 1326 it is mentioned that toll had been removed from the mill and, perhaps another form of the same charge, in the same court it is mentioned that there had been a theft of tithe by the servant of the Rector. Two thefts were mentioned in the court of 1313, thefts of a petty nature. In 1316 Alice, wife of William Sparhawk, was charged with thievery. What must have been a more common type of theft is represented by the court of 1322 wherein it is mentioned that sheaves of the lord's grain were found in the house of Richard Segeley, and two bushels of beans were found in the house of Emma Wodekoc. Very possibly the latter had gleaned wrongly since the court ordered that these beans were to be returned to the village. More often the court is employed to recover damage to persons of property. In 1347 WilliamViker was charged with having trespassed on the property of Richard Segeley for which the latter was awarded 3d. damage, and Viker was bound over by the penalty of a one-half mark.

In 1294 Juliana Bonde was assessed 6d. damages for defaming Richard the Woodward. Albinus Segeley was charged by the village for having overloaded the pasture with 30 sheep from Stukeley. In 1292 there is the case of a pledge recovering a loss suffered by pledging another.

One of the more difficult problems for the student of the village economy is that of identifying the method of tax assessment actually employed. Three court roll entries at Warboys refer to difficulties with the royal taxation system. In 1294 there is a charge against Amicia de Higney concerning royal taxes assessed to her by the hundreder. The claim by John Schut (Scut) in 1333 of loss would also seem to be associated with tax assessment. In the roll of 1347 there are two entries with respect to taxation problems: John Mice was considered non-taxable to the king for the corn he had in the field of Warboys, and it was charged that John Plumbe had removed one of his beasts from an enclosure without license from the taxers.

II

THE SECOND HUNDRED YEARS

According to the main record of village economic activities, the account rolls, no great shift occurred in the disposition of village resources after the Black Death. Much the same number of works were sold in the 1350's as earlier.[1] Manorial administrative adjustments were largely to be found in an increase of villein units *ad censum* from the 1350's.[2] The following table summarizes this account roll information.

At the same time, as we have seen in the previous section, account rolls do not tell us the actual names nor even numbers of tenants holding the varied customary and freehold units. New administrative policies were introduced to Warboys manor late in the third quarter of the fourteenth century, notably the more long-term commutation of work service (the *ad arrentatum* rental) and the leasing of significant portions of the lord's demesne to villagers. With this shift from the more customary arrangement the reeve and his associate beadles seem to have found it necessary to transform the account roll increasingly into a rent roll. As a result, detailed information is available for the names and holdings of tenants from the 1370's. This information falls particularly into two periods, the 1370's and the 1440's. The following table XIII has been constructed to show the actual spread of customary lands among tenants. That is to say, each unit indicates one tenant.

This table serves to indicate something of the dynamics of property holding at the time. There is the tendency towards larger holdings, the two virgate, or more commonly the one and one-half or one and one-quarter virgate tenement in the 1370's. There is also the tendency towards the sub-division of customary holdings, right down to the one-half maltmanland. In between these two extremes come a wide array of combinations, from the one tenant holding three dikemanlands and another two and one-half mondaymanlands, to complex combinations noted at the foot of this table.

[1] *Estates of Ramsey Abbey*, p. 243.
[2] *Estates of Ramsey Abbey*, p. 221 and 270.

Table XII

Changing forms of villeinage tenure over the fourteenth century

	VIRGATES					MALTMAN-LANDS				AKERMANLANDS					MONDAYMAN-LANDS				DIKEMAN-LANDS		
YEAR	Ad Op.	Ad C.	M.D.	Off.	A.	Ad Op.	Ad C.	Off.	A.	Ad Op.	Ad C.	M.D.	Off.	A.	Ad Op.	Ad C.	M.D.	A.	Off.	Ad Op.	M.D.
1354	25¾	8½	–	2	1	6	–	2	–	3	3	–	–	–	27	2	3	–	–	11	–
1359	26¼	6¾	1¾	1½	–	5	1	2	–	2	1	3	–	–	24	3	3	3	–	10	1
1360	26¼	7½	1¼	1	–	5	1	2	–	2	1	3	–	–	24	3	3	3	–	10	1
1362	25	6½	3¼	1½	–	5	1	2	–	2	1	3	–	–	24	3	3	3	–	10	1
1363	23½	5¾	3½	1½	2	4	2	2	–	2	1	3	–	–	20	7	3	2	1	10	1
1366	24¾	3¼	1¼	1½	6½	6	1	1	–	1	–	3	–	2	23	–	2	7	1	10	1
1371	22¾	2	3¼	¾	7½	1¾	1	½	1½	3	–	–	–	3	19	–	3	11	–	10	1
1373	22¼	2½	2½	¾	8¾	1¾	1	½	1½	1	–	–	2	3	17	–	3	13	–	10	1
1374	22	2½	2	1¼	8½	2	1	1	4	1	–	–	1	3	17	–	3	13	–	10	1
1375	21	2½	2	1¼	9	2½	1	½	2½	1	–	–	1	2½	17	–	3	13	–	10	1
1377	20½	2½	1	1¼	11	2½	1	½	3½	1	–	–	1	3	17	–	2	14	–	10	1
1378	21½	2½	½	1¼	11	2½	½	½	3	1	–	–	1	3	17	–	2	14	–	10	1
1379	22½	2	½	¾	11	1	½	–	2½	1	–	–	1	3	17	–	2	10½	–	7	1
1393/4	–	1¾	–	–	13¾	–	½	–	4	–	–	–	–	3	–	–	–	12½	–	–	–

NOTE: Ad op. = *ad opus*; Ad C. = *ad censum*; M.D. = *in manu domini*; Off. = officials, especially reeve and beadle; A. = *ad arrentatum*.

Table XIII

Tenurial structures in the 1370's

Year	v+	IV	¾v	½v	¼v	Akerm.	Dikml.	Mondml.	Maltml.	Number of Combined Units
1371	3 × 1½ 3 × 1¼	7	5	10	8	1 1 × ½	3 2 × 2	13 1 × 1½	4 × ½	 18
1373	4 × 1¼ 3 × 1½ 1 × 2	7	4	10	10	1 1 × ½	3 1 × 2 1 × 3	14 1 × 2½	3 × ½	17
1374	1 × 2 3 × 1½ 3 × 1¼	8	5	10	10	1 × ½	3 1 × 3 1 × 2	14 1 × 2½	1 1 × ½	18
1375	1 × 2 3 × 1½ 4 × 1¼	7	5	11	10	1 × ½	3 1 × 3 1 × 2	13 1 × 2½	1 1 × ½	19
1377	2 × 1½ 5 × 1¼	8	5	11	10	–	2 1 × 3 1 × 2	13 1 × 2½	2	20
1378	2 × 1½ 4 × 1¼	8	6	13	11	–	3 1 × 3 1 × 2	14 1 × 2½	1 1 × ½	16
1379	2 × 1½ 3 × 1¼	8	5	12	11	1 × ½	1 × 3 1 × 2	15 1 × 1½ 1 × 3	1 1 × ½	17

Tenurial structures in the 1440's

Year	v+	IV	¾v	½v	¼v	Akerm.	Dikml.	Mondml.	Maltml.	Number of Combined Units
1442	1 × 2½ 1 × 2¼ 1 × 1½ 2 × 1¼	5	2	13	4	1 1 × 2	3 1 × ½	7 1 × 3 3 × 2	1	 22
1443	2 × 2¼ 1 × 1½ 2 × 1¼	5	2	13	4	1 1 × 2	3 1 × ½	8 1 × 3 1 × 2	1	22

Year	v+	1v	¾v	½v	¼v	Akerml.	Dikml.	Mondml.	Maltml.	Number of Combined Units
1444	1 × 2½ 1 × 2¼ 1 × 1½ 1 × 1¼	5	2	13	4	1 1 × 2	3 1 × ½	5 1 × 3 2 × 2	1	22
1445	1 × 2½ 1 × 2¼ 1 × 1½ 1 × 1¼	5	2	13	4	1 1 × 2	2 1 × 2 1 × ½	6 1 × 3 2 × 2	1	22
1446	1 × 2½ 1 × 2¼ 1 × 1½ 1 × 1¼	5	2	13	4	1 1 × 2	2 1 × 2 1 × ½	6 1 × 3 2 × 2	1	22
1447	1 × 2½ 1 × 2¼ 1 × 1½ 1 × 1¼	5	2	13	4	1 1 × 2	2 1 × 2 1 × ½	5 1 × 3 2 × 2	1	22
1448	1 × 2½ 1 × 2¼ 1 × 1½ 2 × 1¼	5	2	13	4	1 1 × 2	2 1 × 2 1 × ½	5 1 × 3 2 × 2	1	22
1449	1 × 2½ 1 × 2¼ 1 × 1½ 2 × 1¼	5	2	13	4	1 1 × 2	3 1 × ½	6 1 × 3 2 × 2	1	22

Sample combinations:

1375 1 mond. + ½ malt; ¼v + ½ ak.; ½ v + 1½ malt.; ½ v + 1½ mond.; 1 mond. + 1 malt. + ½ ak.; 1 mond. + 1 malt.; ¼ v + 2 mond.; ¼ v + 1 malt.; ¼ v + 1 mond.; ¼ v + 1 dik.; ¼ v + 1 mond.; ¾ v + 1 mond.; 1 malt. + 1 dik.; 1 v + 1 ak.; ½ v + 1 mond.; ¼ v + 1 mond.; 1 dik. + ½ ak.; ½ v + 1 dik.; 3 mond. + ½ ak.

1445 ¼ v + 1 mond.; ½ v + ¼ v + 1 mond.; 1 malt. + 1 dik.; ¾ v + ½ ak.; ½ v + 1 malt.; 2½ v + 1 malt. + 1 mond.; ½ v + 1 malt. + ½ ak.; ½ v + 2 mond.; ½ v + 1 malt.; ¼ v + 1 mond. + 1 malt.; 1 v + 1½ mond. + ½ ak.; ½ v + 1 ak.; ½ v + 1/3 dk.; ½ v + 1 malt.; 1½ v + 2 mond.; ½ v + 1 dk.; ½ v + 1 malt. + ½ ak.; ¾ v + 1 dk.; ¾ v + 1 mond.; ½ v + 1½ mond. + 1 malt.; ½ v + 1 malt.

Figures for demesne renting indicate the same tendencies as have been noted above for customary tenements. It was traditional for more wealthy villeins to seize the opportunity to farm part of the lord's demesne. From the late fourteenth century Reginald Semar and his un-named associates farmed 15 acres, ½ rod of Warboys demesne.[1] However, more novel was the fact that as the lord's demesne began to be rented out in the late fourteenth century, many villagers appear on the rent roll for the first time. For example: John Asplond 2a 1413/14; Robert Bele, 1a 1413/14 and 1421/22; Stephen Bonde, 1 sellion 1371; Robert Bonde, 1a 1404/5 and 1407/8; William Broughton, of Bury, 4a and 1 hedge 1371/79; Richard Broun, 1a 1413/14; Emma Catoun, 1½a 1373/77; John Catelyn, 2¼a 1371; Adam Couper 3a 1407/8; Richard Cost'ne, 6½a with Godfrey Brown and Alice Higney 1407/8; Richard of Ely, 2¼a 1371/79; Robert Gildersowe, 1a 1371/79 and 1393/94; John Hacon, 1 piece 1407/8; Thomas Hyde, 1a 1413/14 and 1421/22; Juliana Lenot, ½a 1373/77; John Miller, 1a + 3a 1413/14 and 1421/22; John Northborough, 2½a 1404/5; John Norreys 1a + 1r 1373/79; John Palmer, 1 sellion 1371; William Raven, 4a 1371/79; Richard Sabyn, 4a 1374/79; Robert Sist'ne, 5a + 1r 1404/5; Richard Sist'ne, 1 headland 1407/8; John Sywell, 3a 1393/94 and 1404/5; Robert Taylor, 4a 1393/94 and 1404/5; William Waren and Emma his wife, 1 piece of land in 1378/79, 1393/94 and 1404/5; John Wright, 3a 1413/14 and 1421/22. In constrast only three individuals came under the same category in the 1440's: John Gilleis, 1 place 1442/49; William Hyde, 1 hedge 1442/49 and Robert Slough, 1a 1442/49.

This transformation by the 1440's is to be explained by the fact that such small units of land were taken up by the engrossing movement. The engrossing movement is evident in the increased size of the larger tenement by the 1440's along with the increased number as well as size of the combined units and the corresponding decline in number of small subdivisions held, beginning with the one-quarter virgate. To the enlarged combinations of small units of former villeinage were also added bits and pieces from the lord's demesne. For example: John Berenger jun. held along with units of ½v, ¼v, 1 mondaymanland, 1 meadow, 1a, 1 sell, 1 butt, 1 butt; John Catoun held with ½v, 1 malt-

---

[1] A total of 60 acres, ¼ rod, 1 furrow, 1 hedge and one headland were farmed out in thirteen units from the lord's demesne in 1371. Beyond the above mentioned 15a ½r, 12a were held by 3 individuals, 3a by two, 5a 1 r by two, 4½a by two and the remaining units by single individuals. Farming from the demesne gradually increased to 114a, ¾ rod, 2 furrows, 1 hedge, 1 headland and 1 piece of land by 1394. By this latter date the farmed parts of the demesne were held in thirty-three units, all additions from 1371 having been granted to individuals.

manland, $\frac{1}{2}$ akermanland, units of 1a + 3a + 2a + 1r; Robert Hunter, held along with 1/3 dikemanland and $\frac{1}{2}$v, $\frac{1}{2}$ ten. + 1 pigsty + $1\frac{1}{2}$a + 1a + 3a + $\frac{1}{2}$ ten (10/-) + 5a + 2a + 1 meadow; John Plumbe jun. held along with $\frac{1}{2}$v + 1 maltmanland + $\frac{1}{2}$ akermanland, units of 7a + 3a + $1\frac{1}{2}$a + a tenement worth 2/8d.; John Shepherd held along with 3 monday-manlands units of 1a + 1a + 1a 3r; William Sharpe held along with $\frac{1}{2}$v + 1 maltmanland + $\frac{1}{2}$ mondaymanland, units of 1 tenement (8/-) + 3a + 1a + 3a + 1a + 1a + 2r + 1a + 2r + 1a (with croft).

The following list summates this whole process by showing a decline in number of tenants from the 1370's to the 1440's of almost twenty-five percent. Appended to this chapter is a table (XIV) listing the properties of the above tables under names of tenants.[1]

Number of tenants holding property from
1371 to 1379 and 1442 to 1449

YEAR	NUMBER	YEAR	NUMBER
1371	92	1442	79
1373	93	1443	79
1374	94	1444	76
1375	93	1445	77
1377	94	1446	76
1378	97	1447	75
1379	99	1448	76
		1449	77

FORMAT FOR TABLE XIV

v.	= virgate	bed.	= beadle
mess.	= messuage	bail.	= bailiff
aker.	= akermanland	sell.	= sellion
mond.	= mondaymanland	jun.	= junior
malt.	= maltmanland	sen.	= senior
dik.	= dikemanland	cap. mess.	= capital messuage
ten.	= tenement	cot.	= cotland
r.	= rod	med.	= meadow
a.	= acre		

[1] For greater brevity, members of the same family with common first names are not listed separately in Table XIV but are indicated by date in brackets.

Table XIV

Table showing property held in Warboys from
1371 to 1455

1E	**FIRST PERIOD** 1371 to 1379	**SECOND PERIOD** 1393 tn 1422	**THIRD PERIOD** 1440 to 1455
ɪ, Robert	ɪv. 1371-1377		
ɪnder, John, son of John	½ malt. 1371		
		½v. 1393/94, 1404/5, 1407/8	
ɪworld, William		1 mond. 1407/8, 1413/14	1 mond. 1442-1449
ɔnd, John		2a. 1413/14	
'homas		¼ ten. 1421/22	
ɪobert			3 butts + 2a. 1442/49, 1454/55; 1 dik. + ¼v. + ¼v. 1449
ʋilliam			¼v. + 1 mond. 1442/49
ɡate, John		2¼(4½) a., with John Rede, 1393/94; 4a. with John Waryn, 1393/94, 1421/22; 6a. 1407/8, 1413/14; 4a. with Richard Plumbe 1413/14, 1421/22	2a. 1r. 1442-49, 1454-55
ʋode, John	4a.(12a) + 12a. 1r. (5a. 1r.), 1371/79; 1 dik. 1371/78	4a.(12a.) 1393/94	
ɩatherine		1 dik. with Mary Wyne, 1413/14, 1421/22	½ dik. 1442-1449
ʋilliam		1 mond. 1421/22	
nger, John	½v. 1371-1375		
ohn jun.		1 mond. 1413/14, 1421/22; ¼v. 1421/22 ¼v. 1421/22	1a. 1442/49, 1454/55; ¼v. 1442/49; 1 mond. 1442/49
ohn sen.		1 med. 1413/14, 1421/22 with Thom. Berenger	1 med. + 1a. + 1 sell + 1 butt + 1 butt 1442/49, 1454/55; ½v. + ¼v. + 1 mond. 1442/49
ohn, of Caldecote			½v. + ¾v. 1442/49
ɩichard			¼v. 1442/49
ʈhomas			12a. + 4a. 1r. + 2a. 1442-1449, 1454/55; ¼v. + 1 mond. 1442/49
ʈhomas jun.			1 malt. + 1 dik. 1442/49
ʋilliam	½v. 1377/79		2a. + 1a. + 1 sell 1442/49, 1454/55
ʋilliam sen.			½v. 1442/49

179

NAME	FIRST PERIOD 1371 to 1379	SECOND PERIOD 1393 to 1422	THIRD PERIOD 1440 to 1455
Berenger, William jun.			ten. (3/—) + ½a. 144 1454/55; 1v. + ¼v. 49, 1½a. 1444/49, 145
—, William, son of Bailiff			½v. 1442/49
Baron, Alice			1 dik. 1442/49
—, John	¼v 1371/79; ½ aker. 1371/79	¼v. 1404/5; ½v. + ½v. 1407/8; ¼v. + ½v. + ½v. 1413/14; 1¼v. + ¼v. 1421/22	
—, Richard	½v. 1371/75. (¼ malt. 1373; ½ malt. 1374/75); 1 malt. 1371/75	¼v. + ¼v. 1393/94, 1404/5; ½v. 1404/5; ¼v. + ½v. 1407/8; ¾v. + ¼v. 1413/14; ¼v. + ½v. + ¾v. 1421/22	
—, Thomas		1 mond. 1404/5, 1407/8, 1413/14, 1421/22; ¼v. 1413/14, 1421/22	½v. 1442/49; ¼v. + ½ 1442/49
—, William	1 v. 1371/79	½v. + ¼v. 1393/94; ¾v. + ½v. 1404/5, 1407/8, 1413/14; ½ aker. 1413/14; 1v. + ¼v. 1421/22; ¼v. + ½ malt. 1421/22	
—, William jun.		½ aker. 1393/94, 1404/5, 1407/8	
Bele, John			1 mond. 1442/49
—, Robert		1a. 1413/14, 1421/22	
—, Thomas		1 mond. 1404/5, 1407/8; ¼v. + ⅓v. + 1a. 1413/14, 1421/22; 1v. (with Jn. Catoun & Jn. Shakestaff), 1421/22	
—, Thomas sen.		1 mond. 1413/14	
—, Thomas jun.		1 mond. 1407/8, 1413/14; ¼v. + 1 mond. 1421/22	
Bennesson, John		½v. + ½v. 1413/14; 1v. 1421/22	½v. 1442/49
—, Matilda		½v. 1413/14	
—, Nicholas		1v. 1421/22	1v. 1442/49
—, Richard	1v. 1371/79	½v. 1393/94; ¾v. 1413/14; 1 dik. 1413/14; 1a. 1413/1414, 1421/22; ¾v. 1421/22	½v. + ½v. + ½v. + ½ ½v. 1442/49
—, widow of Richard		½v. 1404/5, 1407/8	
—, William			1 malt. 1442/49
Benet, John (1371-1410) (1418-1449)	1 mond. 1371/79; ½ malt. 1375/77; 1a. 1374/79	1 mond. 1393/94; ¼v. 1393/94, 1404/5, 1407/8; 1a. 1393/94, 1404/5, 1413/14, 1421/22; 1a. 1421/22	½v. + ½ malt. 1442/49 ½ malt. 1442/46; 1 ma 1447/49

E	FIRST PERIOD 1371 to 1379	SECOND PERIOD 1393 to 1422	THIRD PERIOD 1440 to 1455
, wife of John		½ malt. 1413/14, 1421/22	
obert	1v. 1378/79	½ malt. 1407/8, 1413/14, 1421/22	
homas		1 mond. 1404/5, 1407/8, 1413/14. 1421/22; 3a. + 2½a. 1413/14, 1421/22	
homas		3a. + ½v. + 2 mond. 1413/14	
, John		½ mond. 1407/8	
e, Andrew	¼v. 1371/79; 1 mond. 1371		
ohn (1369-1377) (1429-1458)	¼v. 1377/79		4a. 1442/49, 1454/55; ½v. + ½v. 1442/49
obert		1a. 1404/5, 1407/8; ¼v. 1413/14; 2a. + 1a. + 1½a. + 3r. + 1a. 3r. + 2a. 1413/14, 1421/22; 1a. 1413/14, 1421/22; 1a. + 1 dik. 1421/22	
ichard		¼v. 1421/22	
tephen	1 sell. 1371		
William (1353-1379) (1400-1449)	1 mond. 1371/79; 1a. 1373/79	6a. + 4a. 1413/14, 1421/22	3a. + 6a. 1442/49, 1454/55; ¼v. + ¼v. 1442/49
John	1 mond. 1371/79		
ler, Hugh			½v. 1442/49
, John		5a. 2½r. + 1a. + 5a. 1r. + ½r. med. + 4a. + 1r. + 2½a. 1407/8; 1 place + 18a. freehold 1413/14, 1421/22; 1 place + cap. mess. + 11a. + 4a. + 2½a. + 3a. + 1a. + ½a. + 5a. 1r. + 5a. + 2½r. + perch + 2½a. 1413/14, 1421/22; 24½a. (7 places) + med. 1413/14	1 place + 18a. freehold, 1442/49, 1454/55; 2 mond. 1442/49
alph	1 mond. 1371/79; 1a. 1r. 1377/79	2½a. 1393/94, 1404/5, 1407/8	
pton, John		½v. + 3a. 3r. 32p. of med. + 1a. + 2a. 1413/14, 1421/22	
nying, John	1¼v. 1371/73; ¾v. + ¼v. 1374; 1¼v. 1375; 1v. 1377; 1¼v. 1378		
ohn sen.		1v. 1393/94	
ohn jun.		1v. 1393/94	

NAME	FIRST PERIOD 1371 to 1379	SECOND PERIOD 1393 to 1422	THIRD PERIOD 1440 to 1455
Bron, Robert (alias None)		½v. 1413/14	
Bronnote, John		1 mond. 1404/5, 1407/8	
—, William		¼v. + 1 mond. 1404/5, 1407/8; ¼v. 1413/14	
Broughton, William, of Bury	4a. + 1 hedge 1371/79		
Broun, Agnes			1 cot. + 1 cot. + 1 c[...] 1442/49, 1454/55; ¼v[...] 1442/49
—, Godfrey		1a. 1r. 1393/94, 1404/5, 1413/14; ¼v. + ¼v. 1407/8; 6½a. (with Ric. Cost'ne and Alice Hygeney) 1407/8; 3 cots. + 2½a. 1413/14, 1421/22; 2½a. 1413/14; 1a. 1413/14, 1421/22	
—, John			¼v. 1442/49
—, Richard		1a. 1413/14, 1421/22; ¼v. 1421/22	
—, Robert		2 cots. 1413/14, 1421/22	
—, William	½v. 1371/78; 1 mond. 1371; 1½ mond. 1371/78		
Buckworth, William	1v. 1378/79		
Buntyng, Thomas			1v. + 1v. + ½v. + 1 malt. + 1 mond. 144[...]
Brynewater, John		1 cot. 1404/5, 1407/8, 2 sell 1407/8; 2 cots. 1413/14; 2½a. + 2 sell 1413/14, 1421/22; 1 dik. 1413/14, 1421/22	
Carter, John	1 dik. 1371; 1 malt. 1374/78; 1 mond. 1371/78; ½ aker. 1371/75; ½ malt. 1371/73		
Catoun, Emma	1½a. (3a.) 1373/77		
—, John & wife Joan	6½a. + 3a. 3.r. 1378/79	6½a. + 3a. 3r. 1393/94, 1404/5	
—, John (1370-1442,49) (1413, 1416, 1440/49)	1a. 1r. 1374/79; ½ aker. 1379	½ aker. 1393/94, 1404/5, 1407/8; 1 cot. 1413/14, 1421/22; ⅓v. 1413/14; 1v. (with Jn. Shakestaffe & Thom. Bele) 1421/22	1a. + 3a. + 2a. + 1r[...] 1442/49, 1454/55; 1 r[...] 1442/48; ½v. 1442/49[...] ½ aker. 1442/49
—, Margaret		1 freehold. 1413/14, 1421/22; ½ aker. 1413/14; ½v. + ½ aker. 1421/22	

182

ME	FIRST PERIOD 1371 to 1379	SECOND PERIOD 1393 to 1422	THIRD PERIOD 1440 to 1455
yn, John	2¼a. (4½a.) 1371		¼v. + 1 mond. + ¼v. + 1 mond. 1442/49, 1454/55
man, John	2½a. 1378/79; ½ malt. 1371/73; 1 mond. 1371/79; 1 malt. 1371/79	2½a. 1393/94 ½ ten. 1413/14, 1421/22; 1½a. 1413/14, 1421/22; 1 malt. 1404/5, 1407/8, 1413/14, 1421/22	
imon			½ ten. (7/—) + 2a. 1442/49, 1454/55; ¼v. + ¼v. + 1 malt. 1442/49
l, Alice		1 mond. 1393/94	
'homas	½v. 1378		
e, John			3 cot. (10/—) + 22a. + 3 sel. + 1 cot. 1442/49, 1454/55; ½v. 1442/49
, Agnes	¼v. 1379		
e, Robert chaplain		½v. + 2 mond. 1404/5, 1407/8; 3a. 3½r. 1407/8	
, John jun.		1v. 1404/5	
obert	1 sell 1373/79; ½v. 1373/77	1 sell 1393/94; 2 mond. 1393/94; 3a. 3r. + 32 ft. med. 1393/94; 2a. 1393/94, 1404/5, 1407/8; med. (6s. 8d.) 1404/5, 1407/8; 3a. 3r. + 20 ft. med. + ½v. 1404/5, 1407/8	
er, John	1v. + ¼v. 1371/79		
ville, Richard			1v. 1442/49
Villiam		1¼v. (with Jn. Hichesson), 1393/94; 1v. 1404/5; ½v. + ½v. 1407/8; 1v. 1413/14, 1421/22	1a. 1442/49, 1454/55; ½v. 1442/49
ne, Richard		6½a. (with God. Broun & Alice Hygeneye), 1407/8	
er, Adam		3a. 1407/8	
, John		1 mond. 1393/94; 2 mond. 1404/5, 1407/8, 1413/14, 1421/22	
ohn sen.		3 mond. 1413/14, 1421/22	
ohn jun.		2 mond. 1404/5; 6a. 3r. + 3a. 3½r. 1407/8; 1v. + 1 mond. 1413/14; 1 mond. 1421/22	
ar, John	½v. 1379		

NAME	FIRST PERIOD 1371 to 1379	SECOND PERIOD 1393 to 1422	THIRD PERIOD 1440 to 1455
Derworth, Gilbert	2 mond. 1379		
—, Hugh	¼v. 1371/79; 2 mond. 1371/79; 2a. 3¼r. 1377/79	3a. 3¼r. + ½r. med. 1393/94, 1404/5; 6a. 3r. 1404/5	
—, William		1 mond. 1404/5	
Dicon, Thomas	1 mond. 1371/79		
Edward, John		½v. 1393/94; ¼v. 1404/5, 1407/8	
—, Henry	½v. 1371/79; ¼v. 1371/79	¼v. 1393/94	
—, Thomas		1v. 1404/5, 1407/8, 1413/14; 1¼v. 1421/22	1¼v. 1442/43, 1448/4●
Ely, Richard of	2¼a. (4½a.) 1371/79		
Eyr, Richard		½v. 1413/14, 1421/22	
—, Thomas		1v. 1413/14	
Fisher, Robert	1 mond. 1377/79; 2a. 3½r. 1371/75; 1 malt. 1379	1 mond. 1393/94	
Flemyng, John	¾v. 1371/79	2½a. 1407/8; ¼v. + ½v. 1413/14; ¾v. + ½v. 1421/22	
—, William	¼v. 1377/79	1 sell. 1393/94; ½v. 1393/94; ½v. 1404/5	
Fot, Hugh	1 mond. 1371/75		
Fine, John jun.	½v. 1371/75; 1v. 1371/75		
—, John sen.	½v. 1371/77		
Fordyngton, Hugh		1 malt. + 1 mond. 1413/14; 1 malt. + 1 mond. + 1 mond. 1421/22	1½a. 1442/49, 1454/55 ¼v. + 1 mond. + 1 n● 1442/49
Forester, John	½v. 1377/79; 1v. 1377/79	½v. 1393/94; ¼v. 1404/5	
Gaze, Robert	1 mond. 1371/79		
Gerold, John	¼v. 1371/79; ½ malt. 1371/73; 1 malt. 1374/78; 4a. 1377/79; ½v. (bail.) 1379		
—, Robert	½v. 1377/79; 1 dik. 1377/79	½v. 1393/94; ¼v. 1393/94; ¾v. 1407/8, 1404/5	
Gildesowe, Robert	1a. 1371/79	1a. 1393/94	
Godfrey, John, son of	6a. 3r. 1371/79	6a. 3r. 1393/94	
Gosse, Thomas	3a. 1½r 1378/79; 1 mond. 1379		
Gylis, John			1 place 1442/49
Hacon, John		1 piece 1407/8	
Harsene, John	½v. 1371/79 (sen. from 1378)	4a. (12a.) 1393/94; 1 ten. 1404/5, 1407/8	
—, John jun.	¼v. 1371/79; 1 mond. 1371/79		
—, William		½v. 1393/94	
Hide, Thomas		1a. 1413/14, 1421/22	
—, William			4a. + 1 hedge 1442/4● 1454/55

	FIRST PERIOD 1371 to 1379	SECOND PERIOD 1393 to 1422	THIRD PERIOD 1440 to 1455
(Hrrsson, esson), John, of	¼v. 1371/75; ¾v. 1377/78; ¼v. 1379; ½v. (bed.) 1379		
ɪn jun.		¼v. 1393/94	
son, John	1¼v. 1371/79	1¼v. (with Wm. Colville) 1393/94	
ɔmas		1½ mond. 1413/14	
Hy), John jun.		2 mond. 1407/8; 1 mond. 1404/5	
ɪn sen.		1 mond. + 3a. + 3a. 1413/14; 1 dik. 1413/14, 1421/22; ½v. + 1 malt. 1413/14; 2a. + ½a. 1413/14, 1421/22; ½v. + 1 malt. + 1 mond. 1421/22	
ɪn, of Wolney		1 dik. + 12a. 1413/14, 1421/22	
ɪn		¼v. 1404/5, 1407/8	
chard	2 dik. 1371; 3 dik. 1373/79; 4a. (12a.) 1371/79; 5 ½a. ½r. 1371/79	4a. (12a.) 1393/94; 12a. 1404/5, 1407/8 (with John Attewode); 5a. 1393/94; 5a. 2½r. 1404/5; ½v. 1404/5, 1407/8	
non	20/= land 1379	20/= land, 1393/94, 1404/5, 1407/8, 1413/14, 1421/22; 3a. 1393/94, 1404/5, 1407/8; 4a. 1413/14, 1421/22; 6a. + 6a. 1413/14, 1421/22	
non jun./sen.		1 dik. + 11a. + 2a. 1413/14, 1421/22	1 ten. 22/=) + 2a. + 12a. 1442/49, 1454/55
non jun.			2a. 1442/49; 1454/55; 1 dik. + 2a. 1442/49; 1 dik. 1445/8; 1 cot. 1442/49, 1454/55
ɡ, John			
, (Hny, Hvy), ɪ sen.	1v. 1377/79	2v. 1393/94; 2v. 1404/5, 1407/8; 1v. 1413/14, 1421/22	
ɔn jun.		1v. 1404/5, 1407/8, 1413/14, 1421/22	
d, William		½v. 1404/4, ¼v. 1407/8; 1v. 1407/8; ½v. 1413/14, 1421/22	
er, (Hunter), ert			½ ten. + 1 pigsty + 1½a. + 1a. + 3a. + ½ ten. (10/—) + 5a. + 2a. + 1 med. 1442/49, 1454/55; ⅓dik. + ½v. 1442/49

NAME	FIRST PERIOD 1371 to 1379	SECOND PERIOD 1393 to 1422	THIRD PERIOD 1440 to 1455
Hunter, Thomas	½v. 1371/79; 1v. 1371/79	1v. 1393/94; 4a. ½r. 1404/5	
Horewode, John			1 aker. 1442/43; ½v. + 1½ mond. 14 ½ aker. 1442/49
—, Richard			1 aker. 1421/22
—, William			½v. + 1 aker. 1442
Hygeneye, Alice		6a. (with Richard Cost'ne and Godfrey Broun) 1407/8	
—, William	½v. 1371/79		
Jekkisson, Agnes, wife of John	¼v. 1371/79		
Kaye, Richard	1 mond. 1371/79		
Kaunt, Thomas	1 mond. 1371/79; 1r. 1377/79	1r. 1404/5	
Lambehird, Robert	½v. 1371/75; ¼v. 1371/77		
Launshill, John	½v. 1379	1 mond. 1404/5	
Laveyn, Richard			1 malt. 1442/43; 1 m + ½v. 1442/49
Leheir (Theheir), Thomas	¼v. 1378; 1v. 1379		
Lenot, Emma	1 mond. 1379		
—, John jun.	¼v. 1371/75; 1 dik. 1371/75		
—, John sen.	1 mond. 1371/75		
—, John		¼v. 1421/22; ½v. + 2 mond. 1413/14; 1½a. + 3a. 3r. 1413/14, 1421/22; 1a. 1413/14; 2 mond. 1421/22	
—, Juliana	½a. (3a.) 1373/77		
Lirtebrook, William	¼v. 1371/77; 1 mond. 1371/78		
London, Robert			1 place + croft 144 1454/55; 1 aker. 144
—, William			1 ten. + 8a. 1442/49 1454/55; ¼v. + ½v. 49
Lone, William	½v. 1371/75		
March (Merch) John, of Bury		4a. + 1 hedge 1393/94, 1404/5	
Martin, John		¼v. 1404/5	
Miller, John		1a. + 3a. 1413/14, 1421/22	
Molt, Godfrey	½v. 1371/77		
—, John (1333-1379) (1402-1455)	¾v. 1371/77; 1 mond. 1371/79	¼v. 1404/5; ¼v. + ¼v. 1407/8; 2½a. 1413/14, 1421/22	½a. 1442/43; 1½a. 14 1454/55

…E	FIRST PERIOD 1371 to 1379	SECOND PERIOD 1393 to 1422	THIRD PERIOD 1440 to 1455
…John jun.	½v. 1378; ¼v. 1379	3a. ½r. 1393/94	
…hn sen.	½v. 1378/79		
…chard	½v. 1371/79; ½v. (bed.) 1378		
… Robert	1¼v. 1377		
…l, Robert			½v. 1442/49
…m, John	½v. 1378/79		
…an, Thomas		½ ten. (15/—) 1393-94, 1404/5, 1407/8, 1413/14, 1421/22; ¼v. 1413/14; ¾v. + 1v. 1421/22; ½v. 1413/14; 5a. 1413/14, 1421/22; 5a. + ¼v. 1404/5, 1407/8; ½v. 1407/8	1v. 1442/49
…omas, jun.			½ ten. (15/—) + 5a. + ½ ten. (10/—) 1442/49, 1454/55
…hn			1a. + 1½a. 1442/49, 1454/55; ¼v. + 1v. + ¼v. + 2 mond. 1442/49
…bourgh, Henry		½v. 1404/5, 1407/8, 1413/14	1 mond. 1442/49
…ugh	¼v. 1371/79; 1 sell. 1373/79; 1 mond. 1379	½ mond. 1393/94; 4½a. 1393/4, 1404/5; ½v. 1421/22	
…hn		2½a. 1404/5	
…ys, John	1 med. 1373/77; 1a. 1r. 1377/79		
…e, Richard	1½v. 1371/75; 1v. 1377; 1½v. 1378/79; ½v. (reeve) 1377; 1 med. (¾d.) 1374/79	½v. 1393/94, 1404/5, 1407/8; 1a. 1413/14, 1421/22; ½ mond. 1413/14, 1421/22	
…chard jun.	½v. 1378/79; 1½ mond. 1379	1½ mond. 1393/94; 1 mond. 1404/5, 1407/8	
…chard sen.		2a. of med. 1393/94	
…e Hill, John …tehill)	½v. 1377; 1 malt. 1377; ½ malt. 1377/79	½ malt. 1393/94	
…hn & wife Agnes		3a. 3½r. 1393/94	
…obert		20/= land 1393/94, 1404/5, 1407/8; 2½a. 1393/94, 1404/5	
…r, Robert	1 malt. 1377/79; 3a. 1377/79	1 malt. 1393/94; 3a. + 1 malt. 1404/5, 1407/8	
…illiam	½ malt. 1371/75	1 mond. 1404/5, 1407/8; ½v. 1413/14, 1421/22; 1 mond. 1413/14, 1421/22	1 mond. 1442/43
…nar, John		1 mond. 1413/14; 2a. + 1½a. 1413/14, 1421/22; 1 mond. 1421/22	

NAME	FIRST PERIOD 1371 to 1379	SECOND PERIOD 1393 to 1422	THIRD PERIOD 1440 to 1455
Owndill, William			3r. + 1a. + 1½a. 14 1454/55; ¼v. + 1 c ¼v. 1442/49
Pakerel, Alice	1 dik. 1373/78		
—, John	2 dik. 1371/79		
—, Juliana	1 dik. 1371		
Palmer, John	1 sell. 1371		
Person, John			½v. + ½v. + 1 dik. 49, 1454/55
Pilgrym, Nicholas	¼v. 1371/78; 10/— land 1379		
—, William		1 headland 1393/94, 1404/5; 1 malt. & 1 mond. 1393/94	
Prestecosyn, Henry	½v. 1378/79	½v. 1393/94, 1404/5, 1407/8	
—, John	¼v. 1378/79; 1 malt. 1377/79; 1 mess. 1377/79	¼v. 1393/94; 1 mess. 1393/94; ¼v. + 1a. 1404/5, 1407/8	
Plumbe, John	½ malt. 1371/73; 1 malt. 1374/79; ½ aker. 1377/79	3a. + 1½a. + 1a. + 4a. 1413/14, 1421/22	
—, John jun.		¼v. 1404/5, 1407/8; 1 mond. 1404/5; 1v 1407/8	7a. + 3a. + ten. (2/ 1½a. 1442/49, 1454/5 ½v. + 1 malt. + ½ a 1442/49
—, John sen.		½ aker. 1393/94, 1404/5, 1407/8, 1421/22	
—, Richard (1365-1410) (1400-1458)	½ malt. 1371/73; 1 malt. 1374/79; 1 aker. 1374/79	1v. 1404/5, 1407/8; 1 malt. 1393/94, 1404/5, 1407/8; 4a. (with Jn. Attegate), 1413/14, 1421/22; 3a 1413/14, 1421/22	2 mond. 1442/43; 1 1443/49
Raveley, John	1 aker. 1371/79; 1 aker. (offic.) 1373/79	1 aker. 1404/5, 1407/8	
—, Robert		1 dik. + 1½a. + 1½a. + 2a. 1413/14, 1421/22	
—, William jun.			½v. 1442/49
Raven, Richard	½v. 1371/78; ½v. (bed.) 1375; 1 aker. 1371, 1373/79; ½v. (reeve) 1379		
—, Robert			¼v. 1442/49
—, Thomas	1v. 1371/77		
—, William	4a. (12a.) 1371/79		
Rede, John jun., & wife Amicia	2a. 1r. 1378/79; 2¼a. (4½a.) 1371	2a. 1r. 1393/94; 2¼a. (4½a.) 1393/94	
—, John		4½a. 1404/5	

ME	FIRST PERIOD 1371 to 1379	SECOND PERIOD 1393 to 1422	THIRD PERIOD 1440 to 1455
sson, Richard			1a. 1442/49, 1454/55; 1 dik. + ¾v. 1442/49
g, William	¼v. 1373/79		
, Agnes, fe of Robt.	½v. 1371		
ere, Robert	1 mond. 1379		
n, Richard	4a. 1374/79		
, John			1 mond. 1442/49
William		10/— + 2a + 5r. 1413/14, 1421/22	
, Agnes	½v. 1371/77; 1 mond. 1371/75		
Richard	¼v. 1371/79; 1 mond. 1371/79		
Thomas jun.	½v. 1371/79; 1 mond. 1377/79		
Thomas	1 mond. 1373/77; 1 mond. 1378/79 (sen.)		
ar, Reginald	15a. ½r. with assoc. 1371/79	15a. ½r. with assoc. 1393/94	
Richard	1v. 1371/77, ¼v. 1371/78; ½v. (reeve) 1378		
Roger		15a. ½r. 1404/5, 1407/8	
Thomas	½v. 1377/78		
William	½v. 1371/75; ¼ malt. 1371/73; ½ malt. 1374; med. 1371/74		
ne, Robert		5a. 1r. 1404/5	
Richard		1 headland 1407/8	
Roger	2½a. ½r. 1371/79; (5a. 1r.) 1371/79	½ aker. 1393/94, 1404/5, 1407/8; (5a. 1r.) 1393/94	
kestaff, John		¼v. + ½v. + 1 mond. 1413/14; ¼v. 1421/22; 1v. (with Jn. Catoun & Thom. Bele) 1421/22; 1 mond. 1421/22	land + 1a (¾d.) 1442/49, 1454/55; ¼v. + ½v. + 1 mond. 1442/49
kestaff, William		½v. + 1 mond. 1407/8; ½v. + ¼v. + 1 mond. 1413/14; ¾v. + 1 mond. 1421/22	2½a. 1442/49, 1454/55; ½v. + ¼v. 1442/49
p, William		½ ten. + 1 malt. 1413/14; 1a. + 3a. 1413/14, 1421/ 22; 1 malt. 1421/22	½ ten. (8/—) + 3a. + 1a. + 3a. + 1a. + 1a. + 2r. + 1a. + 2r. + 1a. (croft), 1442/49, 1454/5; ½v. + 1 malt. + ½ mond. + 1 mond. 1442/49
pherd, John			1a. + 1a. 1442/49, 1454/ 55; 1a. 3r. 1442/49; 2a. 3r.
371-1379)	1 v. 1371/79		

NAME	FIRST PERIOD 1371 to 1379	SECOND PERIOD 1393 to 1422	THIRD PERIOD 1440 to 1455
Shepherd, John (1434-1458)			1454/5; 1 mond. + 1 mond. + 1 mond. 1442/49
—, Nicholas		1 mond. 1413/14, 1421/22	
—, Richard		1 malt. + 2 mond. 1404/5; 1 malt. + 1 mond. 1407/8	
—, Roger	½ aker. 1375/79; 1 dik. 1371/79	1 dik. + ½a. + ½a. 1413/14, 1421/22	
—, William		½ ten. 1421/22	
Slough, Robert			1a. 1442/49, 1454/55
Smart, Simon	¼v. 1371/79	1½v. 1393/94, 1404/5; ¼v. 1404/5, 1407/8	
—, William		½v. + ½v. 1413/14; ½v. 1421/22	½v. 1442/49
Smith, Roger (alias Raven as from 1442)		1a. 1413/14, 1421/22; ½v. 1421/22	1 ten. (5/4d.) + 1 cot (4/—) 1442/43; med. 1442/49, 1454/55; ½v 1442/49
—, William (1363-1375) (1392-1455)	1v. 1371/75	3a. 1½r. 1404/5, 1407/8; 15/—(½ ten.) 1413/14, 1421/22; ½ aker. + 1 mond. 1413/14; 3a. 3½r. + ½ aker. + 1 mond. 1413/14, 1421/22	3a. 3r. 1442/43, 1454/
—, Walter		½v. 1421/22	
—, Robert (alias Raven)			½v. + ½v. 1442/49; 1 4/— + cot. 1444/45, 1454/55
Son, John	1 mond. 1371/78		
—, Robert	½v. 1371/77; 1 dik. 1371/79		
—, Thomas	1 mond. 1377		
Sqwyr, John		1 mond. 1413/14, 1421/22	
—, William		1 mond. 1407/8	
Stratton, Nicholas, chaplain	½ ten. 1379		
Strugge, William			1 mond. 1442/43
Sutor, Hugh	¼v. 1371/75		
Swan, Bartholomew	1 mond. 1371/79; 1 headland 1371/79	1 mond. 1393/94	
—, John sen.		¼v. 1393/94	
Sywell, John		3a. 1393/94, 1404/5	
Taylor, Godfrey	¼v. 1378/79		

(E	FIRST PERIOD 1371 to 1379	SECOND PERIOD 1393 to 1422	THIRD PERIOD 1440 to 1455
r, Reginald			1 dik. 1442/49
ichard		¼v. 1393/94; 1 mond. 1404/5, 1407/8; 4½a. 1407/8; 1 mond. 1413/14, 1421/22	
obert		4a. 1393/94, 1404/5	
amisson, William	½ aker. 1371/75		
y, Robert	¾v. 1371/75; 1¼v. 1373/79		
r, John	1 mond. 1371/79; ½ mond. 1371; 1½ mond. 1373/78; ½ mond. 1379		
ı, John	¼v. 1371/79		
:n, William & e Emma	1 piece of land 1378/79	1 piece of land 1393/94, 1404/5	
›hn		4½a. with Jn. Attegate 1407/8	
›ester, Henry		1 mond. 1393/94	
ugh	½v. 1377/79	½v. 1393/94	
obert	ten. 1371/74		
/illiam, of Bury		4a. + 1 hedge 1407/8; 4½a. + hedge 1413/14, 1421/22	
ington, John	1v. 1371/79	1v. 1393/94	
homas	½v. 1377/79; 1 mond. 1377/78		
e, John			3½a. + 1½a. 1442/49, 1454/55; 2 aker. 1442/49
:s, John (1365-1412) (1429-1449)	¾v. 1371/75; ¾v. 1378/79 (snr.); ¼v. 1377; ½v. (bed.) 1377	½v. 1413/14, 1421/22	½v. 1442/49
›hn jun. (1375-76, 1384-1428)	½v. 1378/79	½v. 1393/94	
ichard	1 aker. 1371/73		½v. + 1v. 1442/49
'homas			½v. 1442/49
/illiam	¼v. 1371/79; ¼v. 1371/77		
mot, John	1 mond. 1379	½ mond. 1393/94	
e, John			2a. 1442/49, 1454/55; 1 mond. 1442/49
ekoc, William		1 mond. 1404/5	
ehill, John		1 mond. 1407/8, 1413/14, 1421/22	
e, William 'ebster)		2 mond. 1413/14, 1421/22	
ohn			1a. 1442/49, 1454/55; 2 mond. 1442/49

NAME	FIRST PERIOD 1371 to 1379	SECOND PERIOD 1393 to 1422	THIRD PERIOD 1440 to 1455
Wolney, Henry	½ aker. 1371/78; 3 mond. with Elena wife of Henry 1371/79	1 mond. 1393/94	
Woodward, (Wodeward), Walter		forge + 1a. 3r. + 1a 1413/14, 1421/22	1 cot. (former forg 4/6d) + 1a. 1442/49 1454/55
Wrangil, William		½v. + 1 mond. 1404/5	
Wright, John		3a. 1413/14, 1421/22	
—, Robert & wife Agnes	15/— (½ten) 1379	15/— (½ ten.) 1393/94, 1404/5, 1407/8	
Wroo, Thomas			1 malt. 1442/49; ½v. 1442/49
Wynde, John		1 mond. 1407/8	
Wyne, Mary		1 dik. (with Katherine Attewode) 1413/14, 1421/22	
Wytleseye, John (alias Everard)		1 mond. 1413/14, 1421/22	

Chapter VI

LABOUR RESOURCES OF WARBOYS

The student of Warboys is much better informed about the labour than the landed resources of the village. The mid-thirteenth-century extent describes in great detail the amount and nature of the work owed by a virgater for his land:

> ... for one work he will cut 25 bundles of reeds, which with his own cart he will carry to the *curia* and this will be allowed him as two days work.
>
> From the feast of St. Michael to Hokeday, every week he will work on Monday, Tuesday and Wednesday whatever work task is assigned to him; he will do also if necessary the carrying works to Ramsey or wherever he is ordered to carry in the hundred on Thursday, Saturday and Sunday; and his carrying load will be one ring in the hundred, and outside the hundred and county three virgaters together carry the same amount.
>
> Each Friday of the same weeks throughout the year, beyond Christmastide and five weeks in the autumn, whether he has a plough of his own or ploughs joined with others, he will plough one half acre. In the same fashion he will work each week from Hokeday to the time of the harvest in the same day whatever job is assigned to him for the whole day.
>
> From wheat and rye he will cut 24 sheaves, and from barley, oats, peas, beans, 30 sheaves.
>
> And whether on level ground or in an old ditch he must ditch or enclose from the feast of St. Michael to Hokeday, ditching and enclosing being up to none; from Hokeday to the feast of St. Michael ditching and enclosing are for the whole day.
>
> And if he must collect thorns, from the feast of St. Michael to Hokeday, he collects and carries three bundles to the *curia*; from Hokeday to the Gules of August, four; from the Gules of August to the feast of St. Michael throughout the whole day he collects and carries one bundle.
>
> And if through the above time he does not have to carry, he collects four; from the Gules of August he collects and carries; and he works through the wohle day to the feast of St. Michael, and does this for whatever work falls to his lot. He harrows in winter through the whole day, and in lent likewise, allowing that he goes out for his meal and after his meal returns.

In the second week after the feast of St. Michael he will plough a half acre, which is called wodebene, either by himself if he should have a plough or joined with others for one work. In the third week he will plough at the sowing of wheat, by himself one half acre, and this is allowed for two works...

In the time of weeding, he will weed throughout the whole day.

He will mow in Chevere for one day, will gather hay for another day, and on the third day will carry one cartload of hay to Warboys, or one half to Ramsey, and this is not allowed to him for work, but he and his associates receive from the Abbots purse 6d. for 'sythale'. In other meadows he will mow up to none, and after none if necessary, he will gather hay; and ...

Through a whole day he will gather and carry from Wolfheye one cartload of hay or of corn for one work.

From the Gules of August to the feast of St. Michael on every day of the week beyond Saturday he will provide one labourer, on festival days this is not required. At all boonwork days of the autumn he must come with his whole family, except for his wife; if he should have four labourers or more he himself holds the rod over his workers; if however he should have three then he himself must work with these, unless he should be of such an age or debility that he is not able to work. And the lord requires in the autumn as many boonworks as he wishes, and the day after the first boonwork he must provide two labourers himself he supplying the cost of their meals...

Moreover he will carry in autumn with his cart from all the fields except for Wolfheye and Twocroft three cartloads of corn for one work. From Wolfheye he carries one, and from Twocroft he carries two cart loads. He will thresh at the making of the four quarters for thraves of wheat annually, and this is not allowed him as a work. He will harrow also in winter and lent two days each year, and this is not allowed for work. He will weed throughout the year for one whole day, for what is called a loveboon, and this is not allowed him for work, from stubble he must cut as do other workers in the autumn.

He also collects one 'bolla' full of nuts for one work, should these nuts be sufficiently abundant. And he collects wood at Warboys or from the woods of St. Ives to make a enclosure 11 feet long... and with two virgaters as associates he keeps watch (at the fair of St. Ives) for one work...[1]

Exactly what work was performed by the villagers in any one year remains however a question. The extent itself indicates that work might be sold (*ad censum*) for amounts varying with the seasons of the year (one winter work at a halfpenny ,one summer work at one penny, one work or one penny halfpenny in the autumn). In the extant account rolls of

[1] *Carts*, I, 309-312.

the mid-thirteenth century carrying works were entirely commuted. There are few further references to carrying services either performed or commuted from the late thirteenth century. The lord employed a carter intermittently in the mid-thirteenth century, and as a full-time annual employee from later in the century. A small number of carrying services to Ramsey were performed into the fifteenth century. Nor are there references in any of the earlier accounts to ploughing works performed or commuted. Perhaps these were entirely performed by the lord's ploughamn, although with the more detailed *opera* accounts after the Black Death it is clear that some of the winter *opera* were expended on ploughing and ploughing boons were an annual affair.

The arrangement actually employed for the demesne for manors of Ramsey Abbey from the late thirteenth century was described in the document dated 1293-1294. For Warboys, this document has the following description:

> *Works* of 36¼ virgates, 7 virgates held by maltmen and akermen, and 33 mondaycroft with two one-half crofts. Each virgate does in each week for 44 weeks between the feast of St. Michael and the Gules of August, three works and beyond this four works.
>
> Each maltman and akerman does each week over the same time four works and four extra works.
>
> Each mondaycroft does 1 work per week.
>
> The sum total of all the works 7342, and these are worth in winter halfpenny. And in summer halfpenny farthing.
>
> *Autumn Works:* Each of the above virgaters does in each week between the Gules of August and the feast of St. Michael four works and an extra five works. And each of the maltmen does per week four works and and extra ten works.
>
> And the mondaycroft does one work per week.

This 1293-1294 document does not seem to be a new accounting departure for the enumeration of works, but rather a simplified version of accounting for use at the central office of the lord. For rather than the two seasons indicated in this document there were really indicated in the mid-thirteenth century extent four seasons. These four seasons are clearly employed in references to sale of *opera* with the better series of account rolls available from the first half of the fourteenth century. That is to say the winter, summer, autumn and post autumn seasons as may be seen in the following list of Works Sold at Various Seasons.

YEAR	WINTER	SUMMER	AUTUMN	POST AUTUMN	TOTAL
1306/7	1248	920	215	?	(2383)
1318/19	1942	1037	377	101	3457
1325/26	$2032\frac{1}{2}$	$914\frac{1}{2}$	405	?	$(3351\frac{1}{2})$
1329/30	2154	$1039\frac{1}{2}$	222	53	$3468\frac{1}{2}$
1335/36	$1608\frac{1}{2}$	$1228\frac{3}{4}$	387	373	$3597\frac{1}{4}$
1342	$2442\frac{1}{2}$	$1203\frac{1}{2}$	360	$284\frac{1}{2}$	$4289\frac{3}{4}$
1344/45	1421	$1292\frac{1}{2}$	454	252	$3419\frac{1}{2}$
1346/47	1335	$1334\frac{3}{4}$	272	201	3142
1347/48	2265	1100	243	80	3688
1348/49	2053	1089	$257\frac{1}{2}$	$170\frac{1}{4}$	$3569\frac{3}{4}$
1353/54	1465	1384	207	287	3343
1354/55	$1276\frac{3}{4}$	$688\frac{3}{4}$	192	$219\frac{1}{2}$	2377
1359/60	1291	$26\frac{1}{2}$	$113\frac{1}{4}$	230	$1660\frac{3}{4}$
1360/61	882	652	207	188	1929
1362/63	1115	364	369	325	2173
1363/64	647	$518\frac{1}{2}$	$240\frac{1}{2}$	116	1521
1366/67	$749\frac{1}{2}$	$447\frac{3}{4}$	165	$53\frac{3}{4}$	1416
1371/72	$433\frac{1}{2}$	$706\frac{1}{4}$	$234\frac{1}{2}$	198	$1572\frac{1}{4}$
1373/74	$573\frac{1}{2}$	385	$228\frac{1}{2}$	183	1370
1374/75	525	364	$253\frac{1}{2}$	$107\frac{1}{2}$	1250
1375/76	$550\frac{1}{2}$	11	$212\frac{1}{2}$	76	849
1377/78	$329\frac{1}{2}$	$413\frac{1}{2}$	$250\frac{1}{2}$	72	1065
1378/79	$653\frac{1}{2}$	193	199	77	1122
1379/80	$524\frac{1}{2}$	$374\frac{1}{2}$	$245\frac{1}{2}$	$75\frac{1}{2}$	$1219\frac{1}{2}$
1393/94	$673\frac{3}{4}$	284	173	106	$1236\frac{3}{4}$
1404/5	1283	451	$135\frac{1}{2}$	$97\frac{1}{2}$	1967
1407/8	$998\frac{1}{2}$	$508\frac{1}{4}$	303	56	$1865\frac{3}{4}$

While there is no evidence, therefore, that the method of allocating work owed from the villagers changed in the fourteenth century, or indeed had changed since the time of the 1251 extent, only from the 1330's do any detailed *opera* accounts survive for Warboys. These *opera* accounts list the number of properties of different sizes owing work for each of the four work seasons, then in separate paragraphs for each season are listed work obligations excused for official tasks, feast days, and illness, followed by detail of work actually performed, and concluded by numbers of works sold. In Table XV these accounts have been synopsized for the years for which they are extant over the fourteenth century. There follows a sample list of units of land owing *opera*. (The Disposition of Villeinage Tenements)

The *ad hominem* nature of villeinage had a paradoxical benefit for the serf when various forces in society mitigated burdens upon individual lives. Presumably the right to serfs of free Sundays was guaranteed by their religion much prior to the fourteenth century, although as may be seen in the above quotation from the extent, some carrying services might be expected on Sundays. In any case, the more propertied the villein, the more he was excused because of religious festivals and illness. It is indeed remarkable that the virgater who was obliged to supply several men at boonworks (etc.) was not simply required to substitute for himself when ill. Perhaps it is equally remarkable that the rest of the vill were not required to substitute *opera* for the ill, given the number of villagers, and the fact they were asked to take over vacant land, to marry when widowed, etc.!

Table XV

Disposition of work[1]
(percentages in brackets)[2]

YEAR	TOTAL WORKS OWED	ALLOWED FOR FEASTDAYS	ALLOWED FOR ILLNESS	PERFORMED	SOLD
1335/36	8640½	868½ (10)	54	4121½ (48)	3597 (42)
1342/43	9857	775 (8)	70	4723¾ (48)	4289¾ (44)
1344/45	8547¾	1162 (14)	49	3917¼ (46)	3419½ (40)

[1] Despite the regular claim by the account roll that the sum of the works allowed for feast days and illness in addition to works performed and sold equal the total works owed, the figures rarely tally exactly. Some of the larger aberrations are explained. For example over 1348/49 270 works had to be allowed for tenements that had fallen into the lord's hands during the plague; over 1353/54 it is merely stated that the 743 works not allowed, performed or sold were 'on account'. The only large unexplained item are the more than 500 un-accounted works for 1373/74. Un-accounted works in other years were as follows: 1354/55 120, 1359/60 37, 1363/64 8, 1366/67 11, 1379/80 133, 1404/5 112, 1407/8 49. For 1360/61, 1374/75 and 1393/94 the total of works allowed, performed and sold were slightly in excess of those owed. The remaining years were equal.

[2] Fractions are not calculated in percentages; percentages are rounded to the nearest number. The performance percentage may be high by about .5% since an 'allowance' of about 3 works per virgate for 'benseg, foddercorn, work on vines' has for convenience been left in this total figure.

YEAR	TOTAL WORKS OWED	ALLOWED FOR FEASTDAYS	ALLOWED FOR ILLNESS	PERFORMED	SOLD
1346/47	9186¾	863+ (9)	228	4952¼ (50)	3142¾ (34)
1347/48	9284¼	627¾ (7)	262¼	4706¼ (51)	3688 (40)
1348/49	8851¾	801¼ (9)	236	4026 (45)	3569¾ (40)
1353/54	7964¼	549 (7)	52½	3527 (44)	3103 (39)
1354/55	6768½	579½ (9)	–	3933 (58)	237 (35)
1359/60	6683½	430½ (6)	5	3815¾ (57)	2394¾ (36)
1360/61	6701	632 (9)	24	4126 (62)	1929 (29)
1362/63	6486	573 (9)	48	3692 (57)	2173 (34)
1363/64	5902½	388½ (7)	104	3881½ (66)	1521 (26)
1366/67	6425¾	614¾ (10)	19	4365½ (68)	1416 (22)
1371/72	5406	393¼ (7)	–	3441 (64)	1572¼ (29)
1373/74	5197½	498¾ (10)	–	2823 (54)	1374 (26)
1374/75	5072¼	374 (7)	–	3478 (69)	1250 (25)
1375/76	5016½	301 (6)	13½	3852 (77)	849 (17)
1377/78	4669½	422½ (9)	73½	3108½ (67)	1065 (23)
1378/79	5017	462½ (9)	17	3415 (68)	1122 (22)
1379/80	5038	433½ (9)	–	3253½ (65)	1219½ (24)
1393/94	4693½	412½ (9)	135¼	2914½ (62)	1236¾ (26)
1404/5	4591¼	424 (9)	15½	2073¾ (45)	1967 (43)
1407/8	3997¼	421⅚ (11)	10	1652⅓ (41)	1865¾ (47)

1335-36: 35¼ virgates *ad opus*, one of which held for service by reeve and beadle

9 semi-virgates, *ad opus* to maltmen, except for lands for four ploughmen for service and one-half virgate of Thomas Raven *ad censum*

29 mondaymanlands *ad opus*, except *ad censum* two mondaymanlands and 2 one-half crofts, and one cotmanland

1342-43: 35¼ virgates *ad opus*, one of which held for service by reeve and beadle

8 maltmanlands and 2 akermanlands, except four akermanlands for service

31 mondaymanlands *ad opus*, except one mondaymanland and two one-half crofts *ad censum*

1344-45: 35¼ virgates *ad opus*, one of which held for service by reeve and one-half virgate for beadle

9 maltmanlands and 3 akermanlands, except three akermanlands for service

31 mondaymanlands *ad opus*, except two one-half mondaymanlands and one mondaymanland *ad censum*

1347-48: 35¼ virgates *ad opus*, one of which held for service by the reeve an done-half virgate for beadle

8 maltmanlands and three akermanlands, except three akermanlands for service

31 mondaymanlands *ad opus*, except two one-half mondaymanlands and one mondaymanland *ad censum*

Since labour obligations on the land remained of a fixed amount per unit of property over the late thirteenth and early fourteenth centuries it is possible to calculate obligations owed by specific tenants. That is to say, variations in obligation came from the changeable liturgical seasons, and as seen above, from the incidence of feast days. Over the 1330's and 1340's these variations were as follows, the plus figures indicate workdays beyond the full week as well as boondays:

YEAR	YEAR

1335-36

Virgater

89 (28 wks at 3 works, + 5)
47 (15 wks at 3 works, + 2)
26 (5 wks at 5 works, + 1)
12 (3 wks at 4 works   )

Total 174

Semi-virgater Maltman

59 (28 wks at 2 works, + 3)
31 (15 wks at 2 works, + 1)
16 (5 wks at 3 works, + 1)
6 (3 wks at 2 works   )

Total 111

Mondayman

29 (28 wks at 1 work, + 1)
15 (15 wks at 1 work   )
6 (6 works over 5 wks   )
2 (2 works over 3 wks   )

Total 52

1342-43

Virgater

97 (30 wks at 3 works, + 7)
42 (13 wks at 3 works, + 3)
26 (5 wks at 5 works, + 1)
12 (3 wks at 4 works   )

177

Semi-virgater Maltman

64 (30 wks at 2 works, +   4)
27½ (13 wks at 2 works, + 1½)
16 (5 wks at 3 works, + 1)
6 (3 wks at 2 works   )

113½

Mondayman

30 (30 wks at 1 work   )
13 (13 wks at 1 work   )
6 (6 works over 5 wks   )
2 (2 works over 3 wks   )

51

1344-45

Virgater

89 (27 wks at 3 works, + 8)
47 (15 wks at 3 works, + 2)
28 (5 wks at 5 works, + 3)
12 (3 wks at 4 works   )

Total 176

Semi-Virgater

59 (27 wks at 2 works, + 5)
31 (15 wks at 2 works, + 1)
17 (5 wks at 3 works, + 2)
6 (3 wks at 2 works   )

Total 113

Mondayman

28 (27 wks at 1 work   + 1)
15 (15 wks at 1 work   )
5 (5 wks at 1 work   )
3 (3 wks at 1 work   )

Total 51

1347-48

Virgater

100 (31 wks at 3 works, +   7)
39 (12 wks at 3 works, +   3)
26 (5 wks at 5 works, +   1)
12 (3 wks at 4 works   )

177

Semi-Virgater

66 (31 wks at 2 works, +   4)
26 (12 wks at 2 works, +   2)
16 (5 wks at 3 works, +   1)
6 (3 wks at 2 works   )

114

Mondayman

31 (31 wks at 1 work, + 1)
12 (12 wks at 1 work   )
6 (5 wks at 1 work, +   1)
2 (2 works over 3 weeks)

51

Another way of assessing these *opera* obligations was by the *opera* cancelled from illness. For example, Richard Collesson, as the clerk noted in the margin of the 1347-48 roll, was ill for the whole year. For the various seasons Collesson was excused as a virgater for 85 winter works, 34 summer works and 23 autumn works beyond feasts. That is to say, Richard Collesson was excused 142 works for illness, 23 were excused for feasts, and presumably the remaining 12 post autumn works of the 177 were not demanded.

Assuming the tenant to be an able bodied man, therefore, and the *opus* to be one day's work, work demanded of a virgater for the year would be approximately one-half the days of the year, that of the semi-virgater about one-third, and of the mondaymanland tenant about fourteen per cent. To put the obligation in another way, of the 130 actual tenant figure suggested at the begining of the previous chapter, each tenant would owe on an average some 70 days (in an "average" year of 9000 works owed). Certainly, as calculated on the accounts of Warboys, *opera* obligations did not impose a crushing burden upon the labour resources of the village.

Reduction to accounting units does of course obscure many elements of the work obligations as may be seen by looking again at the extent at the beginning of this chapter. Some obligations, such as carrying, must have been exhausting and wearied the villager for his next day's operation. Other obligations, such as ploughing and carting, exploited the capital as well as the labour resources of the tenant. On the other hand, during certain seasons of the year the work day seemed to be short (to none), and some work-tasks, such as the sheaf-quota for corn, do not seem to have been exessive. The heaviest pressure for work in farming is concentrated at certain seasons and even with the extensive labour resources of Warboys there must have been a competitive pinch over short sowing and harvesting periods. But again, the main burden lay upon the larger tenants who, the extent tells us, apparently had three or four men available for a virgate. In any case since we have no information about the specific allocation of *opera* for any named individual, it is not possible to pursue further this question.

The *opera* accounts do provide some insight into the disposition of burdens by the list of actual allocations. The following lists provide a synopsized account of *opera* allocation for two years. From this list it can be seen that the main *opera* demands remained much the same from one year to another. In actual fact, however, there would be much variety in the specific tasks according to fields and seasons. More of the variety can be seen in the differing smaller tasks required from one year to another[1] as with this contrast between 1335/6 and 1342/43:

YEAR 1335/36		YEAR 1342/43	
WORK	**AMOUNT**	**WORK**	**AMOUNT**
Maltsilver	23	Maltsilver	24
Boon	( )	Boon	$17\frac{1}{2} + 105\frac{3}{4}$
Vines	35	Vines	$35\frac{1}{4}$
Threshing	1003 + 12 + 20	Threshing	1206 + 118 + 11 + 27
Harvesting	372 + 610	Harvesting	844
Thatching	141	Thatching	25 + 48
Hedging etc.	240 + 100	Hedging etc.	100 + 123
Sent to Ramsey	256 + 152	Sent to Ramsey	48 + 32 + 166
Manure	42 + 7	Manure	45 + 67 + 24
Cutting hay & wood	760	Cutting hay & wood	$188 + 28\frac{3}{4} + 23 + 14 + 13 + 59$
Hollode	40	Hollode	12
Reeds	138	Harrowing	379
Custody of Church	40	Weeding	100
Meadow	21	Fen	36 + 11 + 53
		Stubble	29
		Various wood repairs	20 + 18 + 30 + 9 + 10
		Watching at the Fair of St. Ives	44
		Cutting & thatching peas	8 + 30 + 7
		Building in Broughton	6

The percentage figures in Table XV above indicate that the allowance for feastdays remained much the same throughout the fourteenth century. The same percentages show almost an equal number of works were sold as were performed prior to the Black Death, whereas the relative amount of work performed increased dramatically over the 60's and 70's as the labour demands of the time were reflected at Warboys. With the heavy farming of demesne from the early fifteenth century the sale of works again rose to the level of those performed. After the Black Death the general category of works performed was noted, but it was

[1] The plus (+) signs in these lists indicate further the variety of units and occasions of demand for these tasks.

not as clearly indicated how many works were allocated to each task performed during the various seasons as had been shown prior to the Black Death. From early in the fifteenth century, the seasonal scheduling of work disappeared to be replaced by an *ad hoc* listing of *opera* for the few remaining tenements at service. For example, for the 1413-1414 agricultural year work performed was as follows: 123¾ works at the ploughing boon, 37 works for harrowing, 18½ works for shearing sheep, 19½ works for cutting fen and 268 autumn works for mowing corn.

We must complement the data on the work owed on the lord's demesne with the fact that the villager also had to work his own property. The total village property was apparently much larger than that of the demesne with villagers holding more than twice as many acres in the open fields, if we are to take the ten hides of the 1251 extent as a rough measure of villeinage and the ploughing (carrucate) obligations in the same record upon the demesne as four.¹ Therefore the villagers would likely require something like three times the above *opera* (Table XV) for their own lands and that of the lord. The work required of the virgate holder, 510 days for the lord's and his own property, (170 + 2 × 170) would be too much for one man for one year. This explains the reason for the virgater having three or four labourers at his disposal; and it explains too, the variety of smaller tenements—one-half virgates, maltmanlands, mondaymanlands, akermanlands and other cotlands. In addition, of course, the villager would do many more things about his own property than were required by his formal villein obligations noted above. This is not only to be seen as the obligations of maintaining a household, but even more in the fact that the virgater and other such villagers would not have the specialized services of shepherds, smiths and others available to the lord.

Beyond the villagers who actually held property there is the question of apparent residents of Warboys who had no direct association with land. The good series of account rolls for the 1370's has made it possible to be virtually certain of the names of all land holders at that time. All the more surprising, therefore, is the discovery that more than twenty-

---

¹ In fact the villagers may have held more than three times as many acres of arable. Around 1400, some 315 acres were being sown on the demesne and about 115 acres were farmed, suggesting a traditional demesne of around 430 acres. As we have seen in the previous chapter, the villeinage acreage in the Hundred Roll amounted to more than 1300 acres, and some of the villagers always leased from, and would certainly have found some employment on, the 250 acres of freehold in the village.

five families in Warboys at this time were not represented as holding land. Specifically, the following names[1] from the generation table are not found in the 1370's land table of the previous chapter:

Alot	London
Ategate	Milner
Attehill	Newell
Asplond	Newman
Bele	Onty
Bettes	Page
Bigge	Randolf
Botiller	Robyn
Bokelond	Sande
Brampton	Sarrison
Bronnote	Skyner
Brynewater	Sperner
Chaumon	Thacher
Dally	Thresher
Elliot	Vernon
Haugate	William

The same phenomenon would seem to have obtained for the early part of the century. While we do not have a list of property holders prior to the 1370's, it is clear from references to *opera* delicts and major obligations of responsibility of the villager (especially as juror) who were property holders from the court roll evidence of the earlier period. From this court roll information the following[2] were apparently land holders around 1300:

Agath, Robert	Brun, Henry
Albyn, Robert	—, John
Attewode, Roger	Bugge, Nicholas
Attehall, Stephen	Catoun, Richard
Benet, Hugh	Cecilia, Godfrey, son of
—, Reginald	Clerk, Robert
Berenger, Robert	—, Godfrey
—, William	Derward, Richard
Bonde, Martin	Eydon, Hugh of
—, Richard	Faber, William
Bronnyng, Robert	Fine, Robert

[1] Several of these families – Augustyn, Chapman, Onty, Randolf – may not have been resident in the village at this time.

[2] As we have seen from the Subsidy Rolls names at the end of Chapter III, above a good number of women were property holders. However, these are not identifiable here because their obligations were answered by men so far as the court roll was concerned.

Fine, William
Folyet, John
Galeway, Walter
Gardiner, Ralph
Gerold, Richard
—, William
Godwin, Richard
Gosse, Robert
—, Simon
Grendale, Alan of
Haliday, Robert
Harsine, Robert
—, Godfrey
Haugate
Herbert, Godfrey
Hygeneye, John of
Hyrst, Ivo of
Isabella, Henry
Lenot, Benedict
—, Robert
London, William
Lone, Nicholas
—, Simon
Long, William
Lucas, William
Margarette, Simon
Martin, (not clearly)
Mercator, Henry
Miller, Ralph
Molt, Godfrey
Noble, Richard
Nunne, William
Osbern

Pakerel, William
Pilche, Godfrey
Plumbe, Nicholas
Prat, John
Pilgrim, William
Ponder, John
Puttock, Simon
—, John
Raven, John
Rede, John
Reeve, William
Robyn, Richard, son of
—, Simon, son of
Rolf, William
Smart, Robert
Scut, John
Segeley, Albinus
—, John
Semar, Albinus
—, Henry
Thurburn, Ralph
Thurkyld
Top, William
Unfrey, John
Walter, Nicholas, son of Walter
—, John, son of Walter
Walsh
Wennington, Robert of
Wilkes
Wodekoc, Richard
—, William
Wrench, Ralph

Most of the above persons would be involved in major properties, that is the virgate or one-half virgate.[1] In short, this court roll information would seem to reveal almost as many of the larger land holders as the 1251 extent, or the rent roll data of the 1370's, so that we may be assured that only a few individuals (non -"family" names) and freemen escaped the list. The list is undoubtedly less complete for smaller land holders. From the above list the following were likely small holders: Richard Derward, Godfrey Harsene, Haugate, Lenot, William Lucas, Osbern, Pilche, Martin, Pilgrim, Thurkyld, Walsh, Wennington, Wilkes and Wrench.

[1] This is confirmed for several of these familes by the properties of those ill before and during the Black Death. Cf. List of Illness. Ch. 5.

The pool of available labour upon which the more needy landed villagers could draw cannot be equated, however, with the non-landed people of the village. For sons of well-landed families simply to labour for someone else in the village was not enough when the family resources failed to meet the needs of numerous sons. In the extent of 1251, and again in the above list of apparent land holders around 1300, it is evident that several families were able to establish two branches on separate properties. Indeed the Gerold family may have had three branches with substantial holdings around 1300. But more common was the tendency for the supernumerary sons to leave the village. The following is a list of the sons of landed families who do not seem to have inherited property. While our records do not show that all of these left the village their involvement in village life seems to have been so brief and peripheral that we may likely assume that most did depart:

Albyn, Henry, son of
—, John, son of
Attewode, Robert (left)
—, Richard
—, Adam
Berenger, William, son of John
—, Richard, son of John
—, Roger
Bonde, Luke (left)
—, Nicholas
—, Benedict (left)
Bronnyng, Simon, son of Simon
—, Godfrey
Broun, Lawrence (left)
—, Nicholas (left)
—, Richard (left)
Bugge, Richard (left)
—, William, son of Ralph (left)
—, Godfrey (left)
Catoun, Henry, son of Richard (left)
Cecilia, Stephen, son of
—, John, son of
Dike, John
Faber, Richard, son of Henry (left)
—, Stephen, son of Henry (left)
—, Hugh, son of Henry (left)
Folyet, Richard
—, William
Gardener, Godfrey (left)
—, Richard

Gardener, Nicholas
Gerold, Simon (left)
Godwin, Andrew, son of Richard
Grendale, Richard of
Herbert, William (left)
—, John
Isabella, Richard, son of Henry (left)
London, Ralph, son of William (left)
—, Stephen, son of William (left)
—, William, son of William (left)
Margarete, Richard, son of Simon
Noble, Richard, son of Richard (left)
Pilche, Hugh (left)
—, Richard (left)
—, Robert, son of William (left)
Pilgrim, Stephen (left)
Raven, William
—, Nicholas
Robyn, William, son of
—, Maurice, son of
—, Thomas
Scut, Godfrey (left)
—, William, son of Godfrey (left)
—, Henry
—, Robert (left)
Top, Valentine (left)
—, Godfrey, brother of Valentine (left)
Wennington, John, son of Robert (left)
Wodekoc, John
—, Richard

This phenomenon would seem to have continued over the second quarter of the fourteenth century. For example at that time Maurice Bonde, Paul Bonde and John, son of Robert Bonde appear to have left; Benedict Faber certainly left and William Catoun probably left.

On the other hand, there is every evidence that smallholders held tenaciously to their little foothold in the village. Such families as the Walsh, Wennington, Wilkes and Lenot were to survive for many generations at Warboys. Seemingly these people were content to work their own properties and eke out enough for their families by working for the lord or their more affluent fellow villagers. Of course, at times these smallholders would be forced to leave the village, as may be seen with the Pilche and Pilgrim families above. Very likely, in fact, many more members of these less important people did leave the village but their chattels would be so insignificant that the courts did not even bother to record their departure.

A third category of labour at Warboys was that of professional services and special skills. These may be grouped under five general headings. First, administration of the lordship, second, asministration of the demesne proper, thirdly, the *famuli*, fourth, skilled services, fifth, local specialists for villagers' needs. The first group included the steward, the clerks of account, the woodward and from time to time special officials concerned with sowing etc. Except for the woodward who seems to have kept some foothold in the village, these were all outsiders and not of immediate interest for our story of Warboys. The account roll gives much the same information about these people over the two hundred year period: that is to say, the expenses of the steward when his court sessions were held, the expenses of the clerks when the accounts were drawn up, and for the woodward the regular annual stipend of 4/— plus 6/8d. for his robe.

The chief officials for the demesne administration proper were the reeve and beadle. There is no mention of a sergeant in the mid-thirteenth-century account rolls for Warboys, but by the en dof the century a sergeant appears regularly at the stipend of 4/— per year in cash along with payments in kind. The tasks of the sergeant are not clear, although he seems to have eaten at the lord' expense along with the woodward, reeve and beadle during the heavy harvest season period of work. From the mid-fourteenth century the sergeant was called a bailiff, and from this time his task was clearly to take over financial administration from the reeve. Enough is known about the work of reeves and beadles from manuals on estate management,[1] as well as specific writings on the estates of Ramsey Abbey[2] that detailed descriptions are not necessary for these officials at Warboys. These men were well rewarded by discount of their rents as well as food at the lord's expense and livery of corn during the harvest season. Perhaps a cook should be included among this category of administrators, for certainly he was a busy man when he cooked for the above officials during the harvest season and for scores of villagers at the time of the boon work. The cook apparently lived off the general expenses allowed for the lord's hall during the early part of our period from the mid-fourteenth-century he was paid the annual stipend given to *famuli*, that is 6/—. Very possibly a local clerk should be added to this administration group. For, over the late thirteenth and early fourteenth century 5/— were paid annually to the clerk of the account. However, whether this was a clerk from the village, or a special clerk from Ramsey, that is one from the first administration group, is not clear.

The *famuli* were full time servants on the lord's demesne. The line of distinction between these servants and the previous category certainly is not clear in so far as method of payment is concerned. For the ploughman, too, received land at a discounted rent for their services, and the dairyman was sometimes to be found eating at the lord's hall in the early fourteenth century. The personnel of the *famuli* did not change greatly over the two centuries. In the mid-thirteenth-century there were 3 ploughmen, a cowherd, a pigman, a shepherd and a maidservant (dairymaid?). At the end of this century the *famuli* were listed as 1 carter, 3 ploughmen, 1 cowman, 1 pigman, 1 shepherd and 1 dairymaid. Numbers of shepherds had increased to 2 by the second quarter of the fourteenth century. After the Black Death the number of shepherds increased again, while the number of ploughmen fell to 2. Over 1360/61, for example, the *famuli* were listed as 1 carter, 2 ploughmen, 1 cowman, 3 shepherds, 1 pigman and 1 cook. The composition of the *famuli* had not changed greatly by the early fifteenth century when large-scale leasing of the demesne began. Over 1407/8, for example, there were 1 carter, 2 ploughmen, 1 shepherd, 1 pigman, 1 cook and a servant of the bailiff.

The fourth group, that of skilled services, usually embraced the craft of the carpenter, the smith and the thatcher. The account rolls detail

---

[1] *Walter of Henley and other Treatises*, ed. Dorothea Oschinsky, Oxford, 1971.
[2] *Estates*, under Reeve.

the expenses allocated to these services for extraordinary needs as well as regular annual requirements. Sometimes the unusual needs seem to have been subcontracted so that we are unable to distinguish wage stipend from other costs. For example, over 1254/55 a new sheepfold was constructed, but the account roll only states that 27/11d. were allocated for "lumber, reeds, nails, wage labour, carpentry, roofing and building of a certain new wall and other things". Or, over 1325/26 it is stated that a stipend of 9/9d. was paid to John of Caldecote and his associates for carpentry on the grange of Chatteris. This same John and associates were paid the sum of 21/10d. for cutting timber and shaping, it for a grange over 1329/30. In the same year a carpenter of the lord was paid the round sum of 16/3d. to re-build the kitchen and bakehouse. Occasionally however, more detail was given, as for 1318/19 when we have the following list of costs for building a new sheepfold and perhaps other walls: 1 thatcher for 17 days —3/6½d. (at 2½d. per day); 1 carpenter for 5 weeks, bringing timber from St. Ives—7/6d. (18d. per week); 1 carpenter for 15 days as assistant—3/—; 1 carpenter for 3 days—9d.; the work on shaping the timber for the sheepfold—2/—; 1 man to repair wall of the garden etc. for 14 days—2/11d. (2½d. per day); 2 carpenters cutting and shaping timber for 14 days—7/— (6d. per day); 1 carpenter for 3 days—9d.; 1 carpenter for 5 days—15d.; 1 thatcher for new sheepfold for 20 days—4/2d.

The more regular use of the skilled services was for the maintenance of ploughs, the shoeing of horses and the thatching of stacks of corn. Over 1329/30, for example, a carpenter was paid 2/10d. for building a new plough and re-building others. The smith was paid an annual wage of 3/— in the mid-thirteenth-century but from the end of the century he seems to have been enployed on piece work. For example, over 1318/19, the smith was paid 20/— for the irons for 4 ploughs and the front shoes for 4 stots and both front and back shoes for 2 other stots. Over 1329/-30, the smith was paid 27/— for irons for the plough and shoes for carthorses. At the end of this century the picture seems to have been much the same, since over 1407/8 the smith was paid 28/10d. for the iron for 3 ploughs and for shoeing horses. Thatching was a less well-paid skill, over 1256/55, thatching of stacks only paid 16d. And over 1329/30, 1 thatcher was paid 2d. a days for 5 days for thatching the grange.

One of the most disappointing aspects of the account roll as a source for social history is the anonymity of the *famuli*, carpenter, smiths, and thatchers. On the other hand it is indicative of the full-time professional roles of these services that they should assume the designation of surname. From the thirteenth century surnames appear for Woodward (and Forester), Reeve, Pigman, Shepherd, Akerman (ploughman), Carpenter, Carter, Clerk, Cook, Cowherd, Thatcher and Smith. Most of these would seem to have been full-time or almost full-time for the persons involved. A good number of other specialized names appeared in the village from this time, very likely offering their services to the villagers since there is no reference to them in the lord's account. Such were Gardener, Hayward, Merchant (Mercator), Miller, Potter, Skinner, Taylor, Tanner and Thresher. It is clear from the court rolls and the above Generation Table (III) that many of these specialists were not solidly rooted in the village. There is little evidence for their having acquired standard village holdings and for the succession of the immediate family to what property they did hold in the village.

It is a well-known fact of peasant society that the peasant should be capable of performing a wide variety of tasks. The list of *opera* performed by peasants cited at the beginning of this chapter illustrates this versatility among the people of Warboys. To a degree, therefore, one is surprised by the number of special craftsmen that the lord had to hire full-time or part-time. But it must be remembered that these specialists did not represent a significant proportion of the labouring population at Warboys. At the two boonworks of 1360-61, for example, these were respectively 88 and 314 workers in addition to the *famuli*. It must be kept in mind too that by far the greater variety of tasks were performed by villagers in routine working of their own properties. This resource could not only be exploited by the lord for the many needs of his demesne but it also provided the villager with opportunities for piece-work bonuses. Rather than increase of *opera* for special needs, the Warboys accounts showed a preference for hiring someone, presumably from the village. For example, over 1254-55, 3s. 10d. were paid out for winnowing and 6d. for a keeper of the calves; over 1306-7, the reeve and his "boy" were given 2s. expenses for bringing 80 lambs from M'Cheford to Ramsey; over 1318-19, 12d. were paid to someone for carting stone for twelve days and another 6d. for repairing the cart for this; during the 1325-26 year someone was paid 16d. for cutting forage for one week; over 1329-30, 2s. 10d. were paid for transporting reeds from the marsh and 10s. 3d. for digging 80 perches of ditch; in 1336, six rings of corn were paid for carrying timber; from later in the fourteenth century special wages were paid for herding the lord's beasts in the marshes (2s. in 1407-8).

PART IV

CHANGE IN THE SOCIAL COMPLEX
AND PERSONALITIES

Chapter VII

THE WHOLE VILLAGE

Previous chapters have been concerned with presenting the main data available for the study of the people of Warboys. We now turn to the question: what human story do these data tell? First of all, it is clear that the local community of Warboys survived with much vigour throughout the whole of the 1250-1450 period. But it is equally clear that Warboys changed drastically at various times over these two hundred years. The changes came both from internal structures and relations in the village, as well as from the fact that Warboys was far from being uninfluenced by the outside world. This is only to say that the story of Warboys requires both a multi-level and a short run perspective. In the following pages we shall endeavour to reveal this by analyzing change at Warboys in terms of total village community, family groups and individuals.

A modern village of only 1, 720 in 1966, despite the affluence of fen agriculture, Warboys was at its peak population of our period around 1300. To the 629 people identifiable from court rolls over 1290-1318 must be added about 300 women if the sex ratio may be assumed to be fairly even. Since no children under the age of puberty are noted in the court rolls, some additional 25%, or 230 children must likely be added to acquire an approximation to the true population of the village. This comes to a population of over 1150, and while some of these were outsiders their number is almost balanced by those not listed in the court rolls.[1] The pressure of such a population upon village resources must have been great for this is almost one mouth to every acre of arable available to the villagers. There is no evidence that the lord responded in generous fashion to this situation, for the evidence from account rolls indicates that by the late thirteenth century, in contrast with the mid-thirteenth-century, entry fines had been pushed up.[2] Many young men,

---

[1] Cf. Chapter II above for court roll data, and Chapters III and IV for data concerning isolated individuals and mobility.

[2] *Estates*, pp. 248-249.

agressive members with more successful family backgrounds, left the village with or without licence of the lord to seize opportunities in a region they were quite familiar with. What happened to the many isolated individuals we cannot say.

Yet, the village was more unconsciously "open" at this period than at any later time, so that it is not easy to record this pressure. Outsiders from many places had come to reside for at least a brief stay in the village. Nearly every court roll recorded a number of outsiders (or *ignoti*, and or *malefactores*) received, both by lesser members of the vill seemingly careless of the law as well as by main villagers eager for cheap labour from the transient. Control of gleaning,[1] the main village welfare technique of the time, does not yet seem to have become strict. Of some 70 cases of fines for gleaning wrongly before the Black Death only 15 were before 1316; similarly, of 18 persons fined for receiving some unnamed person who gleaned wrongly, only one fine was recorded before 1316. Few were out of tithing, and personal pledging—that extension of the tithing system into all areas of village life—provided a clear dependence zone for the isolated individual so that evictions for even petty theft as well as gleaning wrongly were rare. No difficulty was experienced in finding pledges among responsible people in the village. Of nearly 1400 personal pledges noted between 1290 and 1347, fewer than 50 were pledged by people outside the main village family. Within these main families, pledging was concentrated in the most responsible individual, and his pledging role was clearly not framed by blood relationships[2]. This core of pledging responsibility was of course focussed in the village administration, with official (i.e. personal name of official not even given) pledging by the beadle more than 200 times and by the reeve more than a 150 times.

The social and legal discipline of Warboys shifted noticeably from the time of the famine in the second decade of the century. In line with the economic retrenchment from this time[3] was a generally stultified atmosphere. Court roll data suggest a fall in population by as much as 15% over the second quarter of the century. In 1316 alone 7 main

---

[1] The best illustrative study of gleaning in village society is still that of F. M. Page, "The Customary Poor Law of Three Cambridgeshire Manors", *Cambridge Historical Journal*, III, No. 2; and by the same author, *The Estates of Crowland Abbey*, Cambridge, 1934, pp. 108-112.
[2] This can be readily established by contrasting numbers in families in Table II with numbers of pledges by leading members of the same family in Table III of my article 'The Concentration of Responsibility in Five Villages', *Mediaeval Studies*, 1966, pp. 98-99, 113.
[3] *Estates*, Chapter Eight.

villagers were fined for receiving those who had gleaned wrongly while the courts adopted the unusual practise of not bothering to mention most of the numerous "evil gleaners" of this year. In 1316, too, several from substantial families (Stephen Le Bonde, Beatrice Bishop, Emma Bishop, Emma Hayward) were indicted for gleaning wrongly. Over the next three decades the number of illegal gleaners remained higher than before the famine and continued to appear from all levels of society. Over the next three decades, too, whether from recalcitrance by the villagers (8 of 10 citations for receiving *extra decenna* were after 1316), or simply tighter tithing control over outsiders, those cited to be out of tithing remain much higher than earlier. On the other hand, control of reception of undesirables—unkown, prohibited, wrong-doers—seems to have succeeded, especially among more important families.[1] There was a gradual increase in tension between the lord and tenant about the payment of services. The following are the charges for neglect of service recorded in court rolls: 1290: 6; 1292: (0); 1294 (1): 2; 1294 (2): 0; 1299: 0; 1301 (1): 0; 1301 (2): 0; 1305: 0; 1306 (1): 0; 1306 (2): 5; 1309: 0; 1313: 0; 1316: 1; 1320 (1): 25; 1320 (2): 13; 1322 (1): 12; 1322 (2): 0; 1325: 7 (+?); 1326: 7; 1331: 15; 1333 (1): 33; 1333 (2): 0; 1334: 33; 1337: 23; 1339: 35; 1343: 14 (+?); 1347: 38. The fen frontier of the village was always the most difficult to police although a gradual frequency in sale of produce to outsiders and other abuses in the fen was recorded: 1290: 7; 1299: 28; 1305: 7; 1313: 2; 1321: 1; 1326: 15; 1331: 11; 1333: 5; 1334: 41; 1337: 7; 1347: 8. But most indicative of all perhaps for the new spirit was the fact that so few villagers left the village from this time. The cumulative total of those leaving Warboys prior to 1316 was 68; those leaving between 1316 and 1347 were only 13.[2] Warboys was indeed much more a closed village at this time!

Warboys nevertheless remained a vital social and economic community. The village had not become tightly closed, nor had it lost its social cohesion. There was still an economic attraction in the village since many families were able to get established there over this time: Alot, Bettes, Bokelond, Bolby, Bryd, Colle (Colleson), Collier, Cosyn, Cous, Dike, Fleming, Hunter, Lawrence, Mice, Moke, Molt, Palmer, Sawere,

---

[1] Reception by less important families was as follows: 1306: 1; 1309: 5; 1316: 22; 1333: 17; 1334: 10; and by main families: 1290: 3; 1301: 3; 1306: 9; 1309: 21; 1313: 19; 1316: 11; 1332: 25; 1333: 14; 1334: 15.

[2] Those leaving earlier in the thirteenth century cannot be established owing both to a lack of court rolls and of surnames in the thirteenth-century extent.

Taylor, Tymme, and Vicory. Family discontinuance[1] in the village did not have a particular bias against the "small" man as the following names of disappearing families indicates: Agath, Baseley, Beadle, Bishop, Brandon, Burg, Capenter, Chose, Clerk, Clervaux, Duraunt, Edwin, Eydon, Feker, Folyet, Galeway, Gardner, Godwyn, Grendale, Hayward, John, Juliana, Katherine, Mably, Mercator, Pigman, Ponder, Reeve, Roger, Sculle, Sparhawk, Thurkyld, Tortorin, and Unfreys. Pledging did not vary much in the long run over the two generations either in number or in social patterns. On the latter point, for example, pledging was much the same in number and variety by the beadle and reeve over the whole period. The total number of personal pledges recorded in various courts before the Black Death were as follows: 1290: 31; 1292: 41; 1294 (1): 70; 1294 (2): 38; 1299: 67; 1301 (1): 23; 1301 (2): 40; 1305: 36; 1306 (1): 45; 1306 (2): 56; 1309: 19; 1313 (1): 73; 1313 (2): 35; 1316 (1): 37; 1316 (2): 45; 1318: 10; 1320 (1): 53; 1320 (2): 49; 1322 (1): 51; 1322 (2): 74; 1325: 59; 1326: 50; 1331: 56; 1332: 30; 1333 (1): 25; 1333 (2): 41; 1334: 48; 1337: 40; 1339: 46; 1343: 21; 1347: 9.

The dislocations at Warboys following upon the Black Death provide an interesting insight into the forces behind the social and economic life of the village over previous generations. Our records detail more directly the economic effects of the Plague: land left without tenants, debts of manorial officials from failure to collect rents and breakdown in the communal farming discipline. The virgates and cotlands rendered vacant by the death of their tenants were filled within a couple of years. A relatively successful amortization of manorial debts was under way by the 1360's.[2] Records are casual about services performed for the lord immediately after the Black Death, perhaps because many were condoned. But when a very detailed accounting was demanded in 1353 some 88 failures to come to work or to work properly were recorded. By 1360 these work failures were reduced to about 30; they remained around the low of 10 over the next decade, fell to one by 1375 and became thereafter an incident in the issue of individual renting arrangements, overshadowed by dilapidation and vacancies, rather than a problem of general concern.

The most striking breakdown in the communal discipline after the Black Death was the disappearance of the personal pledge. Since the pledging of another person was customarily a free option of the indi-

---

[1] Cf. further on this point, below p. 225 ff.
[2] Cf. *Estates*, pp. 254-257.

vidual,[1] we must assume that villagers now no longer wished to support one another in this fashion. Whether as cause or effect of this disappearance of the personal pledge, regular proclamation of the impersonal byelaw with stress on large penalties, increase in the number of byelaws and coercive use of village officials attempted to fill the traditional role of the pledge. The new system never really succeeded, at least in recovering fully the social spirit of the early fourteenth century. A community bordering on the fen expanse, Warboys was not easy to govern at any time, as we have seen with reference to sale of turf and reeds before the Black Death. But, from the time of the Black Death, the problem of the fen frontier increased and spread to the open fields where trespass upon the crops of lord or fellow villager now became endemic and chronic.

After the fen, trespass of the woods for timber, branches or simply forage had been the next most prominent problem, varying considerably from year to year, though increasing in the second quarter of the century: 1290: 1; 1294: 2; 1299: 13; 1301: 6; 1305: 8; 1306: 3; 1313: 13; 1316: 13; 1320 (1): 9; 1320 (2): 13; 1322 (1): 3; 1322 (2): 4; 1325: 9; 1326: 12; 1331: 12; 1333: 20; 1334: 16; 1337: 20; 1339: 14; 1343: (8); 1347: 23.[2] Trespass in the lord's meadow did not occur at all for many years and rarely become very frequent: 1290: 4; 1301: 5; 1306: 1; 1313: 1; 1322: 11; 1325: 2; 1326: 3; 1331: 1; 1333: 6; 1337: 7; 1339: 13; 1347: 3. Trespass in the open fields was more frequent and became somewhat more pressing over the second quarter of the century: 1290: 2; 1294: 2; 1299: 3; 1301: 5; 1306 (1): 2; 1306 (2): 1; 1309: 18; 1313: 4; 1316: 56; 1320 (1): 3; 1320 (2): 4; 1322 (1): 3; 1322 (2): 5; 1326: 7; 1331: 9; 1333: 22; 1334: 11; 1337: 5; 1339: 7; 1343: (8); 1347: 14.

Virtually all trespass in meadow before the Black Death was against the lord rather than other villagers; trespass in the open fields upon grain of the villagers only began to occur occasionally from the 1330's. While the strain upon the lord's properties in marsh, turf and woods only slowly increased after 1348,[3] the most novel feature of trespass from

---

[1] The court stated that the individual had to 'find' a pledge.

[2] Trespass by neglect of ditches was a nagging problem, but never consistently reported in courts: 1290: 1; 1294: 3; 1306 (1): 4; 1306 (2): 1; 1326: 1; 1333: 1; 1347: 4; 1384: 2; 1387: 1; 1390: 5.

[3] Trespass in wood: 1350: 2; 1360: 3; 1363: 13; 1365: 11; 1369 (1): (7); 1369 (2): 9; 1371: 15; 1372: 3; 1372/3: 5; 1382: 13; 1384: 11; 1386/8: 9; 1387/8: 11; 1390 (1): 8; 1390 (2): 18; 1391/2: 16; 1398: 10. Trespass in marsh and turf: 1353: 4; 1360: 2; 1365: 1; 1371: 24; 1372: 11; 1372/3: 20; 1375/6: 30; 1382: 1; 1384: 9.

this time was the fact that trespasses in the open fields remained high, several of the trespasses in the open fields every year were against fellow villagers and personal trespass among villagers with regard to other properties—a rarity before 1348—now became a regular feature of the courts. This new tension may be seen by the following list of total trespasses in the open fields and of lawsuits among villagers for personal trespass damages:

TRESPASS IN OPEN FIELDS				PERSONAL TRESPASS SUITS			
1349:	28	1372/3:	22	1350:	5	1372:	2
1350:	32	1375/6:	19	1353:	8	1372/3:	1
1353:	15	1382:	19	1360:	4	1375/6:	6
1360:	15	1384:	3	1363:	1	1382:	7
1363:	33	1386/7:	25	1365:	2	1386/7:	1
1365:	23	1387/8:	21	1369 (1):	6	1387/8:	3
1369 (1):	38	1390/1:	10	1369 (2):	5	1390(1):	4
1369 (2):	22	1390/2:	28	1371:	8	1391/2:	1
1371:	4	1391/2:	12				
1372:	8						

As a social complex, Warboys was a relatively peaceful village in the first half of the fourteenth century. Violence that did occur was infrequent, and then largely the result of personal confrontation rather than indicative of wider social and economic malaise. The following list of assaults, defamations and hues illustrates how violence was reported in the court rolls:[1]

1290:	1 defamation; 1 murder; 1 hue;
1292:	1 defamation; 1 hue;
1294 (1):	1 hue wrongly;
1294 (2):	2 hues wrongly; 1 hue;
1299:	1 theft and hamsok; 2 assaults; 5 hues; 1 hanging; 3 defamations;
1301:	2 defamations; 1 hue wrongly; 2 hues;
1305:	1 hue; 1 assault; 1 defamation;
1306 (1):	4 assaults; 6 hues;
1306 (2):	8 assaults;

[1] The false or wrong hue would seem to indicate antagonism or some form of fear or tension in the village. Unfortunately we do not know what really lay behind most of the defamation charges.

1309:   3 assaults; 2 hamsoks;
1313:   3 assaults; 3 hues; 1 hue wrongly;
1316:   2 defamations; 3 hues wrongly; 2 hues;
1320 (1): 5 assaults; 2 hues; 2 hues wrongly;
1320 (2): 1 asault; 6 hues;
1322:   1 assault; 16 hues; 1 hue wrongly;
1325:   7 assaults; 12 hues; 4 hues wrongly; 1 hamsok;
1326:   1 assault; 2 hues;
1331:   2 assaults; 12 hues;
1332:   2 assaults; 7 hues;
1333 (1): 1 assault;
1333 (2): 1 assault; 11 hues; 2 hues wrongly; 1 hamsok;
1334:   4 assaults; 7 hues; 3 hues wrongly; 1 hamsok;
1337:   3 assaults; 12 hues; 2 hues wrongly;
1339:   2 assaults; 11 hues; 1 hue wrongly;
1343:   6 assaults; 12 hues: 1 hue wrongly: 1 hamsok;
1347:   4 hues; (1) hue wrongly

From the time of the Black Death, however, the social atmosphere of
the village did not only change from the disappearance of the personal
pledge and the decline in respect for the fellow villager's property.
There was also a marked increase in violence among villagers. In order
to put this in perspective we must first assess the change in personnel
of the villagers at this time. The most notable feature of population
change from 1348 is not simply the disappearance of several family names
from this time, but rather the fact that this disappearance rate continued.
Families were often sufficiently large to survive the Black Death in at
least a few of their representatives. But, by the 1360's and 70's many of
these last representatives were wiped out either by new epidemics or the
normal processes of mortality in a weakened family. Some of the largest
families of earlier generations, such as Walsh, Pakerel and Fine were
able to survive for a longer period. By the 1380's they too had disappeared. The list of families disappearing shortly after the Plague was
as follows (the date in brackets is that of the last appearance in the village
of the family): Bost (1379), Buk (1347), Burbridge (1350), Cecilia (1353),
Chaumon (1360), Clerk (1353), Cowherd (1350), Dike (1353), Fine (1377),
Haliday (1363), Haugate (1372), Henry (1360), Hyrst (1350?), Isabelle
(1347), Long (1347), Lucas (1347), Pakerel (1379), Palmer (1353), Reginald
(1353), Richard (1360), Robyn (1369), Segeley (1347), Sewyn (1363),
Skynner (1369), Sutor (1371), Top (1353), Tymme (1347), Walsh (1382),
Walter (1379), William (1371), Wodekoc (1348).

While decimation by the Black Death is often obscurred by the relative difference in size of families under the one surname, families entering the village would be more nuclear and indicative of the places left to be filled after the Plague. In point of fact, new family names entering Warboys after 1350, as may be seen in the following list, outnumber the family names disappearing by some 30%:[1] Attegate: 1363-1428; Attehill: 1369-1408; Asplond: 1369, 1413-1428; Augustyn: 1369-; Bele: 1360-; Benson: 1360-; Bigge: 1369-1373; Botiller: 1375-; Bronnote: 1369-; Buckworth: 1369-; Brynnewater: 1375-; Carter: 1349-1371; Child: 1378-1379; Dally: 1387-; Edward: 1369-; Elliot: 1353-1369; Eyr: 1382-; Fisher: 1360-; Herresson: 1371-; Hervy: 1369-; Hichesson: 1369-; Jekkisson: 1371-; Lambehird: 1371-1390; Newell: 1369-1371; Newman: 1369-; Norreys: 1350-; Northburgh: 1371-; Oliver: 1360-; Page: 1369-1371; Person: 1387-; Prestecosyn: 1378-; Randolf: 1369, 1448; Raveley: 1363-; Revisson: 1369-; Ropere: 1379, 1391-1392; Sande: 1371-; Sarrisson: 1363-; Son: 1371-; Tasker: 1382-; Thacher: 1375-; Thomisson: 1369-; Thresher: 1360-; Vernon: 1363-1364; Warren: 1378-; Willimot: 1360-; Wolney: 1371-; and Wright 1382.

Along with the considerable change in personnel at Warboys over the decades after the Black Death there came an increase in violence. This is not so noticeable immediately after the Black Death (1349: 2 assaults, 3 hues, 2 wrong hues; 1350: 2 assaults and 7 hues; 1353: 4 hues). There are no more data for the 1350's, but by 1360 the list was long: the hue and cry was raised by Joan Rolf, Margaret Robyn, Hugh Foot, William Thresher, Joan Skynner, Agnes Olyver, Agnes Hygeney, Joan Botild, Richard Shepherd and Roger, servant of Cristina Brown; assaults were reported by Joan Rolf on Margaret Robyn, William Chaumson on Joan Skynner, John Alcok on Agnes Olyver, Isabella Rolf on Agnes Hygeneye, Isabella Rolf on John Lenot junior, John Pilgrim on Joan Botild, Richard Livedon on Roger, servant of Cristina Brown, John Baroun on John Mold and Andrew Bonde on John Mold, the hayward. Court roll information is very poor for the rest of the 1360's, but certainly by the mid 70's tension had mounted again with assaults reported by John High on Robert Vicory, Thomas Callon on John Miller, John servant of the Rector on Thomas Colle, Thomas Gosse on Robert Say, John Sperner on John, servant of the Rector and Thomas Gosse on

---

[1] Many of these families did not remain long in the village, as is indicated by the dates following the surnames. A dash after the date indicates that the family remained for more than two generations. Family entries to the village would seem to have fallen off by the 1380's, although Warboys data are not very complete for that decade.

John Sperner. This tension remained at a higher level over the next decade and more. Particularly distressing seems to have been the year after the Peasants Revolt when Juliana Bonde, John Herresson, John Hervy, Thomas Hunter, the constable, Beatrice Wilkes and John Herresson again were involved with the hue and cry; while assaults were reported by John Webster on John Tasker, John Tasker on John Webster, John Swan junior on William Webster, William Gosse on Alice Brown (hamsok), John Lenot on the tasters, Robert Vicory on John Hervy, Robert Vicory on Thomas Hunter, the constable and Robert Vicory on John Herresson.

By this time newcomers were very highly represented among those involved in violence, although not as much as at the neighbouring village of Upwood.[1] More obvious at Warboys was the consistent violence against officials. In the above list, the tasters and the constables were assaulted. For 1360, as we have seen, Andrew Bonde assaulted the hayward; the constable was reported assaulted in every court for which we have complete records over the 1380's (1384, 1387/8, 1390) and in 1391 the beadle suffered an attack on his house. Equally significant, though not reported as assaults here, were the categories of "rebel"—rare prior to 1348—but now fairly regular. In 1360 Andrew Bonde was fined for being "disobedient and rebellious to the lord's bailiff"; 1363, John Mold, John Sanderson and John Lenot hindered work on the lord's demesne and were disobedient to his officials; in the same year, William Olyver, John Chapman, John Bost, John Thatcher (carter), John Baroun, Thomas Hunter, Thomas Willimot and William Smyth were disobedient and unwilling to be taxed and justiceable by their peers; William Olyver was fined for the same disobedience in 1365; John Rewell, John Bost, John Thommisson, Richard High, Robert Rolf, Bartholomew Swan, John Baroun and John Chapman were rebellious in the same way in 1369; in the latter year too, Thomas Newman, Hacon and Milner junior refused to pay the head tax with their neighbours; Henry Wolney, John Chapman, Robert Swan and William Olyver again refused to be judged by their peers and to pay head tax over 1372/73. This category of rebellion almost disappears from the early 1370's as more open neglect of property becomes the focus of individual opposition.

The vitality of the Warboys community in the early part of the four-

---

[1] Cf. my article "Changes in an English Village after the Black Death", *Mediaeval Studies*, 1967, pp. 158-177; it should be noted, however, that the Upwood court roll series are more complete for this post-Black Death generation.

teenth century was such that many activities of the villagers were not personally reported through the court rolls. It is obvious from the court roll, for example, that juro s, tasters and chief pledges worked through-out the year but the court roll merely lists the fines resulting from the work of such officers, not the method or scope of their performance. It is obvious from the court rolls, too, that the villagers must have gathered frequently in large groups in their function as *villata* or in smaller groups of *socii* who undertook various farming enterprises. Perhaps the most striking way of all by which self-government was left to the village community may be seen with reference to the management of open fields and common. The customary manorial regulations of the lord that survived in the extents of surveys did not embrace regulations of the open fields or of the villagers rights in the various type of com-mon.[1] By the second half of the fourteenth century the social ordering of Warboys was less submerged in the "community". Indeed the whole *villata* as a vague entity seems to disappear by this time. By the last quarter of the fourteenth century, too, Reginald Semar and his *socii* are the last group of villagers renting land in such an impersonal fashion. Henceforth the village social order became much more precisely articul-ated by byelaws and corresponding growth in officialdom.

The byelaw had only been enunciated in the courts of Warboys be-fore the Black Death in that area where village regulations had to be proclaimed for the intercommoning of several villages, that is regulation of the fen.[2] The following texts illustrate the nature of this growing concern in the second quarter of the century.

> 1326: The whole homage of Warboys, freemen as well as the rest, request in full court that henceforth it be forbidden to anyone of the township to sell or give away any reeds (trimmed and bundled) in the marsh of Warboys until the reeds (   ) have been collected and bound on his own lands, under penalty of one-half mark to be paid to the lord for each offence against that ordinance in anyway by any of them. And this was granted in full court etc. in the above form.

> 1334: And they say that the whole township of Broughton, both free and natives during the night enter with their carts and labourers into the marsh of Warboys, and throughout the night they cut and carry both the reeds cut and bundled by the people of Warboys as well as their own reeds, to the damage of the lord and of the whole township. It is ordered that this is not to be done again under penalty of one-half mark fine.

[1] For illustrations of the points in the above paragraph, cf. *Tenure and Mobility*, Part II.
[2] The only exception was a unique entry about common concern, the sale of ale at inflated prices, forbidden by common consent of the customaries of Warboys in 1301 (cf. *Tenure and Mobility*, p. 254, no. 4).

As the village recovered from the Black Death some familiar byelaws were re-iterated: in 1353 it was found necessary to proclaim as an ordinance of the *tota communitas* that there were certain closed seasons for cutting reeds and a limit of 500 reeds to the bundle; it was also ordained by the whole community that year that each must make his ditch between Wodemede and Stokkyng. By the end of the 1360's, however, the repeated failure of villagers to respect the open fields brought proclamation of the byelaw to support the field regulations. In 1369 the ordinance about the time of cutting reeds in the marsh was repeated; but ordinances were also given to control pasturing too close to grain, carting grain at night, pasturing before the grain was completely gathered and pasturing among the shocks of grain. However, in line with other attempts to recover the *status quo ante* ordinances about ditches and turf rather than open fields remained the norm throughout the 1370's.

The 1384 court roll gives ordinances on careless pasturing by pigs and colts as well as the chronic control of reeds in the marsh and from this time byelaws for the open fields gradually become a regular feature of the courts.[1] In 1386 the proclamation was directed to the use of stubble. In 1390 three separate proclamations were directed to the control of sheep, colts and "beasts". In 1398 new ordinances were issued concerning the control of sheep and the pasturing of stubble. Whether in the fourteenth century byelaws were issued annually, or were considered of more permanent reference cannot be determined. For fines were actually given in terms of the more modest trespass penalty rather than the penalty threatened under the byelaw. But certainly by the fifteenth century the byelaw would seem to have been repeated annually and became a regular section of the court roll. For example, the 1402 court roll has a long paragraph governing pasturing under four different titles. By 1430 these ordinances were more briefly summarized as follows: that no one tie his animals in the corn stubble before the feast of St. Michael under penalty of 20 pence; and that no colts be allowed to follow the carts in the autumn under penalty of 12 pence; and that no one tie mares among the horses in the fields before the feast of St. Michael under penalty of 12 pence; and that all ditches within the domain be cleaned before the next leet under penalty of 20 pence to the lord and

---

[1] It should be noted, however, that this chronology cannot hope to be precise since the autumn court roll – the main source of information for byelaws – does not survive in great numbers for some decades and not at all for the 1370's.

20 pence to the church; and that no beasts be allowed to come within a *stadium* of the grain that is being removed under penalty of 12 pence.

As the byelaw became more clearly articulated, so too did the election of the officials responsible for its enforcement. The election of custodians of the marsh is only reported in desultory fashion (1369: 5; 1440: 2; 1448: 1). But with every autumn court from the late 1360's we are informed of the election of officials —custodians in the fourteenth century, autumn reeve in the fifteenth century—to maintain discipline in the open fields during the harvest season (1369: 7; 1386: 6; 1390: 6; 1398: 9; 1402: 6; 1405: 6; 1411: 6; 1430: 5; 1434: 4; 1440: 4; 1448: 1 reeve of the field). Whether from the success of this byelaw discipline, or the release of pressures in the village from the new social and economic conditions of the fifteenth century, various violations at Warboys over the first half of the fifteenth century point to a more stabilized society:

	TRESPASSES				VIOLENCE	
DATE	WOODS	DITCH	MARSH	OPEN FIELDS[1]	HUE	ASSAULTS
1400	12	1		8		
1402				12		
1403	9	1	5		1	
1405	9			1		
1410	11		23	3	1	
1411	12			5		
1412	1			15	1	3
1418	8			2	1	
1421	12	8	2	10	2	3
1423	16	1	3	2		
1424	12	3	10		1	1
1427	13			1	1	2 (quarrelsome)
1428	13	7	1	13		1 (and 2 rebels)
1430				3		
1434		4		8		
1440	7	4		3		
1448			12	10		
1455		14		10		2
1458		1		9		

[1] The more personal trespasses among villagers are included in this column but not separated out since they usually relate to open fields, and in any case decline in numbers (1400: 8; 1402: 12; 1410: 3; 1411: 5; 1412: 10; 1421: 5; 1423: 1; 1448: 2).

Chapter VIII

FAMILIES

Families have inevitably entered into the above story of the village community as active or passive influences, particularly with the arrival or disappearance of families at differing rates over the fourteenth century. But each family also had its own history and in the next few pages will be sketched out some of the features peculiar to several groups of families.

Some families clearly suffered from the biological inability to replace themselves, although in the closely inter-related social and economic story of peasant life it is not easy to separate the biological and the economic. That is to say, a number of families did not establish themselves in the village for long because of apparent economic or social insecurity. Such were the Burg, Chose, Edwyn, Folyet, Goldwyn, John, Katherine, Mercator, Pigman, and Sparhawk families. Other families of lesser substance seem to disappear because their sons left to seek better things: Agath, Baseley, Feker, Gardener, Juliana, Mably, Scull and Tortorin. Unmarried daughters stayed on for sometime into the last generation of the Gardener and Scull families. Other families again seemed to have daughters only, as the Beatrice, Emma, Sarra and Agnes of the last Bishop generation, Alice of the last Brandon generation, Beatrice of the last Galeway generation, Alice, Emma and Isabella of the last Hayward generation, Alice of the last Ponder generation and Mable of the last Reeve generation. No children at all were mentioned for the last generation of the Carpenter, Grendale, Roger and Thurkyld families as well as for the likely free families of Clervaux, Eydon and Unfrey.

The variety of information available, and therefore the degree of identification possible, is not so great for the last two generations of the fourteenth century at Warboys. However, some patterns are obvious. Joan is the last person mentioned for the Burbridge family, Letitia for the Cecilia family, Alice for the Clerk family, Matilda for the Isabella family, Cristine for the Palmer family and Agnes and Alice for the Skynner. There are possibly others in this category since the Joan and Juliana of the Cowherd family figure more prominently than a Peter Cowherd who may not have been of the village; and Alice Dyke was more prominent in the last few years of that family than a Richard Dyke. Couples who were apparently childless were the Bost, Robyn, Sutor and Walsh families. Several families marked their attenuation by signs of economic stringency such as debt or trespass even though the last member was a male: Fine, Haliday, Haugate, Pakerel, Reginald, Sedgeley, Sewyne, Top, Walter, William and Wodekoc. Of the remaining one-half dozen families who disappeared over these generations there were no pecularities in their last few years. On the whole, therefore, it would seem that fertility remained a problem for many families after as well as before the Plague, although clearly the decline in some of these families was initiated by the Plague.

The very detailed data available from the Court Book after 1399 makes it possible to obtain a fairly precise picture of family survival at Warboys over the first half of the fifteenth century. The Court Book conveyances indicate whether the party is married and have any children at that time.[1] It is assumed in the following summary that no mention of children in conveyances after the 1430's, along with no corroboration about tenure in the 1440's and 1450's from the very detailed account rolls, means that no further members survived for that family. The following families appear to have ended with childless couples: Altheworld, Bowde, Birchere, Bythewater, Boleyn, Brynnewater, Buntyng, Clerk, Croxton, Dally, Derworth, Everard, Gylys, Ode, Ordemar, Rabyn, Sist'ne, Slough, Strugge, Thacher, Waleys, Webester, Wethe, and Wodehill. Many of these couples were not from old Warboys families and had entered the village only because of the opportunity to take up some land; but there is no evidence that they left the village with or without licence of the lord before the end of their lives. The un-married man, and occasionally the un-married woman seems to have been fairly common in the village and to have ended the following families: Asplond, Asshwell, Barbat, Bere, Burford, Bokelond, Bottiller, Brampton, Brayn, Bronnote, Buckworth, Collesson, Corbet, Hert, Hill, Hobard, Lancyn,

---

[1] Warboys conveyances have the following information:
19 families with one daughter;
 3 families with two daughters;
23 families with one son;
 3 families with one son and one daughter;
 1 family with one son and two daughters.
For wider treatment of this question, though based upon quite different data, see Sylvia L. Thrupp, "The Problem of Replacement-Rates in Late Medieval English Population", *Economic History Review*, 2nd. series XVIII, 1965.

Nunne, Payn, Prestycosyn, Shakestaff, Son, Thorpe, Wethirle, White, Wodekoc and Wynde. From the nature of these entries it is more difficult than from our records of one hundred years earlier to discover when a family failed to survive because daughters only were born. We know only that Margaret Alot and perhaps Agnes Margaret are the last mentioned of their families.

In contrast with the families that failed to survive, the definitive characteristic of most families continuing throughout our period was the appearance of more than one adult male for several generations. This can be more readily seen by tabulation:

FAMILY	MALES PER GENERATION							
	I	II	III	IV	V	VI	VII	VIII
Albyn	2	5	4	1	–	–	–	–
Alot	1	1	2	–	–	–	–	–
Attewode	1	1	4	1	1	4	–	–
Baroun	1	2	1	2	–	–	–	–
Benet	1	1	2	2	2	2	2	1
Benson						2	5	3
Berenger	2	1	5	5	3	3	5	10
Bonde	1	4	11	3	4	2	–	–
Boys	3	1	2	1	–	–	–	–
Bronning	2	3	3	1	1	1	–	–
Brun	5	3	3	2	1	–	–	–
Catoun	1	2	2	3	1	–	–	–
Chapman	1	1	1	2	1	–	–	–
Clerk	1	2	3	2	–	–	–	–
Colle (Collesson)	3	3	2	1	–	–	–	–
Cowherd	1	4	2	1	–	–	–	–
Derward (Derworth)	1	2	1	1	2	–	–	–
Faber (Smith)	4	4	6	1	3	4	–	–
Fine	1	3	1	2	1	–	–	–
Gerold	1	1	3	4	2	1	1	–
Gosse	1	3	1	2	–	–	–	–
Harsine	2	2	2	2	–	–	–	–
Hichesson (Hiche)	3	2	2	1	–	–	–	–
Hygh	1	2	3	3	2	–	–	–
Hygeneye	1	2	3	1	–	–	–	–
Kaye	–	1	1	1	–	–	–	–
Lenot	3	2	2	4	2	–	–	–

FAMILY	I	II	III	IV	V	VI	VII	VIII
London	1	4	3	1	1	1	–	–
Lucas	1	2	1	1	–	–	–	–
Martyn	1	3	2	1	–	–	–	–
Molt	3	4	2	1	–	–	–	–
Nunne	1	3	2	1	3	–	–	–
Pakerel	1	3	6	2	–	–	–	–
Pilche	2	5	4	1	–	–	–	–
Pilgrim	2	1	2	3	–	–	–	–
Plumbe	2	2	4	3	2	5	6	–
Raven	1	2	10	5	2	1	–	–
Raveley	1	3	1	1	–	–	–	–
Rede	1	1	1	1	–	–	–	–
Robyn	2	5	3	1	–	–	–	–
Scut	5	4	2	1	1	2	–	–
Semar	2	3	6	4	3	–	–	–
Smart	1	1	1	1	2	–	–	–
Sperner	2	4	2	1	–	–	–	–
Swan	1	4	3	1	–	–	–	–
Taylor	3	3	1	3	1	–	–	–
Walsh	1	1	3	1	1	–	–	–
Walter	2	3	3	1	–	–	–	–
Webester	3	3	7	2	–	–	–	–
Wilkes	5	3	1	2	4	–	–	–
Wodekoc	1	3	2	3	–	–	–	–

It would be misleading to generalize about the first generation of the above families since information about their thirteenth-century beginnings is not as detailed as later; and for families easily traceable from the mid-thirteenth century, as the Berengers, only the one member can be traced for the first two generations. Furthermore, where families first entered the village in the fourteenth century it was as one member or one married couple. However, for most families there does appear to have been a "bulge" for one or two generations—usually the second and third in our series—and then a falling off. The falling off occurred in most instances of course after the Black Death. There is then a tendency for a bulge to re-appear in the fifteenth century, most noticeable in the larger families (Benson, Berenger, Plumbe, Wilkes), as in the families beginning after the Black Death and not included in the above list (Fleming, Sand). The rapid increase of some families in the early fourteenth century was relieved by several male members (Bonde, Brunne, Clerk, Faber (Smith), Pilche, Scut, Sperner, Swan) or at least one male (Alot, Attewode, Catoun, Cowherd, Gerold, Gosse, Harsine, London, Lucas, Nunne, Pilgrim, Robyn, Semar, Walter) leaving the village. Large numbers left from the hard-pressed Berenger, Plumbe, Raveley, Scut, Semar, Smart and Wilkes families in the early fifteenth century and one male from each of the smaller Albyn, Baroun, Bronning and Raven families.

The blood relationship of all members with the same surname cannot be established for enough families to determine the precise statistical pattern of familial growth and decline. Enough data are available to illustrate larger families: in the first quarter of the fourteenth century Cecilia had sons Godfrey, John and Stephen, Reginald had sons John, Richard and William, Robert had sons Maurice, Richard, Simon, Thomas and William; in the second quarter of this century Godfrey had sons John, Reginald, Richard and Simon, Henry Isabelle had sons John, Richard and William, Lawrence had sons Benedict, John, Richard and Simon, Nicholas had sons Nicholas, Richard and Robert. However, this evidence for several sons was not from the largest and most prominent families. For the latter, such precise identification does not seem to have been considered necessary. On the other hand, there are enough data available about the prominent families such as the Benet's and Berenger's to indicate that more than one son was marrying in each generation. It should be noted too, although women are not as frequently indicated as men, the large family could be a blessing of daughters only— as with the four women in the last generation of the Bonde's, the two of three children being girls in the last Hichesson generation, the seven of eight children who were girls in the fifteenth century Molt's, two daughters of the last Pilche generation, four of six were women in the last Baroun generation and three of four in the last Benet generation.

In addition to the ability to produce heirs, family survival in the complex social and economic environment of Warboys required considerable genetic qualities of leadership, energy and ingenuity. The appearance of these qualities was a consistent feature of village life. The highest level of such abilities was manifested by involvement in a wide variety of responsibility in the village: juror, personal pledge, taster, beadle and reeve. Some examples of this professional ability were Hugh Benet, several times pledging in the 1290's, taster and juror in 1299, juror in 1301, 1305, 1309, taster in 1313, taster and juror in 1316 and juror for several years in the 1320's; Martin Bonde, capital pledge, juror and taster in 1290, juror and pledging in 1294; Richard Catoun, capital pledge and juror in the early 1320's, juror and taster for several years in the 1330's and juror at least in alternate years; Richard Gerold, beadle and juror in 1294, and juror in many following years as well as a multiple pledger; William Pakerel, taster in 1343, juror and taster in 1339, reeve for at least the years of 1329-30, 1335-1336, 1341-42, 1343-44, 1345-46 and 1346-1347; Thomas Raven, juror in 1294, beadle in 1305 and reeve in at least 1318-19 and 1325-1326. A number of families showed a remarkable ability to produce this leadership throughout the whole of our period: Benet, Berenger, Bonde, Brown, Catoun, Gerold, London, Plumbe, Raven, Rede and Semar. It must not be understood, however, that this leadership was maintained for every decade since a "junior" training period was necessary before the more advanced obligations could be assumed. A number of families manifested these abilities for only a generation or so early in our period: Clerk, Haliday, Isabelle, Lone, Pakerel, Pilgrim, Smart, Sedgeley and Top. For most of these families the inability to produce heirs would seem to have been the cause of the decline in their fortunes. A number of other families gradually rose to more prominent positions in the village only by the late fourteenth century: Boys, Baroun, Bronning, Newman, Raveley, Scut and Wilkes. The Newman family only came into the village late in the fourteenth century and may have brought successful experience from elsewhere; but for the other families of this last group it would appear that the new opportunities of the late fourteenth and early fifteenth century finally gave scope to abilities frustrated by poverty at an earlier period.

A more modest ability was manifested by a number of families who were occasionally jurors and personal pledges but who never were able to perform the leading role of such officials as the reeve nor to be a regular recourse as juror and pledge. Throughout the greater part of our period the families Godfrey, Higney, Noble, Rolf, Robert and Walter were of this type. A number of families rose to this position of responsibility for one generation in the early fourteenth century but thereafter declined: Agath, Albyn, Attehall, Cecilia, Galeway, Gosse, Grendale, Harsine, Herbert, Lawrence, Margaret, Mercator, Nicholas, Puttock, Wodekoc and Foliet. On the other hand, a number of families were able to rise to a position of occasional service as jurors later in the fourteenth century: Fleming, Molt, Nunne, Richard, Fine, Hygh, Hunter, Horewode, Henry, Martin, Oliver and Wennington.

It will be obvious from the above that the story of poverty at Warboys varied very much from family to family and from generation to generation. At the same time a good number of families never seem to have "made it" at Warboys over the whole of our period: Attewode, Alot, Bissop, Bost, Bryd, Ellsworth, Dike, Fot, Godwyne, Haugate, Hering, Kaunt, Long, Lucas, Brandon, Bettes, Sculle, Sperner, Swan, Tymme and Vicory. To these families could be added many isolated individuals or one generation families such as the Osbern's and Wrench's in the early fourteenth century and Thomas Arnold and William Frost towards the end of our period. The individual story of these families and their members varies so much that it is difficult to ascribe common characteristics to the group. In view of the cycle of fortunes of the more wealthy families of the village, what is surprising about this group is their persistence in the village where indeed some of these families remained for several generations. We have information about some members of these families leaving the village although undoubtedly the court was rather indifferent to the whereabouts of these poorer people. But despite this ability to move in and out of the village it can be seen from Table III (Chapter III) that some of the poor families noted above in this paragraph remained at Warboys for as long as six generations.

There is further evidence from Warboys that the problem of malnutrition in the medieval village cannot be too closely correlated with the size of tenement.[1] From Table XI (Chapter V) it can be seen that the incidence of illness was actually higher for larger property holders than for the smaller. It may be recalled from our information in the extent and the Hundred Rolls that the actual number of tenants on the small holdings, especially the mondaymanland, was quite large.[2] The following list of the numbers ill, along with the size of their tenements, has been summarized from Table XI. It has not seemed necessary to attempt a summary of the length of periods of illness since these periods did not seem to vary with the size of the holding.

DATE	NUMBERS ILL	SIZE OF HOLDINGS
1342-43	2	1 virgate
,,	2	½ virgate
,,	1	¼ land
,,	1	1 maltmanland
,,	1	1 mondaycroft

[1] For further evidence of the persistence of families upon units of land, apparently too small for subsistence, see E. B. De Windt, *Land & People in Holywell-cum-Needingworth* (Toronto, 1972), Chapter I, especially pp. 42-43, 98-99.

[2] See above, Chapter V, pp. 155ff.

DATE	NUMBERS ILL	SIZE OF HOLDINGS
1344-45	3	1 virgate
"	2	½ virgate
"	1	¼ virgate
"	1	1 mondaymanland
1346-47	3	1 virgate
"	4	½ virgate
"	1	1 mondaymanland
1347-48	7	1 virgate
"	3	½ virgate
"	2	¼ virgate
"	1	1 maltmanland
"	2	1 mondaymanland
"	1	1 cotland + 1 mondaymanland
1348-49	17	1 virgate (including one unit of 1½ virgates)
"	1	½ virgate
"	3	1 maltmanland
"	1	1 maltmanland + 1 monday-manland
"	1	1 mondaymanland
"	1	1 mondaymanland + ¼ virgate
"	1	¾ virgate
"	1	¼ virgate
Rest of the fourteenth century	10	1 virgate (including one unit of 1¼ virgate)
"	9	½ virgate
"	1	¾ virgate
"	1	¼ virgate
"	2	2 mondaymanlands
"	1	1 mondaymanland
"	1	1 maltmanland

As we have seen in Chapter VI above many Warboys families were found not to have any property when the full rent rolls began in the 1370's. By and large these propertyless people were the poorer people noted in the above paragraphs. From this time, however, the opportunities for obtaining property differed greatly from the conditions of earlier generations. As we have seen in Chapter V, Section II, bits and pieces of the lord's demesne became available, many old family holdings were allowed to decay and some members of prosperous families simply deserted the village for better opportunities elsewhere. The resulting cycles of property accumulation or dispersal provide an interesting picture of family properties at the time. In the following table we do not list families where the number of tenants has remained one over the three periods or less, nor do we list the smallholders, especially those that did not remain in the village for long. These data are taken from the detailed Table XIV (Property held in Warboys from 1371 to 1455). It should also be noted in Table XIV that the the average size of properties held by some families, for example the Berenger's, was much larger than the average tenements of a Swan or Wright. Table XVI serves to corroborate the greater family involvement before the engrossing movements discussed in Chapter V. That is to say, in the 1370's more members of 11 families were holding property than later; but by the early 1400's 32 families had more members holding property than before or later. With engrossing, only five families had more members holding property by the 1440's than earlier, and correspondingly, there were 25 of these families without any property in the 1440's whereas there had only been 10 of these families without any properties in the 1370's and six in the early 1400's.

Table XVI

Property spread within families

| FAMILY NAME | NUMBER OF TENANTS IN EACH PERIOD | | |
	1 (1371-1379)	2 (1393-1422)	3 (1440-1455)
Asplond	–	2	2
Attewode	1	3	1
Berenger	2	2	10
Baron	3	5	2
Bele	–	4	1
Benson	1	5	4
Benet	2	5	1
Bonde	4	3	2
Boys	1	2	1
Bronning	1	2	–
Bronnote	–	2	–
Broun	1	3	2
Catoun	3	3	1
Colle	1	2	–
Coleville	–	1	2
Dally	–	3	–

FAMILY NAME	NUMBER OF TENANTS IN EACH PERIOD		
	1 (1371-1379)	2 (1393-1422)	3 (1440-1455)
Derworth	2	2	–
Edward	1	3	1
Eyr	–	2	–
Gerold	2	1	–
Harsine	2	2	–
Hervy	1	2	–
Hichesson	1	2	–
High	2	7	2
Horewode	–	–	3
Lenot	4	1	–
London	–	–	2
Molt	5	2	1
Newman	–	1	3
Northbourgh	1	3	1
Nunne	2	3	–
Of the Hill (Attehill)	1	3	–
Oliver	2	2	1
Pakerel	3	–	–
Prestecosyn	2	2	–
Plumbe	2	4	2
Raveley	1	2	1
Raven	3	–	1
Rede	1	2	–
Scut	4	–	–
Semar	4	2	–
Sist'ne	1	3	–
Shakestaff	–	2	2
Shepherd	2	4	1
Smart	1	2	1
Smith	1	3	3
Son	3	–	–
Swan	1	2	–
Taylor	1	2	1
Warren	1	2	–
Webbester	2	3	–
Wennington	2	1	–
Wilkes	4	2	3
Wright	1	2	–

Quite distinct from the landed families of Warboys, rich and poor, yet closer in replacement and survival pattern to the poor families, were the families deriving their names from employment as artisans or other small specialized occupations. As noted in the previous chapter, the village did seem to support many of these humble service personnel. Indeed the names of some of the families—Carpenter, Chapman, Cowherd, Shepherd, Sperner, Taylor, Webester—remained throughout most of our period. However, beyond the occasional abuse by a shepherd or cowherd, we must depend for identification of this group upon their surnames rather than evidence for their actual performance of the tasks indicated by their names. Moreover, in most cases it cannot be established from the records that this was the same family continuing under the name. We do know that Henry Mercator and his wife lived at Warboys in the late thirteenth century, and that their children William and Emma were at Warboys in the early fourteenth century. But such evidence for blood relationship over merely two generations is rare and perhaps only certain for the Ponder, Shepherd and Taylor as well as Mercator families. Indeed, for many families it is clear that their work enabled them to remain in the village for only a generation or two; such were Carter, Chauman, Gardiner, Haywood, Mercator, Pellage, Palmer, Pigman, Ponder, Sawyer, Skinner, Soper, Sutor, Thatcher, Thresher, Tasker, Tortorin and Wright families. As we shall see, some of the better paid skills such as the carpenter were occasionally undertaken by members of well-established village families. But on the whole our evidence points towards these people as an economic sub-group of the village and perhaps of the region. Certainly some individuals whose names indicate quite specialized tasks—Draper, Roper, Hamemaker—appeared too infrequently at Warboys to attract members of more substantial village families.

For some of these service people, as with the Ponder, Carpenter and Gardiner family around 1300, existence in the village was made more possible by holding a small unit of land in the fields. Such smallholdings by Shepherds, Taylors and others are more traceable, and as we have seen these small units of land were more possible of acquisition in the late fourteenth century. Nevertheless, throughout the whole of our period there is no consistent evidence for these occupational families being able to obtain a good foothold on the land in the manner of such more profitable professions as those of the Clerks, Fabers and Semars. Our evidence is, rather, that these poor people turned to a variety of tasks for their livelihood.[1] This is best illustrated from the court rolls by

[1] See below, Chapter IX, for detailed personal illustrations of this point.

the licencing of butchers. It cannot be contended that the court roll supplies full evidence for all engaged in the butcher trade at Warboys. But the entries are sufficiently numerous to reveal certain patterns. As the following list shows, prior to the Black Death most of those working as butchers have names indicating some small trade or other while from the mid-fourteenth century members of more prominent families became identified with the butcher trade.

LIST OF BUTCHERS FROM THE COURT ROLLS

Chapman, William: 1306, 1307, 1313
Brumewater, (Brynewater) Andrew: 1347
Ponder, John: 1292, 1294, 1299, 1301, 1306, 1313
Soper, William the: (also for a time Haywood): 1299, 1305, 1306, 1313
Shepherd, Robert: 1294
Tabard, John: 1309
Tra, Ralph: 1322
Mercator, Henry: 1294
Mercator, William, son of Henry: 1294-1295
By, Simon: 1387-1388
Catoun, John: 1390, 1391-1392
Catoun, Thomas: 1384
Colle, Robert: 1384
Lenot, John: 1382, 1384, 1387-1388, 1390, 1391-1392
Lenot, John, the butcher: 1365-1375
Sperner, Richard: 1360
Catoun, John: 1400
Chapman, John: 1400
Derworth, William: 1400
Heryng, John: 1400-1421
Horewode, John: 1440
Lenot, John: 1400
Olyver, William: 1423
Plumbe, Richard: 1423
Plumbe, John: 1440
Scharpe, William: 1412

The way by which specialization could supplement the village economy is best depicted by records of fines for breaking the assize of ale. As the following list shows, prior to the Black Death some members of wealthy families, or families that were wealthy for at least a generation, were regularly engaged in brewing of ale: Agnes Berenger, Alice Brun, Alice Catoun, Margaret Clerk, Agnes Gerold, Alice Gosse, Joan Grendale, Annabella Lenot, Emma London, Alice Pakerel, Alice Raven, Cecilia Semar, Hawysia Wodekoc, Cassandra Rolf and Juliana Rede.

Indeed, several of the wealthy families—Albyn, Bonde, Catoun, Clerk, Faber, Gerold, Higney, Lenot, Pilgrim and Raven—had several members involved in brewing. A few members of poorer families—Agnes Bishop, Emma Bryd, Alice Dyke, Matilda Hering, Agnes Martin and Emma Pilche—were apparently employed fulltime in brewing ale. But much more common, and represented in the following list by more than 30 different family names prior to the Black Death, was the appearance of a poorer member of the village as brewing ale for only a few years. These four occupational characteristics of the brewing of ale continued throughout the second century of our period, as may be seen in the following list, although the record of those fined for malpractise in brewing suggests that there were considerably fewer engaged in the trade after the Black Death.

LIST OF BREWERS FROM THE COURT ROLLS

Albyn, Alice, dau. of Robert: 1320
—, Beatrice, dau. of Robert: 1320-1322
—, Matilda: 1343
Attewode, Joan: 1347
Berenger, Agnes: 1339, 1343, 1347, 1349
—, Alice, wife of Robert: 1320
Birgate, Agnes atte: 1350
Bishop, Agnes, wife of Robert: 1290, 1292, 1294, 1306, 1309, 1313, 1316, 1320
—, Emma: 1316
Bonde, Alice: 1331
—, Joan, wife of Hugh: 1322, 1325
—, Juliana: 1290, 1294, 1306
—, wife of William: 1316, 1320
Bronnyng, Joan: 1343
Brun, Alice: 1294, 1299, 1301, 1306, 1313, 1316, 1320, 1322
Bryd, Emma, wife of Richard: 1313, 1316, 1320, 1322, 1326, 1331, 1334, 1337, 1339, 1343
Buk, Amitia: 1322
Burnbrigge, Joan: 1350-1353
Cecilia, Agnes: 1306
—, Beatrice: 1294, 1301
Catoun, Alice: 1301, 1306, 1320, 1322, 1326, 1334, 1337, 1339
—, Beatrice: 1306
—, Cristina: 1292, 1294
—, Hawysia: 1292, 1294
—, Margaret, wife of John: 1322
Chatteris, Alice de: 1299-1316
Chaumon, Margaret: 1306
—, Cristine: 1313, 1316
Chaumonisson, Agnes, wife of Richard: 1353

Chapman, Emma: 1306
Clerk, Alice: 1292,[1] 1299, 1306
—, Alice: 1349, 1350, 1353
—, Margaret, wife of John: 1320, 1322, 1331, 1333, 1334, 1337
Cook, Amitia, wife of Ralph: 1320
Cowherd, Isabella, wife of Henry: 1292, 1294
—, Joan: 1349
—, Juliana: 1347
—, Robert: 1292
Cristine, Mariota: 1292
Dyke, Alice: 1322, 1326 (wife of Godfrey 1326), 1343, 1349, 1350, 1353
Everard, Agnes, dau. of Ralph: 1294
Faber, Agnes, wife of William: 1290, 1292
—, Juliana, wife of Stephen: 1294
—, (Smyth), Mariota: 1339, 1343, 1347
—, wife of Richard: 1301
Freman, Catherine: 1333
Fine, wife of William: 1290
Folyet, Cristina, wife of John: 1292, 1294
Gerold, Agnes: 1316, 1320, 1322, 1331, 1333, 1334, 1337, 1339, 1343, 1347, 1349, 1353
—, Agnes, wife of William: 1326
—, Agnes, wife of Simon: 1337
Godfrey, Alice: 1306
—, Hawysia, dau. of John, son of: 1294
Gosse (Gaze), Alice: 1337, 1339, 1347, 1349
Grendale, Agnes: 1299
—, Joan: 1320, 1331, 1333, 1334, 1337, 1339
Haliday, Margaret, wife of William: 1290, 1294
Hamemaker, Margaret le: 1301
Hey, Emma: 1322 (bread)
Heryng, Matilda: 1289, 1290, 1299, 1301, 1306, 1313, 1316, 1320, 1322
Higney, wife of Robert: 1290
—, Allota: 1322
—, Amitia, widow of Robert: 1299, 1306, 1309, 1320
—, Cecilia, wife of Roger: 1325 (bread), 1326 (bread)
Isabella, Matilda, wife of William: 1347
Jewel, Juliana: 1339, 1343
Lenot, Agnes: 1353
—, Alice: 1333-1334, 1337, 1339, 1343
—, Annabella, wife of Robert: 1309, 1313, 1316, 1320, 1322, 1326
—, Emma: 1349, 1350-1353
—, John: 1350
—, Matilda: 1349
London, Emma, wife of William: 1290, 1292
Martyn, Agnes: 1339, 1343, 1347, 1349, 1350, 1353

[1] Martin Bonde pledged for Alice Clerk and Emma Pilche who were brewing at his house.

Mercator, Emma, dau. of Henry: 1292
—, (H): 1290
Nicholas, Joan: 1334, 1337
Noble, Alice, wife of Godfrey: 1322, 1347
Pakerel, Agnes: 1294
—, Alice: 1289, 1290, 1292
Pilche, Emma: 1292 (in the house of Martyn Bonde), 1294, 1301, 1306, 1313, 1316, 1320, 1322, 1326, 1331, 1333, 1334, cf. of Wistow also
—, Matilda: 1322 (bread)
Pilgrim, Agnes: 1339, 1343, 1347
—, Alice: 1290
—, Cristine: 1294, 1299, 1301
Ponder, Margaret: 1294
Quena de Thyrngg: 1294
Raven, Alice: 1322, 1326, 1331, 1333, 1334, 1337, 1339, 1343, 1347, 1349
—, Catherine: 1343, 1349
—, Joan: 1331
—, Mariota: 1333, 1339
Rede, Juliana: 1333, 1334, 1339
Rolf, Cassandra, wife of William: 1309, 1320, 1322, 1326, 1331, 1333, 1334, 1337, 1339
—, Isabella: 1350, 1353
—, Matilda, wife of Hugh: 1353
Robyn, Beatrice: 1313
—, Margaret: 1347, 1349, 1350
Sedgeley, Alice: 1313
Semar, Cecilia, wife of Albinus: 1288, 1289, 1290, 1292
—, Cristina, dau. of Albinus: 1290
—, Juliana: 1292, 1343
—, the wife of Ralph: 1290
Shepherd, Emma, wife of John: 1322
Soper, Constance: 1294
—, Emma: 1294
Sperner, Cristina: 1294
Sutor, Agnes: 1350
Walter, Juliana: 1347
Wodekoc, Hawysia, wife of Richard: 1289, 1290, 1294
Wymark, Alice: 1306

1360-1398

Allot, Alice, wife of John: 1290
Attehill, Agnes: 1371, 1372, 1375, 1376, 1382
Berenger, Agnes, wife of Richard: 1384, 1387, 1388
—, Mariota: 1372, 1373, 1375, 1376
Boys, Alice: 1382, 1384, 1387, 1390, 1391, 1392
Breuster, Beatrice: 1390
Buckworth, Agnes: 1390, 1391
Burbrigge, Joan: 1360

Catoun, Joan: 1371
Colier, Alice: 1360
Derworth, Katherine: 1382, 1384, 1387, 1390, 1391
Eyr, Rose: 1390, 1391
Godfrey, Nicholas, of Niddingworth: 1360
Hy, Juliana: 1371, 1372, 1373, 1375, 1376
—, Simon: 1390
Lenot, Emma: 1360
—, Joan: 1382, 1387, 1390, 1391, 1392
—, John: 1387
Martin, Agnes: 1371, 1372
Merton, Agnes: 1372
Pilgrim, Alice: 1360
Plumbe, Joan: 1371
Roger, Christina: 1372
Sande, Agnes: 1372, 1373, 1375, 1382, 1387, 1390, 1391
Sutor, Agnes: 1360
Smyth, William: 1391-1392
Swan, Sgnes: 1371
Taylor, Beatrice: 1387
Willimot, Joan: 1371, 1372, 1375, 1384, 1387, 1390, 1391
Wright, Agnes: 1382, 1387

1400-1458

Boys, Alice: 1400, 1403
Brynnewater, Alice: 1400, 1403, 1410, 1412, 1418, 1421
Bukworth, Agnes: 1400, 1403
Chapman, Katherine: 1455, 1458
—, Alice: 1410, 1412, 1418
Cobbe, Emma: 1427, 1428, 1440, 1448
Gooselowe, Juliana: 1455, 1458
Horewode, Agnes: 1427, 1428, 1448
—, Joan: 1400, 1403, 1410, 1412, 1418, 1421, 1423, 1424, 1428
(Hyghell), Margaret: 1403
Newman, Alice: 1448, 1455, 1458
Oundell, Joan: 1455, 1458
Plumbe, Margaret: 1424
Raveley, Agnes: 1410, 1412, 1418
—, Alice: 1424
Sand, Agnes: 1410, 1412, 1418, 1421, 1423, 1424, 1427, 1428
Scharpe, Agnes: 1458
Slough, Margaret: 1424
Smyth, Agnes: 1410, 1412, 1418, 1421, 1423, 1424, 1440
—, William: 1418 (bread)
Taylor, Agnes: 1448
Whete, Alice: 1427, 1428, 1440, 1448
Willymot, Joan: 1400

Chapter IX

INDIVIDUALS

In order that we might envisage Warboys as much as possible as a social entity it has been necessary to tabulate frequency patterns of various sorts in the preceding sections of this chapter as indeed throughout most of the volume. Nevertheless, as noted at beginning of Chapter IV, those court roll data that have remained our main source of information are for the most part indices of individual behaviour. It is of course true that court rolls can not expect to reveal the subjective understanding to be found in biographies or diaries, nor even those insights into *mentalité* derived from literary sources. But the pattern of individual behaviour, above all as seen from court rolls, does diverge in interesting particulars from that expected by economic and familial circumstances. Furthermore, the actual variety of individual personality and family types, at least in so far as these are mirrored in our sources, is much wider than the common patterns to be found at Warboys. In this section we shall deal with these more uncommon patterns of activity among the villagers of Warboys.

Some exceptional careers can provide a point of departure for these studies. One has only to read the estate manuals of the thirteenth and fourteenth centuries to realise that the office of reeve must have been the most important post in the lives of the villagers of Warboys. According to surviving records, the office of reeve was performed by a certain William over 1306-07, by Thomas Raven for at least 1318-19 and 1325-26, and over the second half of the century scattered for brief periods among a greater number of persons: Pilgrim (1348-49), Collier (1353-54), Brun (1354-55), Semar (1359-61), Scut (1362-65), Bronnyng (1366-67), Catoun (1371-72), Wodekoc (1373-75), Raven (1375-76, 1379-80), Nunne (1377-78), Plumbe (1393-94). Unique among the careers of reeves at Warboys, therefore, would seem to have been that of William Pakerel whose account rolls survive for 1329-30, 1335-36, 1342-43, 1344-45, 1346-47 and 1347-48. The arrears at the beginning of these accounts show that he was also reeve for each of the previous years. Since there are references to pledging by William the Reeve in other years of the 1320's and 1330's, and we only know that Roger Raven succeeded him for 1336-37, William Pakerel may well have been reeve more or less continuously for over 20 years.

The Pakerel family were well established at Warboys by the mid-thirteenth century when a William Pakerel, perhaps the grandfather of our William the Reeve, held one virgate. There were several branches of the family by 1290. The Pakerel's shared too in the population explosion around 1300 when Lawrence was said to have sons Benedict and Roger, and a daughter Alice, and Richard had daughters Cristine and Gracia. A Simon, Henry and Nicholas Pakerel were also in the village at this time. Of these many other Pakerel's, only Benedict got well established in the village. Probably the father of our William was that William Pakerel prominent in the 1290's and possibly the reeve at the time. In any case, our records do not show the father and son with overlapping careers as adults. The older William died around 1300 and first references to the younger begin with that "learning process" necessary for operation of the open fields and customary obligations on the lord's demesne. William trespassed on the lord's grain with his beasts in 1316; he was fined for failure to perform work owed to the lord three times in 1320, twice in 1322 and once in 1326. But from this time his activities became consistently orthodox and although he acted as taster for at least two years and as a pledge upon numerous occasions, he was really fully occupied as reeve.

Our notion of the capability of one of these leading villagers is virtually transformed when we see the scope of his activities as reeve. From the account roll that begins "account of William Pakerel, reeve of Warboys, of all his receipts and expenditures ...", we find that William began his year with arrears as high as nearly 15 pounds for two years. He had to account for the money rents and customary rents at all four seasons, including the rent of a *fabrica* and mill; he had to account for the sale of corn, work services, oxen, cattle, sheep, pigs, chickens, hides, skins, wood, reeds and *minutiae*. When Roger Raven succeeded him there was a memorandum for the incoming reeve that he will also account for Gressilver, for apples for the sale of reeds outside the demesne for ploughshare and the "upper" millstone, pannage, nuts, one-half of the farm of the dovecote fines of *gersuma*, letes and perquisites of court, farm of the vaccary and all *incrementa*. William Pakerel normally handled revenues coming to over 50 pounds, and in the 1340's when he shared some of his tasks with a bailiff who was no doubt responsible for the increase in money rents, the total came to over 60 pounds. As well as handing on some of these monies to the lord, William had to purchase cattle and various implements, to repair ploughs, carts and buildings, to look after expenses for the steward, *famuli* and *curia*, to pay wages for hired servants, as well as a wide variety of items from the purchase of salt to ingredients for the care of sheep. The scope of this responsibility carried by the reeve is well attested to by the fact that when he entered his office he was given an indenture listing all the manorial items that were within his care. This indenture survives for Roger Raven who took over from William Pakerel in the year 1336 as noted above. From this indenture we find that he is responsible for the granaries and their contents including not only grain but a dozen utensils of various kinds; in the stable he was responsible for various horses as well as all sorts of carts, stable equipment and ploughs; his care also included all the oxen of every age, the sheep, pigs and fowl right down to the precise number of chickens; there is also a bakehouse with its equipment, a cookhouse with its equipment and the hall itself with various furnishings. From the records one sees William Pakerel as a stolid administrator, guiding Warboys through the seasons and years with a massive fund of sound judgement and yet a ready decisiveness.

There are a fair sampling of men from Warboys for the time of William Pakerel or slightly earlier who appeared to be somewhat of the same administrative status as William. And these fellow villagers also manifested the same legitimating tendencies, that is to say, a few delicts in their earlier years but then as they "became the law" so too they betrayed a consistent conformity to the laws of the village. The following is a synopsis of the involvement of this group of villagers according to the court rolls:

John Catoun: 1331 juror, taster, 1333 juror, taster, 1334 juror, taster, pledge, 1337 juror, taster, pledge (twice), 1339 juror, taster, pledge, 1343 juror, taster, 1347 juror, taster, 1350 juror, taster, 1353 juror, pledge; *Henry Brun*: 1306 right of warren, 1313 right of warren, juror, pledge, trespass in the lord's wood, 1316 pledge, 1320 juror, pledge (7 times), raise the hue, trespass by digging, 1322 juror, taster, trespass on his neighbours' meadow, 1325 taster, pledge, 1326 pledge, failed to perform one work, 1331 juror, 1333 juror, trespass in wood, 1334 juror, failed to perform one work, 1337 juror, trespass with sheep, 1339 juror, ploughed wrongly, 1343 juror, trespass in the lord's wood, 1347 juror; *Richard Bonde*: 1288 capital pledge, juror, 1290 capital pledge, juror, pledge, debt, trespass, 1292 pledge, etc.?, 1294 juror, pledge (5 times), 1299 juror, 1301 juror, taster, pledge (4 times), trespass in the fen, 1305 juror, concord, 1306 pledge (3 times), 1309 juror, trespass by ploughing;

William Berenger: 1294 beadle, juror, 1299 juror, 1301 pledge, 1306 juror, 1313 juror, pledge, 1316 pledge (twice), trespass in the lord's grain with his beasts, 1320 juror, 1322 juror, 1326 trespass in the lord's wood; *Hugh Benet*: 1294 reeve, pledge (twice), 1299 juror, taster, pledge (twice), 1301 juror, 1305 juror, 1309 juror, 1313 taster, pledge (twice), 1316 juror, taster, pledge (4 times), 1318 pledge, 1320 juror, pledge (6 times), 1322 juror, pledge (3 times), 1325 pledge, 1331 pledge, 1333 trespass in wood, defective in threshing, 1334 failure to perform one work; *Robert Albyn*: 1305 pledge, 1309 juror, capital pledge, 1316 juror, pledge, trespass in lord's grain with his beasts, 1320 juror, pledge (5 times), 1322 juror, pledge; *Nicholas Plumbe*: 1294 pledge, 1299 trespass in the lord's grain, trespass in the marsh twice, 1301 pledge, 1306 taster, pledge (10 times), 1316 pledge, 1322 pledge (twice), 1325 pledge, trespass in the lord's wood, 1326 pledge (twice), 1331 pledge (twice), 1332 pledge, 1333 pledge, 1334 pledge, died in 1339; *Roger Raven*: 1322 juror, pledge, 1325 pledge, 1326 juror, pledge (twice), 1331 juror, 1333 failure to perform work, 1334 juror, failure to perform work, 1336 reeve, 1343 juror, debt, 1347 juror, failure to perform work, *John le Rede*: 1313 juror, 1316 taster, 1320 juror, taster, pledge (twice), 1322 taster, pledge, 1326 juror, 1333 juror, 1334 juror, 1337 juror, 1339 pledge, trespass in wood; *Albinus Semar*: 1290 capital pledge, juror, pledge (3 times), 1292 pledge, 1294 juror, right of warren, pledge, 1299 juror, trespass in the lord's grain, trespass wood, 1301 juror, trespass in the fen, 1305 juror, 1306 right of warren; *William Gerold*: 1299 juror, 1301 pledge, trespass in the fen, 1306 pledge (twice), 1309 juror, pledge, 1313 taster, pledge (6 times), 1316 juror, taster, pledge, 1320 juror, taster, pledge (3 times), 1322 juror, taster, pledge, 1325 debt plea, pledge (twice), 1326 juror, pledge; *Nicholas Bronning*: 1316 pledge, 1322 juror, 1325 debt plea, pledge, 1326 juror, 1331 juror, 1333 juror, 1334 to 1336 juror, 1339 juror trespass in the lord's grain.

This is not at all to suggest that conformity was the normal pattern of officials of the village! Rather, as has been pointed out in the earlier sections of Part IV, it was more usual for villagers to reflect economic and social pressures by a more or less predictable variety of deviations. These group deviations still do not reflect the wide variety of responses to various pressures among individuals. For some this came later, for others at a wide variety of periods in their active lives, as may be seen in the following examples: *Richard Gerold*: 1292 juror, 1294 juror, pledge (5 times), fined to relieve himself of the post of beadle, trespass in the lord's wood, 1299 juror, 1316 juror, 1320 juror, pledge (twice), trespass by digging, 1322 juror, 1326 failure to perform a work, trespass with his pigs, 1331 juror, 1334 juror, failure to perform a work, trespass with his sheep, ploughed wrongly; *John Clerk*: 1305 juror, 1306 his grain was trespassed upon, 1309 juror, 1313 pledge, 1316 juror, pledge, 1320 juror, pledge (4 times), raise the hue, 1322 juror, pledge (3 times), 1325 raise the hue, was accused of assaulting and drawing blood, pledge, 1326 juror, pledge (twice), failure to perform one work, 1331 juror, pledge (twice), 1332 pledge, 1333 juror, pledge (twice), 1334 juror, trespass in the lord's wood, pledge, debt plea, 1337 juror, twice failed to perform work, 1339 failed to perform work, trespass in the lord's wood, 1343 juror; *Robert Berenger*: 1313 pledge, trespass in the marsh, 1316 trespass with his beast on the lord's grain, 1318 hue and cry was raised on him, 1320 juror, pledge (twice), three times failed to perform work, trespass in the lord's grain with his beasts, 1322 was charged with debt, disputed over property boundary, 1325 failure to perform one work, 1326 pledge, failure to perform work twice, trespass in the lord's wood, 1331 failed to perform work, trespass on neighbours with his beasts, 1333 juror, failed to perform work, 1334 failed to perform work, 1337 failed to perform work, trespass with his sheep, 1339 failed to perform work, raise the hue, entered a debt plea, was twice charged with debt, 1343 failed to perform work, 1347 failed to perform work and died. Among these ostensibly more propertied people the following had patterns much like the above three: Robert Smart, Simon Lone, Henry Semar, Richard Semar, Godfrey Noble, Thomas Raven, Robert Gosse, Godfrey, son of Cecilia, Godfrey, son of Richard.

Yet another group, with less official responsibility, had wide patterns of aberrations. Some, such as Richard Noble and Henry Isabelle, seem to fall into decline in their later years: *Richard Noble*: 1290 juror, ploughed wrongly, 1294 juror, 1301 pledge (3 times), received wrongly, 1306 juror, pledge (twice), 1319 taster, pledge, 1313 juror, taster, defaulted, 1316 pledge (twice), trespass in the lord's grain with his beasts, had a son out of demesne who did not report; *Henry Isabelle*: 1290 juror, 1294 juror, debt, 1299 juror, trespass on a neighbour, 1301 indicted for contempt for the twelve jurors, did damage in the marsh, 1316 did not have one he pledged, 1320 failed to perform work twice, trespass in the lord's wood, did not have (his son?) Richard Isabelle who was out of demesne. Others with similiar patterns in the court rolls were Reginald Benet, Godfrey Dyke, John Palmer, John Sedgeley, Richard Sedgeley and Hugh Higney.

This tendency to exhibit less conformity to village laws was to be found for those performing less important official jobs in the village as well as for those performing the more important offices infrequently. Some examples may be taken from the tasters and haywards: *Thomas Raven junior*: 1325 pledge (twice), taster, trespass on neighbours twice, 1326 taster, debt, trespass on a neighbour by his ditch, pledge (twice), 1331 taster, pledge (twice), 1332 pledge (3 times), raise the hue, and had the hue raised on him, 1333 pledge (twice), 1334 taster, pledge (twice), failed to perform work, 1337 taster, 1339 taster, pledge (3 times), failed to perform work, 1343 taster, false plea, 1347 taster, pledge, failed to perform work, trespass twice, 1350 juror, pledge (4 times), 1353 juror, failed to perform work; *John Bronning*: 1326 raise the hue, 1333 had the hue raised on him, 1337 had the hue raised on him, drew blood, raise the hue, 1339 had the hue raised on him, 1347 trespass in the lord's wood, 1349 juror, had the hue raised on him, taster, constable, failed to perform work, affeerer, 1350 taster, raise the hue, trespass three times, failed to perform work, Much the same patterns may be found in the court records of the tasters Robert Agath and Benedict Pakerel. The hayward could be a quite insignificant person in the village. John, son of Cecilia, elected hayward in 1325, had gleaned wrongly in 1316, the hue raised on him in 1325, charged with a debt in 1326, trespass on the lord's grain and was trespassed upon in 1333. Godfrey Pilche, hayward a decade and more earlier seemed to be of the same type.

An entirely different rationale lay behind the difficulty that the village court had with another social and economic group. These were the wealthy freemen of the district who came into conflict with the jurisdictional power of the village court in a great number of ways. Alexander Chamberlain, who had pledged twice in the village court in 1294, in the same year was charged with having taken 6 loads of wood illegally and was to be pursued on this charge in the court of Wistow. The same Alexander had been charged in 1316 with allowing his animals to damage the lord's grain; one russet tunic had been taken to distrain him to pay the fine for this, but since he had not paid more was to be taken. John of Cranfield, custodian of the wood of Warboys, was fined 40d. in 1290 for contempt in the village court since he had not come to make his presentation. In 1316, too, John of Elton, chaplain of Wistow and Robert Bulloc, a regional official of the lord were charged with taking wood wrongly at night. In the same court master Lawrence of Sutton was charged with trespass by his animals, distress had been taken and more was ordered to be taken. Similar charges about abuse of the woods were made against William of London in 1299, Alan of Grendale in 1301 and

Robert of Wennington in 1292. Some of these suits must have caused considerable tension, as with Robert Gray of Niddingworth who had been distrained to pay for damage in the woods in 1305 and was being distrained further on the same charge some two years later.

Freemen also abused local rights in the marsh; in 1299 the local court was so annoyed at the trespasses by Ivo of Hurst that he was forbidden further entry to the marsh. Freemen holding village property also had to be watched closely in order that they did not exploit this to the gain of their holdings elsewhere. For example, in 1318 William Fine was charged with taking timber from his holding at Warboys to his freehold. In 1313 John of Higney and Richard Godwyne were charged with the same type of dilapidation. Sometimes the servants of such persons were charged, as with Richard Pilche, servant of John of Temesford, who was charged in 1305 with trespass in the woods. Another type of intrusion was represented by William Waleboy who abused inter-village commoning in 1313 by overloading the pasture with sheep.

Some of these frictions centred about certain families. One of these was the London family. In 1290 Ralph the son of William London was charged with taking wood from Warboys at night at his father's request. Perhaps in relation to the same charge, the wife of William of London and her servant defamed the forester, John of Cranfield, and William the Reeve. In this same court Ralph the son of William of London was charged with murdering Henry the son of Albyn and his chattels were to be seized. Very likely it was another Ralph the son of William of London, who in 1299 was charged in the court of Broughton with cutting and carrying away by night 17 oak trees. Another such family were the Higeney's, and especially Amicia, widow of Robert of Higeney from 1294. Amicia began the year 1294 by being fined 2/— for raising the hue wrongly against John of Higeney and Alexander the Chamberlayn. Later in the same year John of Higeney entered a plea against Amicia; she was charged with taking the crop of one rod of wheat belonging to Ivo of Hurst and with carrying away one cartload of dredge from the land of Ralph the Miller. In this court of November 1294, Amicia was also fined because Emma the daughter of Ralph Miller had raised the hue against her and because Amicia had wrongly raised the hue against Alan the Hundreder since the latter had claimed 40d. for which she had been fined before the royal justice Gilbert of Kirkeby. After this very active year, Amicia appears in the court rolls for some two decades under the prosaic fines for brewing wrongly; however, she continued to be in trouble as may be seen by the involvement by a hue and cry in 1299, four concords, a trespass and a debt in 1305, and with an assault upon John Of Higeney in 1306.

The Millers at Warboys seemed to have fulfilled the role assigned to them by Chaucer. The court of November 1320 stated: "it is established that Nicholas the Miller knocked down the building next to the mill, carried away the timber and burned it. He comes and fines (2/—) with pledges Hugh Benet and the Beadle to rebuild before next Easter. Nicholas the Miller (is charged) with carrying away and selling 2/— worth of timber given to him to repair the mill; this 2/— he is to pay to the lord, Robert Lenot is his pledge and he is fined 4/—. Since the same Nicholas in the presence of the steward showed grave contempt for the bailiff and others in the court, he is fined 12d, with Robert Lenot as pledge". In 1322 William Fine was charged as miller for deliberately not keeping honest servants, but removing them and hiring evil ones to the harm of the village. Nicholas the Miller appears again in the court of 1325 and is fined for allowing his servants to take toll wrongly to the harm of the village. The same Nicholas in 1326 had been distrained by a hatchet and an adze, and more was to be taken until he replied to the charge against him by John Clerk. In 1331 Nicholas the Miller still appears to be unreformed since he is fined 2/— for trespassing in the lord's wood and 6d. for employing a defective millstone.

Another interesting complex centred about the parish church although it is difficult to distinguish the various references to rectors, parsons, chaplains and servants of these as well as villagers who had begun to take their surname from such employment. The following is a simple list of the court roll references for this group: Walter of Edyham, parson of the church of Warboys, 1292 (?); John Clerk, chaplain of Warboys, 1292 trespass; William, chaplain of Warboys, 1292 trespass with his dog; John, chaplain of Wistow, 1316 had the hue raised on him, and he did not appear; master Reginald of St. Albans, 1306 trespass in the hedge; John of Elton, chaplain, 1316 cut the lord's woods wrongly; Lord Ralph, rector of the church of Wistow, 1292 enter a plea of debt; Philip the chaplain, 1318 pledge; Lord Robert, chaplain, 1326 sold land; the parson of Warboys, 1299 loss by theft; John de Hernston, chaplain, 1347 enters a debt charge; William, chaplain of the parish, 1350 has the hue and cry raised on him by the bailiff for rescueing some property from the bailiff as charge; the rector of the church 1349 trespassing with his beasts. Other entries are likely concerned with servants or those with the surname of parson: William Parson, 1294 failure to perform work, 1320 failure to perform work; William, servant of the parson of Warboys, 1292 raised the hue wrongly; John Parson, 1294 outside the village with licence; Simon Parson, failure to perform work in 1333, 1337, 1339, 1343, 1347 and owing suit to the mill 1337, charged with trespass in 1339; John Parson, 1334 cut in the marsh too soon, 1337 had the hue raised against him; Stephen, servant of the parson, 1290 pledge; Stephen Parson, 1294 had the hue raised on him; Peter, servant of the rector accused of theft in 1326.

Despite the heavier fines, distresses and other pressures by the court, the poor as well as the more wealthy villagers of Warboys and the district were not easy to control. One indicator of this was the forceable recovery, or 'rescue' as it was called in the court rolls of various animals inpounded by the bailiff and other officials. In 1301 Godfrey Wodekoc recovered his ox, and Ralph Scut recovered his cow, both animals having been seized for trespassing in the lord's wood. In 1313 Gilbert Nunne recovered some unidentified animal from the hayward. The hayward was also the victim of recovery of animals by Richard Sewyne and William, servant of Thomas atte Halle in 1316. In 1318 Reginald Walsh, servant of Philip the chaplain, took seven pigs from the lord's park. William Attewode re-seized some unidentified chattel from an official (beadle?) Godfrey Wodekoc in 1320. Robert, the son of William Rolf recovered a horse from the beadle in 1322. The bailiff charged in the court of 1334 that John Bottiler of Broughton, had recovered animals seized from him for trespass. Although the parchment is damaged at this point, among several men at least William Smart and William Lone can be identified as having broken into the lord's park to recover animals in 1347.

On the other hand, there is no evidence that the court fines at Warboys were assessed according to what the traffic would bear. It has been discovered for other villages of England in the thirteenth century that the court fines, quite heavy in the early thirteenth century, had become more frequent but normalized into small fines by the late thirteenth century.[1] The same pattern of small fines was to be found for the villages belonging to Ramsey Abbey. The court would seem to have relied upon the system of pledging with the gradual increase of distress and fine rather than a statutory fine valued in terms of the type of offence. As we have seen distresses and fines gradually became heavier for the wealthier villagers and freemen of the district. Fines did tend to be heavier for court

[1] A. N. May, *The Franchise in Thirteenth-Century England. With Special Reference to the Estates of the Bishopric of Winchester.* Unpublished Ph. D. thesis, Cambridge, 1970.

officials themselves, especially when the royal statute was involved. At Warboys, the jurors were sometimes fined 12d. each for not fulfilling their obligations, especially concerning keeping the watch. Fines were particularly heavy for not responding to the hue and cry, or not presenting in court that a hue had been raised. For example, in 1306 the village was fined 13s. 4d. for not presenting the hue raised by Joan Grobbe upon Alice Pilche who had assaulted her. The lord's officials too might be subject to heavier fines, as in 1325 when it was reported: "And they say that Godfrey Beadle is an inopportune servant of the lord and of the community since he takes various small things from the customaries in order to cancel the work they owed to the lord to the grave damage of the lord. Therefore etc. 40d. the reeve is the pledge". On the other hand, John Albyn was only fined 3d. on each occasion for refusing during several years of the 1320's to act as juror. As will be seen below fines tended to be singularly small and uniform for such a wide variety of offences as assaults, defamations and trespasses. These various charges at Warboys involved, therefore, a wide cross section of the community rather than a special economic group. It is impossible to assess the wide variety of trespasses on fences, walls, trees, gardens, fields, etc. that we find in the court rolls. Nor is it possible to assess what lay behind the vast majority of the pleas, concords and even the hue and cry since specifics were rarely given for these entries. However, a fairly clear picture emerges from the fines for defamation and assault.

Defamation charges appear fairly regularly in the court rolls in the early fourteenth century. In 1292 Elena Scut was fined 6d. for defaming Simon Gerold and assessed 6d. damage. Juliana Bonde was not fined for defaming Richard Woodward in 1294 since she was poor, but she was charged 6d. for damages. Agnes Wymar escaped a fine for the same reason in 1299, but was assessed 2d. damage for defaming Robert Clerk. In the same year Richard Gardner and Godfrey his brother paid a 1d. damage and 6d. fine for defaming Roger Carpenter. 1299 also saw John Ponder paying 1d. damage and 3d. fine for defaming John Higeney. In 1301 Matilda Bugge was twice fined 6d. and assessed 3d. damage for defaming Matilda Herring and John Ponder. In the same year Henry Isabelle was fined 12d. for cursing the jurors in the presence of the steward. The court of 1305 has the interesting entry: "The jurors convict John Ponder for wrongly defaming Thomas Raven the beadle saying that he was useless in the service of the lord as well as attributing other enormous things to his damage of 6d. which he is to pay to him and for the transgression etc. 6d. with Simon Gerold as pledge". In 1316 Richard

Sedgeley paid 6d. damages and 6d. fine for defaming William Fabion. In the same year Annabella, wife of Robert Lenot, paid 3d. in damages and 3d. fine for defaming Phillipa wife of Roger Shepherd.

In the early fourteenth century sixpence was the most common fine for assaults too, while damages for assault were somewhat surprisingly not as frequently assessed as damages for defamation. In 1299 Robert Clerk assaulted Alice daughter of Stephen of Wynton, was fined 6d. and paid 3d. damages; in 1305 Beatrice Fot assaulted the son of Richard Godwyne, was fined 3d., with 2d. damages; in 1306 Richard Pilche, assaulted Henry Pakerel was fined 6d. and 18d damages; in 1306 Richard the son of Reginald, assaulted Richard Attewode, was fined 6d. and 3od. damages; in 1306 Juliana Bonde assaulted Matilda Fine, in the latter's home and was fined 6d.; in 1306 Richard Pilche, assaulted Henry Pakerel with a knife, and was fined 12d.; in 1306 Stephen the son of Cecilia assaulted Hugh Pakerel, and was fined 6d.; in 1306 John the son of Hugh, of Eydon, was charged with assaulting Alice Derworth; in 1306 John of Higeneye assaulted Godfrey Burg, and was fined 6d.; in 1309 the pledge of Richard Pilche was fined since the latter had assaulted Richard the Couper, and had not appeared; in 1309 Robert the Couper had broken into the house of Godfrey Gardener and his pledge too was charged 6d. since he had not appeared; no fine was assessed for the assault of Robert of Stratford on Agnes Cowherd in the same year and in that year also the pledge of Beatrice Puttock was fined 3d. since she did not appear in court for assaulting Thomas Raven; the pledge was fined for the same amount in 1313 since Richard Carter had not appeared after assaulting Reginald Clerk; in the same year John Godfrey was fined 18d. for assaulting Simon Lone; in 1320 pledges were found for Matilda wife of Paul Bonde who had assaulted her own daughter Margaret and for Reginald Walshe who had assaulted John Gosse, servant of the hayward, but no fines were assessed; no fine was assessed John Gosse in the same year for assaulting Roger Foliet, although he had to pay 3d. damages; in 1322 Roger Berenger attacked and drew blood from Richard the son of Reginald and paid 3d. for each of the charges; in the same year Matilda Cowherd paid 6d. and 12d. for attacking and drawing blood from Simon Bryd; a fight between two parties seems to be implied by the 3d. fine and 3d. damages charged to Simon Bryd in 1325 for assaulting Nicholas Pilche, while the latter paid the same amount for assaulting Simon Bryd; Henry Pakerel was also fined 6d. for assaulting John Bronning in 1337 and the latter paid in turn 6d. for assault and an additional 12d. for drawing blood upon the same Henry; a quarrel between Michael Bryd and John the servant of Stephen Bonde in the same year brought in the beadle as pledge but not fine upon either party.

When one moves from the area of personal damages to that of property the fine seems to have been less important still in the function of the court. This can be seen most clearly in relation to pleas for the recovery of debt. For many of these, there is no evidence whatsoever for a fine, although it may be possible that the plaintiff paid a small fee to have the court take action. Since these suits concerned with the recovery of debt contain a great variety of data about the economy of the village, as well as the function of the court, many of these are listed here. In 1290 Alexander Woodward recovered 15d. from Richard Bonde for the rent of one acre and 15d. from Robert Bishop for the rent of one acre of meadow; in the same year Ralph Fine the hayward recovered six sheaves of oats owed as cornbote by Walter the son of Ralph Thurbern; in 1290, too, Mabel the widow of Godfrey formerly the reeve of Caldecote recovered a debt of 12d., a half-ring of grout and three sheaves of wheat for grain damaged by his cattle from Lawrence Pakerel. John Robert of Broughton recovered 4/4d. from Robert Cowherd, owed to him for malt purchased, in the court of 1294; in the same court the reeve Hugh Benet was fined 6d. for not raising 10/— that Robert Smart, Robert Clerk, Ralph Fine and Thomas le Feker owed to John of Higeney. The same John of Higeney collected 6d. from Cecilia Benet in the court of 1299, but in October 1301 the court had to order that this amount had to be raised from Cecilia. In 1305 the executors of Robert Chose, perhaps from Fenton, entered a debt plea against Emma le Sopere for 4/10d. owed from the purchase of malt; in the same court John the Ponder was fined 3d. for not having delivered one ring of peas owed to Richard Wodekoc. In 1306 the court ordered William Fine to pay the 20d. owed to William Gerneys and the fine was condoned; but the same court fined William Scut 4d. for not having paid the 6d. owed to William High. In 1313 Richard the son of Catherine was fined 3d. for not having given six sheaves of oats to the lord for fodder corn and William Wodekoc was fined 3d. for not having given two sheaves for fodder corn. Through the court of 1316 Godfrey the son of Richard recovered 4/6d. from Alice of Chatteris and the latter was fined 3d. for withholding this amount; in the same court John of Higeneye was fined 3d. for the 2/10d. he owed William Fine and William the Cowherd was fined 3d. twice for the bushel of wheat owed to Ralph Scut and another bushel owed to Robert Edwin. Through the court of January 1320 Robert Smart recovered 4/6d. from Robert Nunne, 18d. being paid immediately, 12d. in lent and 2/— at

Easter; at the same court Richard Puttock recovered one ring of wheat and 12d. from Thomas Puttock but this does not seem to have been paid, since in November of the same year Thomas Puttock was fined 10d for damages and 6d. as a court fine for failing to honour an agreement with Richard for part of a messuage, six rings of wheat, two rings of barley, one ring of beans and 12d. The court of January 1320 granted to William Bumbel that Richard Cissor owed him 6d. a year and was behind 3 years in payments; by the same court Simon Noble recovered a one-third interest in an oven formerly belonging to his father from his brother Godfrey. The court of January 1322 imposed the heavy fine of 40d. upon Thomas Haugate for not having paid 11/9d. owed to Thomas Puttock; by the same court Benedict Lenot was fined 3d. for the 3d. debt owed to John of Ellsworth.

From the 1320's fines were much more commonly associated with recovery of debt as were also damages for loss of the use of capital. For example, in October 1322 Alice Raven was fined 6d., and assessed 3d. damages for the two bushels of dredge owed to Reginald Semar; in the same court William Nunne paid a 6d. fine and 1d. in damages for the 2/2d. owed to Richard Wilkys. The village may have had its money-lenders. In this same court of October 1322 William Cowherd recovered a debt of 3/4d. from Beatrice, the wife of Simon Robyn (3d. fine), 2/— from Benedict Lenot (3d. fine), 16/6d. from Robert Berenger (6d. fine), 8d. from Richard Pilgrim (6d. fine and 2d. damage). In the court of December 1339 William of Higeney reached an agreement about debt with Nicholas Miller, recovered 2/—. half-penny farthing from Robert Berenger for one debt and 3d. as the remainder of another 2/— debt owed by Robert Berenger, 2/1d. from John Tymme. In the same court William of Higeneye and his wife were said to have owed 18d. to Robert Berenger 17d. to John Tymme and 12d. to Simon Dyke. Indeed on the whole the debt structure widened and involved more villagers from the 1330's into the 1340's.

While most of the debts reflect petty business arrangements among the Warboys people themselves, as we have seen from some of the above debts for the purchase of grain, there was undoubtedly much commerce with neighbouring villages. One text from the court of 1326 will be presented to illustrate this type of inter-village indebtedness:

Thomas Raven senior and Thomas his son junior came into court and acknowledge that they owe William the son of John Raven of Hurst for Henry Above the Town 50/= of sterling to be paid to the same William at the 3 terms designated below, namely, 1 mark at the feast of the Annunciation of the Blessed Mary next, and 1 mark at the feast of Pentecost next following and the remainder at the next feast of All Saints without any delay. And therefore these are fined 6d. for wrongful indebtedness, the pledge Robert Raven. And for this acknowledgement made through the above Thomas and Thomas for Henry above the Town, the said William son of John Raven relaxes and quitclaims to the same Henry all actions which in any way he might be able to have against him by reason of the above debt or of any other debt following upon the will of the said John his father".

Another group of individuals who reveal interesting features about a wide cross section of village life are the servants, usually called the *garcon* and *ancilla*. We have already made reference to a number of these in the context of the clergy and other prominent freemen of the district. But there is enough evidence to deduce that a wide variety of people employed servants at Warboys, although undoubtedly some of these would only be for casual labour. Further references to more important servants would be John, servant of the forester of Somersham accused of assault and drawing blood in 1332, Reginald, servant of the farmer of Wolfeye charged with trespassing the lord's wood in 1331, Thomas, servant of the bailiff who raised the hue wrongly on Thomas, servant of John Keston in 1334, Henry of Broughton, servant of the farmer of Wolfeye, who in 1306 carried off a cartload of forage belonging to Richard Plumbe, William, servant of Lawrence Woodward who raised the hue wrongly on John Unfrey in 1316. Servants of less important villagers were represented by the following: William, servant of Simon who raised the hue in 1332, John, servant of John Mousichet who raised the hue wrongly in 1325, Paul, servant of John Ponder who trespassed in the lord's wood in 1294, John servant of Robert Agath who raised the hue twice in 1320 because he was assaulted and defamed, John, servant of Henry Brun who was fined 6d. in 1318 for having the hue raised on him. Godfrey, servant of Hugh of Eydon who was wrongfully subject to the hue in 1313, Richard servant of Godfrey Noble, who raised the hue in 1322, Alan, servant of Richard Plumbe who raised the hue in 1306, a servant of Thomas Puttock who trespassed in the lord's wood in 1331, a servant of Thomas Raven who trespassed in the lord's wood and on another occasion raised the hue in 1325, Godfrey (H) *manupastus* of Nicholas Buk who in 1290 defamed Stephen the servant of the parson, the *manupasti* of Robert Bonde who in 1326 were fined 6d. for trespassing in the lord's fields, William, servant of Ralph Bonde who in 1334 assaulted and drew blood from Robert, the son of Thomas Robyn, Beatrice, servant of William Clerk, who was the subject of a hue in 1347.

The very fact that most of these servants were not even given a surname indicates that they were on the periphery of village social life. Hence, many references to servants indicate poverty. For example, John, servant of Richard Lucas was fined 12d. in 1318 for gleaning wrongly by taking the sheaves of his neighbours; the *ancilla* of Thomas? in 1343 gleaned wrongly; Matilda, servant of John Molt who was fined 6d. in 1339 for gleaning wrongly. It was stated in 1301 that the *manupastus* of Nicholas Lone who trespassed in the lord's wood was too poor to pay the fine. The servants of the more prominent villagers seemed to face the same temptations as with Adam, servant of Lawrence Woodward, charged with gleaning wrongly "since he took 50 sheaves of grain and hid these in the woods, and the jurors say he has from these sheaves and others five bushels of wheat. The steward orders that these be distributed to pay for the repair of paths and other ways in disrepair". Another interesting entry occurred in 1326: "And they say that Peter, servant of the rector took seven sheaves of wheat from Sampson Faber which had been given to him stolen from the grain tithing for this same Sampson and valued by the jurors at 3d. And that he delivered to the same Sampson a native and villein of the lord 6/— in redemption of the same theft. Therefore he is in mercy etc. and since the same Sampson made this fine without the bailiffs of the lord and their counsel therefore he is in mercy 12d."

Another number of individual actions standing apart from economic and social groupings may be recognised as those fined under the ancient title of leyrwite. These fines for sexual misbehaviour were usually imposed upon women pregnant outside of marriage. This problem of identification is further illustrated by the fact that for nearly 60 cases of leyrwite at Warboys before the Black Death the male partner could only be named in three instances. Names of those fined for leyrwite from more prominent families were Emma Bonde 1320, Matilda Bonde 1339, Cristine, daughter of Robert Clerk with William, son of John of Fenton 1294, Agnes Faber widow 1309, Agnes Fine 1301, Alice, daughter of Ralph Fine 1322 and 1325, Phillipa Fine 1347, Agnes Gerold 1334, Allota Lenot 1320, Margaret Lone 1347, Alice, daughter of Lawrence Pakerel 1290, Gratia, daughter of Richard Pakerel 1305, Agnes Palmer 1337 and 1343 (with Richard Fot), Agnes Rede 1333, Cassandra Rolf 1325, Agnes Wilkes 1331 and 1339, Agnes Scut 1309 and 1326. Although only Juliana Sperner, fined for leyrwite in 1294, was said to be too poor to pay the fine, the number of those charged with this offence spreads over into the poorer families too: Alice Gosse 1313, Emma Hey 1301, Alice, daughter of William Lucas 1306 and 1313, Agnes, daughter of Ralph

Cowherd 1305, Agnes, daughter of Simon Cowherd 1322 and 1325, Alice, daughter of John Ponder 1305, Matilda Gardener 1322, Beatrice Puttock 1299 and 1339, Alice daughter of Juliana Sculle 1305 and 1306, Beatrice Sculle 1320, Cristine Sperner 1290, Matilda Sperner 1322, Margaret Sperner 1294, Agnes Top 1334, Alice Top 1337, Juliana Blosme 1301, Joan Taylor 1320, Margaret Powel 1320, Mabel Decoun 1337, Margaret, daughter of Stephen Gouler 1299 and 1301, Alice of Chatteris 1299, Emma Smult 1294, Juliana Trill 1322, Gratia Wyton 1306 and 1313, Alice Bumbel 1339 and 1347, Alice Cous 1339, Agnes Kaye 1333, Alice Brandon 1332. In view of the great activity recently discovered for ecclesiastical courts of this region for a later generation in the fourteenth century,[1] it is surprising to find so few references to marital problems in the village court. In 1337 John Tymme was fined for receiving Richard Reynold who was accused of adultery. Adultery charges likely lay behind the fact that Richard Smith had lost chattels in the ecclesiastical court in 1334 and William Raven in 1326, but this is the full extent of such information.

While many families and individuals were non-conformist in so far as regulations of the village court were concerned, other families and individuals were simply unruly by any standards. One such family, taken from what must have been the more wealthy members of the village, was the Rolf family. William Rolf, who died in 1325 and had held one virgate, had led a fairly respectable career as juror in the years of 1305, 1313 and 1316. However, for the remainder of the century the Rolfs were nearly always in court on the charge of some violence, transgression or another. The very year of the death of William Rolf, his wife Cassandra was charged with immorality. Their son Robert first appears in the court of 1320 charged with assaulting William, the son of Robert Smart and with defaming the same William. In 1322 the same Robert forceably recovered a horse that had been taken by the beadle and was fined heavily (40d.) for causing 3d. damage to the property of Hugh of Higeney. Robert perhaps left the village at this time. A John, son of William, was ordained in 1326 but, whether the same John or not, a John Rolf kept up the family tradition in the 1330's by drawing blood from William Thresher and drawing the hue and cry upon himself. Perhaps the family became rather impoverished over the 1330's and 1340's since the wife of John Rolf gleaned wrongly in 1343. In any case the Rolfs were back in

[1] Michael M. Sheenan, "The Formation and Stability of Marriage in Fourteenth-Century England: Evidence of an Ely Register", *Mediaeval Studies*, XXXIII, 1971, pp. 228-263.

form after the Black Death since John and Isabella both let blood in a fracas in 1350. Isabella drew blood from both Agnes of Higeney and John Lenot junior in 1360; in the same year Joan Rolf drew blood from Margaret Robyn and was fined 12d. for leyrwite. We have already noted that the Rolf name was prominent among the 'rebellious' villagers in the next decade or two.[1] From this time some of the Rolfs moved abroad and carried their peculiar spirit with them, as with William Rolf who drew blood from five different persons at Upwood.[2]

Another aggressive and mutinous family, though much poorer than the Rolfs, was the Kaunt family. Henry Kaunt first comes to our attention in 1292 when he was fined 12d. for having left the lord's fee without licence. Henry was still not staying on the fee by 1294 since in that year Simon Gosse and William Lucas became his pledges "that he will remain a resident and that he will perform the customary service owed for the messuage that he holds from the lord". Henry apparently did stay at home from this time since he was fined late in 1294 for trespassing upon the property of one of his neighbours. Nicholas Kaunt first comes to our attention in the court of 1299 when it was ordered "that Nicholas Lone under penalty of 12d. have Nicholas Kaunt in his tithing to reply for the fact that he was presented in the view of Broughton as a vagabond skulking by night under the porches of the villagers and fishing by night in waters of the villagers". What effect this prescription was to have is difficult to see since the court of 1299 had begun with an entry to the effect that Nicholas Kaunt had been presented in the last view as useless and disobedient to his capital pledge Nicholas Lone. It was also noted in this court that Nicholas Kaunt had trespassed in the lord's wood. Our next extant court roll, that of October 1301, has an entry: and to Nicholas Kaunt since he was unwilling to remain at Warboys under direction for the autumn work, as was determined at the last court, but went into the county of Cambridgeshire and there remained all autumn (therefore he is fined) 6d. with pledge Lawrence Kaunt. Nicholas Kaunt then seems to have remained at Warboys and lived there according to his fashion, in 1306 charged with damage to the turf of his neighbours in the marsh and with selling turves to outsiders, trespassing in the lord's wood in the same year, in 1313 charged with adultery with an outsider and with receiving someone who had gleaned wrongly, and 1316 again charged with trespassing with his animals.

[1] See above, p. 220-221.
[2] "Changes in an English Village after the Black Death", *op. cit.*, p. 164.

The women of the Kaunt family did their part for the family image, Juliana being charged with pregnancy outside of marriage in 1320 and 1331, and Alice with pregnancy outside of marriage in 1347.

Much more common were those villagers of Warboys troubled in many ways simply because of poverty. The Bishop family allows us to trace the effects of poverty. Robert Bishop first comes to our attention in 1290 for owing a debt; he was charged with another debt in 1292; in 1294 he was excused for a fine imposed for trespassing in the lord's wood since he was poor. Agnes, who is spoken of as the widow of Robert Bishop in the November court of 1294, had her fine for bad brewing condoned in that court and again in the court of January for poverty. Agnes continued to eke out an existence by brewing until 1320 at least. Perhaps the children of Agnes and Robert, a Beatrice and Emma Bishop were fined in the court of 1316 for gleaning wrongly. Last mention of the family comes in 1339 when a Sarra Bishop was fined for gleaning wrongly.

The Bryd family were not as poor as the Bishops and therefore reacted against their situation more vigorously. The first male, Richard Bryd, comes to our attention in 1316 when he failed to come to court to answer to the hue and cry. Among his charges were for a false plea in 1320, assaulting, drawing blood and hamsok in 1325, trespass in the lord's wood in 1331, having the hue raised on him several times over the 1330's. Simon Bryd who entered to a small property in 1324 had been charged in the ecclesiastical court of 1320, involved in charges of the hue and cry, drawing blood, contempt of court, false plea in 1322, in several cases of assault and drawing blood in 1325 and again in 1331 while in the meantime trespassing in the marsh, refusing to perform work and trespassing in the lord's wood. This Simon Bryd was described in the account roll of 1344-1345 as a fugitive and his name thereafter drops from the records. The same problems hovered about the female members of the family as Cristine Bryd was charged with debt, stealing grain and having been bloodied by an attack in 1331, with gleaning wrongly in 1332, trespass in 1334, with raising the hue since she was attacked and lost blood in 1343. The family carried through the Black Death in the same fashion since we know that William Bryd was the subject of a hue and cry three times, forceably recovered some chattels taken for trespassing on the parson in 1350, and in 1353 was again charged with trespass, allowing his building to dilapidate and refusing three times to come to autumn works.

With no more resources than perhaps the warren for which licences were noted in the 1290's the Fot family reflect a parallel performance in the courts to the Bryds. Godfrey Fot who had the right of warren was charged with several sorts of trespass over the 1290's. William, the son of Godfrey Fot left the village without licence in 1294, was charged twice with trespass in the woods in 1306, once with the same trespass in 1309, was out of tithing in 1322 and prohibited the village that year but he seems to have wandered back on occasion since his last entry is for trespassing in the lord's grain at night in 1333. Beatrice, the wife of William, was charged with assault in 1305, had the hue raised on her in 1306 and leaves the picture charged with gleaning wrongly in 1339. The second generation continued in the same fashion, a Hugh Fot being charged with assault in 1333, several times involved in the hue and cry over the next decade and failed to come to work in 1353. In 1343 an Alice Fot was charged with assault, drawing blood and causing the raising of the hue and cry.

Contrasts in the lives of these poor families would be determined by the number of male and female members of the family and the corresponding ability of the family to gain a livelihood elsewhere. The Nel family seems to have been as much at home at Ramsey as at Warboys. Our records open for this family in 1294 with reference to a Richard Nel at Ramsey without licence and the court gives an order to arrest him. In 1299 the order is repeated with the words that "his pledges were to have him". The 1299 Richard was referred to as senior and there seems to have been another Richard at Ramsey who trespassed in the lord's wood in 1301 and was a pledge of the Richard Nel at Ramsey over 1305 and 1306 when the latter seems to have been licenced to be abroad since he paid two capons. The court of 1309 had the entry: No one to receive Hugh (Richard?) Nel, Bartholomew Sperner or Lawrence Sperner who are put out of tithing of Richard Nel. Richard Nel again paid the capons to remain at Ramsey in 1313. But he does not seem to have honoured this in the following years since there is an entry in 1316: "and they say that Richard Nel and Agnes his wife are usless and wrongdoers and not worthy to remain in the village. And then William the Reeve came and became their pledge that henceforth they should behave themselves. Their fine is condoned since they are poor". It is interesting that the pledges of poor individuals such as Richard Nel do not seem to be fined for their non-appearance. It is obvious that the court is threatening to exclude such persons from the village rather than forcing their re-entry. In any case, further references to the Richard Nel's disappear after 1316, and one may assume that they did not survive the famine of the following years. However, one branch of the family did continue over the next generation since there are references to a John Nel over a period of 25 years. He obviously had property, although not very much, and was represented in the courts by the usual entries of trespass, assaults, hue and cry along with many refusals to perform the work service for his land.

The Pilche family may be taken as a contrast with the Nel family. The Pilches were more numerous and retained an active core at Warboys apparently because of the many women in the family. There were some male children but most of these seemed to have left Warboys and remained away: Hugh Pilche at Hemington from 1299, Richard Pilche at Bury from 1299 although he seems to have been back in the village from 1301 to 1306, Robert, son of William went to Kent in 1301. The family had only small property at Warboys since we know that Nicholas received a one-half croft in 1303. This Nicholas was the subject of the hue and cry in 1320, had been presented in the ecclesiastical court in the same year and was involved in a multiple bloody assault charge in 1325. A Bartholomew Pilche had been a butcher in the 1290's and a Godfrey Pilche hayward for several years after 1300. Godfrey's son John appears frequently in the court over the 1330's and 1340's with the usual entries associated with the poverty-stricken: hue and cry, assaults, debts and taking carts of outsiders into the marsh. Emma Pilche predominates among the members of this family at Warboys since she was an ale brewer from at least 1292 to 1334. Many of her sister Pilches did not fare so well: Matilda was involved in trespass, gleaning wrongly and leyrwite; Alice was charged with assault and also with being pregnant outside of marriage on two occasions; Sarra was charged with trespassing in the woods. The Pilche women figure less prominently in the second quarter of the century, perhaps because there were fewer of them, since there are references only to a Margaret who was owed a debt in 1339 and a Beatrice, tenant of a mondaymanland, who was ill in 1347.[1]

The Sperner family have left us a social pattern much like that of the Pilche's. Four of the women come to our attention first as being pregnant outside of marriage: Cristine in 1290, Juliana and Margaret in 1294, Matilda in 1322. Cristine also did some ale brewing; Juliana was said to be too poor to pay a fine; Margaret refused to help with any of the

[1] From the detailed records of Ramsey it can be discovered that the poorer and troubled families that came there from Warboys — Bryd, Nel, Pilche, Sculle — continued in the same mode of existence. On the other hand, members of wealthier families from Warboys — Fine, Faber, London, Pakerel — took up land and became involved in trade at Ramsey.

autumn work in 1301. There was also a Phillipa Sperner at this time who trespassed on several occasions in 1306 and gleaned wrongly in 1316. Of the Sperner males Robert went away to Waresley, Hunts, without licence from 1292, Bartholomew to Colne with licence from 1294 although the last reference to him in 1320 says that he has now refused to pay his licence; Lawrence Sperner was at Reach, Cambs, without licence from 1299. One male, Richard, did stay on at Warboys trying to subsist with the usual trespasses and gleaning. A second generation of the family appeared from the 1320's when a Stephen was accused of trespassing in the woods and he reappeared in the 1330's in relation to hue and debt charges.

It has already been noted that some members of poorer families had at least part-time employment as butchers, brewers, haywards and keepers of warren in the woods. From surnames it is possible to isolate many families of these petty tradesmen. They appear to be poor but aggressively unconcerned with conforming to the village laws. One of these, Hugh the Webester, was apparently resident of the village for sometime although his court roll entries were entirely negative: 1316 received unkown persons who are not in tithing and an unidentified woman who had been prohibited the vill; 1325 was involved in and bloodied during an assault so that he raised the hue and cry and it was raised on him; 1331 pledge; 1334 received outsiders of evil reputation and came to an agreement over some difference; 1339 raised the hue; 1347 received William Bewford out of tithing. Clearly in most cases these tradesmen were not more permanent residents of the village and indeed do not indicate any family attachments there. A simple list of their names and the court roll entries will indicate their pattern of involvement in the village: John, son of Richard the Webester 1320 wrongly charged in the court; Robert the Webester 1331 stole grain, 1334 trespassed in the lord's wood, 1337 pledge; John Webester 1332 a common forestaller; Walter Webester 1334 trespass, 1347 out of tithing, William Webester 1339 concord; Agnes, the daughter of Alexander Webester 1343 trespass, trespassed upon and wrongly charged him for it. Members of the taylor trade betrayed the same social pattern: Godfrey Taylor 1332 assaulted and bloodied Nicholas Taylor, 1333 owed a debt; Agnes, daughter of Nicholas Taylor 1339 gleaned wrongly; Robert Taylor 1334 not in tithing; Roger Taylor 1347 trespassed in the grain; Henry Taylor 1347 trespassed in the wood.

There are to be expected of course all sorts of variety among this group of people. The Chaumon (Chapman) family seemed to have been more established in the village where Margaret Chaumon was involved in brewing over 1305-6 at least. A William Chaumon had trespassed in the lord's wood in 1320 and let his building decay in 1325; it cannot be established whether this was the same William who was owed a debt in 1343 and in 1347, identified as William Chaumon Taylor, was out of tithing. Other members of this family were involved in brewing and they may have had small properties. The Cowherd family present another pattern first coming to our attention with Robert Cowherd out of tithing in 1294 and complaining of a trespass in 1316. Agnes, the daughter of Ralph the Cowherd was fined for leyrwite in 1305, raised the hue because of an assault in 1309 and was again charged with immorality in 1325. Nicholas, the Cowherd had been distrained in 1315 to be put in tithing, trespassed in the lord's wood in 1320 and received someone out of tithing in 1322. Matilda Cowherd was attacked in 1322 so that she bled and raised the hue. Some of this family may have gradually acquired property since Simon the Cowherd refused to perform a work in 1320 as did Emma Cowherd in 1326. Certainly by the late 1330's this family was becoming more important—if one family it was--since they performed minor roles as jurors, became involved increasingly in brewing[1] and from debts owed to them by 1350 would seem to have acquired some wealth.

Those poorer persons who resorted to theft for survival were simply put out of the village. The court of November, 1306, had a presentation by the jurors that Stephen Gagon was a malefactor since he took geese and chickens from the villagers, so that he is to be seized if he should come on the fee. There is no evidence that Stephen had been a resident of the village. Undoubtedly there were many of these people wandering about, as with another unusual name appearing in the court of 1313: "and they say that Agnes Malitraz does not deserve to stay in the village because she gleans wrongly taking sheaves and other small things; therefore she is prohibited the village; and Allan Haugate who received her is fined 3d. with pledge Ralph Haugate". Another entry in this same year deals with a more familiar family name from the district: "and they say that Eleanor Baroun is of the same sort; therefore she is prohibited the village and Ivo of Hurst who recieved her is fined 3d." A fine upon those who received these "undesirables" was the main technique for keeping them out of the village. Another example can be taken from the court

[1] Unfortunately there are so many explanations for fines for bad brewing or the sale of weak ale that these fines — varying from 6d. to 2s. — do not indicate the wealth or importance of the trade for the brewer.

of 1316: "And they say that Margaret Fine received a certain Thomas Galyon, nor is he worthy to remain in the village, therefore she is fined 3d. with William Fine as pledge; and the village is prohibited to the same Thomas Galyon". Of course, if such persons came from the village they might be able to make restitution by fine and find someone who would be their pledge. An example of this can be taken from the January court of 1320 wherein Beatrice Puttock was accused of stealing many small things and therefore prohibited the village with the caution that no one receive her under penalty of 20/=. Actually, the court continues with the remarks that she comes to court and pays a fine and presents two pledges John Derward and John Catoun that she will henceforth behave herself.

Except for strictly economic matters, the variety of information available about the people of Warboys declined drastically after the Black Death. As a consequence, less is known from this time about aberrations of various members of families. For example, there are many fewer references to fines for leyrwite: Joan Rolf 1360, Alice Rolf 1363, Joan, daughter of Robert Berenger 1365, Agnes Bonde 1375, Margaret Harregate 1369, Emma Albyn 1382 and 1386, Emma Lone 1386, Emma, daughter of John (?) 1400, Joan Alot 1410. There are even fewer references to servants: Robert, servant of Robert Albyn 1365, the servant of John Collier 1365, Simon, the servant of Thomas Hunter 1372, the servant of John Lenot 1369, John, servant of the rector 1375, Thomas, servant of William Buckworth 1382, Richard, servant of Robert Colle 1382, William, servant of John 1391, Thomas, servant of John Chapman 1398.

Disappearance of the personal pledge from court roll records was the main reason for this change in the nature of surviving social information. The pledge was replaced by greater emphasis upon the fine and the byelaw. Nominally the fines increased considerably, as may be seen by the severe penalties threatened under the byelaws. *De facto*, however, fines were usually much smaller, especially later in the century as the lord was faced with unfavourable supply conditions for labour and tenants. We have noted already in the above chapters of Part IV, as well as in Chapter V Section II, the resourceful acquisition of property by poorer families in the later fourteenth century and the ensueing concentration of land by various families and individuals. With the fifteenth century many Warboys people took advantage of new trade opportunities. Some of these were local, as the butcher trade seemed now to attract more prominent villagers: John Catoun 1400, John Chapman 1400, William Derworth 1400, William Scharpe 1412, John Heryng 1400 to 1421, John Lenot 1400, William Olyver 1423, Richard Plumbe 1423, John Plumbe 1440, John Horewode 1440. However, for many of the new trades the individuals involved increasingly moved away from the village. The story of John Raven the tanner, of John Plumbe *medicus*, John Berenger *medicus*, John Berenger master carpenter and William Plumbe master carpenter does not centre about Warboys. Even more, as we come to those villagers who went to Ramsey or St. Ives to learn the trades of smith and tanner, or as far abroad as Lavenham for the new wool industry, the social history of the people of Warboys enters a new and a more regional phase.

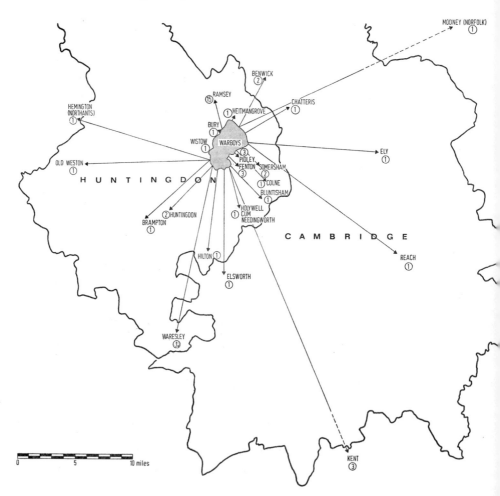

Map I: Warboys people who left the village between 1290-1339

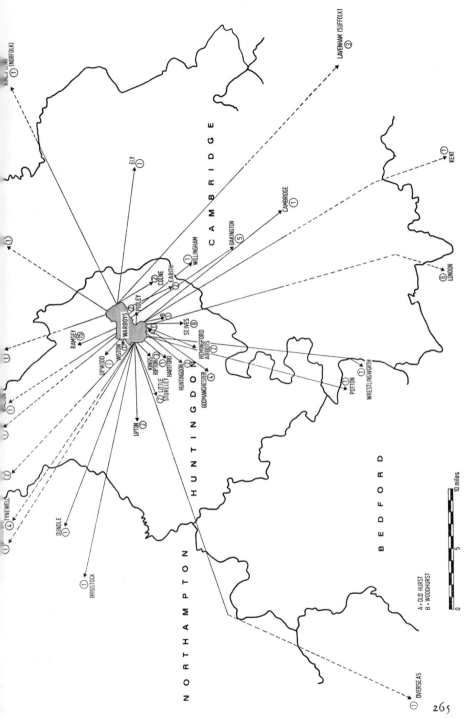

Map II: Warboys people who left the village between 1400-1458

BIBLIOGRAPHY

Manuscript Sources*

LONDON: British Museum

Compotus Rolls Additional Rolls 34903, 34904, 39669, 39795, 39889, 39797, 39798, 39799, 39800, 39801, 39802, 39803, 39805, 39807, 34900, 39809, 39811, 39804, 39806, 39808, 39810, 39812, 39813, 39814, 39815, 39816, 39817, 39818, 39819, 39820, 39821, 39822, 39823, 39824, 39825, 39826, 39827, 39907, 39828, 39829, 39830, 39831, 39832, 39833, 39834, 39835, 39836

Charters Additional Charters 34176, 34177, 34182, 34183

Court Rolls Additional Rolls 39754, 34335, 34597, 34894, 39755, 39850, 34774, 34895, 39756, 34342, 34910, 34324, 34897, 34896, 39757, 39758, 34918, 39759, 34777, 34898, 39760, 39761, 34363, 39470, 34919, 39762, 34899, 39853, 39856, 39763, 39764, 39857, 39860, 39473, 39765, 39858, 39766, 34306, 34901, 34902, 39474, 34815, 34814, 34817, 39862, 39768, 39769, 39770, 39864, 39865, 34370, 39480, 39771, 39772, 39773, 39774

LONDON: Public record office

Charters Ancient Deed A 5156

Court Rolls Series Sc 2 Portfolio 179 nos. 10, 11, 20, 31, 34, 35, 39, 40, 42, 43, 45, 47, 48, 49, 53, 55, 59, 62, 68

Subsidy Rolls Series E, Portfolio 179 nos. 122/4 and 122/7

Secondary Sources Referred To

Cartularium Monasterii de Rameseia. Ed. W. H. Hart and P. A. Lyons. 3 vols. Rolls Series 79. London, 1893.

DeWindt, E. B., *Land and People in Holywell-cum-Needingworth*, Toronto, 1972.

Hogan, P. M. *Wistow: A Social and Economic Reconstitution in the Thirteenth and Fourteenth Centuries*, Unpublished Ph. D. thesis, University of Toronto, 1971.

May, A. N. *The Franchise in Thirteenth-Century England. With Special Reference to the Estates of the Bishopric of Winchester*, Unpublished Ph. D. thesis, Cambridge, 1970.

* Records are listed under each grouping in chronological order; the dates are indicated as these documents are employed in the text.

Oschinsky, Dorothea, *Walter of Henley and other Treatises*, Oxford, 1971.

Page, F. M. "The Customary Poor Law of Three Canbridgeshire Manors", *Cambridge Historical Journal*, III, no. 2.
— *The Estates of Crowland Abbey, Cambridge*, 1934.

Raftis, J. Ambrose. "Changes in an English Village after the Black Death", *Mediaeval Studies*, XXIX, 1967.

— "The Concentration of Responsibility in Five Villages", *Mediaeval Studies*, XXVIII, 1966.

— *The Estates of Ramsey Abbey: A Study in Economic Growth and Organization*, Toronto, 1957.

— "Social Structures in Five East Midland Villages", *Economic History Review*. 2nd series. XVIII, 1965.

— *Tenure and Mobility: Studies in the Social History of the Mediaeval English Village*, Toronto, 1964.

Rotuli Hundrdorum tempore Henrici III et Edwardi I. Ed. W. Illingworth and J. Caley. 2 vols. London: Record Commission, 1818.

Sheehan, Michael M. "The Formation and Stability of Marriage in Fourteenth-Century England: Evidence of an Ely Register", *Mediaeval Studies*, XXXIII, 1971.

Thrupp, Sylvia L. "The Problem of Replacement-Rates in Late Medieval English Population", *Economic History Review*, 2nd. series XVIII, 1965.